Environmental, Social, and Governance (ESG) Investing for Sustainable Finance

nova
science publishers
www.novapublishers.com
New York

Business, Technology and Finance Series

The Basel III Endgame: Navigating Financial Regulations and Uncertainties
Reinaldo Montgomery (Editor)
ISBN: 979-8-89530-902-5
eBook ISBN: 979-8-90134-004-2

FinTech for Sustainable Financial Market Innovation
Neha Kamboj, PhD, and Vinita Choudhary, PhD
ISBN: 979-8-89530-930-8
eBook ISBN: 979-8-90134-012-7

Digital Engagement and Optimization – Systematic Reviews on Social Media, SEO, and Business Strategy
Bonginkosi A. Thango, PhD, and Lerato Matshaka, PhD
eBook ISBN: 979-8-89530-736-6

Asset Allocation: Theory, Recent Developments and Beyond
Cemile Özgür, PhD, and Vedat Sarikovanlik, PhD
ISBN: 979-8-89530-649-9
eBook ISBN: 979-8-89530-721-2

Deepfake Technology Dilemmas: Mastering Managerial Navigation
Sanjay Taneja, PhD, Mukul Bhatnagar, Swati Gupta, PhD, Pawan Kumar, PhD, Sanjeet Kumar, PhD, and Ercan Ozen, PhD
ISBN: 979-8-89530-549-2

More information about this series can be found at

Veena Grover
Editor

Environmental, Social, and Governance (ESG) Investing for Sustainable Finance

nova science publishers
www.novapublishers.com
New York

DOI: https://doi.org/10.52305/BKXE5215

Library of Congress Cataloging-in-Publication Data
ISBN: 979-8-90134-138-4 (Hardcover)
ISBN: 979-8-90134-219-0 (eBook)

Published by Nova Science Publishers, Inc. † New York

Contents

Chapter 1

An Introduction to Sustainable Finance

Sonal Trivedi[1,*]
and Veena Grover[2]
[1]School of Business, Manav Rachna University, India
[2]Lloyd Business School, Greater Noida, UP, India

Abstract

In a century characterized by climatic urgency, social inequalities, and worldwide economic transformation, classic finance is simply not sufficient anymore. Welcome Substantial Finance—the revolutionary financial way that brings sustainability, ethics, and long-term effects into making financial choices. This article describes the growing applicability of substantial finance as the driver of sustainable economic development, overcoming the conflict between profitability and duty. With a combination of policy analysis, literature review, and a case study in real-world application, the study examines how significant finance mechanisms—like impact funding, green bonds, and ESG investing—are transforming corporate conduct and capital markets. It also analyses the contributions of technology, financial institutions, and governments to such practices. Findings underscore that although finance is still unfolding, its potential to channel global capital toward the United Nations Sustainable Development Goals (SDGs) is tremendous. Yet, challenges like patchy regulations, greenwashing, and data deficiencies still hold back large-scale uptake. This research not only underscores the strategic value of sustainable finance to contemporary economies but also delivers practical recommendations to policymakers and financial executives. As we move toward a future propelled by growth and

* Correspoding Author's Email: trivedi.sonal86@gmail.com

In: Environmental, Social, and Governance (ESG) …
Editor: Veena Grover
ISBN: 979-8-90134-138-4

accountability, substantial finance is at the vanguard of impactful, quantifiable results.

Keywords: SDG, sustainable finance, sustainability, ESG, green bonds, impact funding

1. Introduction

1.1. Background of the Study

In the rapidly changing global economy of today, finance is not merely about profits, numbers, and balance sheets—it's about purpose, sustainability, and long-term value creation. The conventional model of finance, with its emphasis on short-term returns and shareholder primacy, is slowly giving way to a wider, more encompassing vision: Substantial Finance (Clark, Feiner, &Viehs, 2015; Serafeim, 2020). This new strategy brings together environmental stewardship, social responsibility, and sound governance (ESG) into capital decision-making. It seeks to use capital to support the United Nations Sustainable Development Goals (SDGs).

With climate change growing stronger, social inequality on the rise, and resource shortages destabilizing the economy, the world's financial system is at a turning point. Institutions, investors, and governments are increasingly recognizing the imperative of redefining the purpose of finance—not only as an engine of growth but as a driver of beneficial societal change. This paper aims to discuss how meaningful finance is a bridge of critical importance between economic growth and sustainable development, remaking the way capital is mobilized and allocated across sectors (Climate Bonds Initiative [CBI], 2022; IFC, 2021).

1.2. Research Problem

Regardless of increasing momentum, significant finance is still under deployed and poorly comprehended. There is a lack of transparency on its fundamental principles, sparse regulatory convergence, and patchy implementation across markets (UNEP FI, 2020). Furthermore, sustainable finance is still perceived by many organizations as a compliance cost, not a strategic opportunity. This disparity presents the essential research question:

How can substantial finance be efficiently utilized to encourage sustainable economic development, especially in a globalized world propelled by both economic performance and moral responsibility?

1.3. Objectives of the Study

The key objective of this study is to examine the definition, application, and operational use of substantial finance as drivers of sustainable development. Particular objectives include:

- To define and put into context the notion of substantial finance
- To analyse its fundamental tools (e.g., ESG investing, green bonds, impact investing)
- To assess its efficiency in fostering sustainable economic growth
- To determine challenges, constraints, and future prospects in this area
- To study real-world applications through a targeted case study

1.4. Research Questions

This research is informed by the following main questions:

- What is substantial finance and how is it different from mainstream finance?
- How does substantial finance enhance sustainable economic progress?
- What are some of the techniques and mechanisms which are used under substantial finance?
- What are some challenges that are delaying the implementation of substantial finance processes?
- What policies or guidelines can maximize its adoption throughout the world?

1.5. Scope and Limitations

The current paper emphasizes mainly on use of massive finance in sustainable development, referencing examples across developed and developing economies. The subject matter touches upon ESG lending, climate-related instruments, and institutional policy measures. Yet, the paper does not exhaustively cover micro-finance, informal finance mechanisms, or regional rules because of space limitations.

Although the study features one or more case studies, it is not an empirical survey-based report or statistical analysis. The results are mainly qualitative, drawing on secondary data, policy documents, and written financial practices.

2. Literature Review

2.1. Overview of Substantial Finance

Substantial Finance is not only a financial innovation—it's a philosophical shift. At its essence, it upends the conventional "profit-first" worldview by instilling sustainability, ethics, and long-term social value into the world of finance. Substantial finance encompasses activities such as environmental, social, and governance (ESG) investing, impact investing, green bonds, and socially responsible lending (UNEP FI, 2020; EY, 2021). Academics such as Elkington (1997) and Porter & Kramer (2011) have underlined the fact that companies and capital providers now have to work with a double mandate—to make returns and to produce genuine societal contributions.

This form of finance speaks to the triple bottom line: planet, people, and profit (Amel-Zadeh & Serafeim, 2018). It channels capital into initiatives that combat climate change, decrease inequality, enhance governance, and create resilient economies—hence its significant contribution toward the UN Sustainable Development Goals (SDGs).

2.2. Historical Development

The origins of significant finance lie in socially responsible investing (SRI) during the 1960s and 70s, when investors started excluding companies that produced arms, tobacco, or supported apartheid governments (BlackRock,

2020; Morningstar, 2021). But the idea took serious traction in the early 2000s, especially following the United Nations Principles for Responsible Investment (UN PRI) launch in 2006.

Some of the major milestones in its evolution are:

- 1990s: Emergence of ethical and green mutual funds
- 2005: UNGC "Who Cares Wins" report supported the inclusion of ESG considerations in capital markets
- 2006: Launch of UN PRI with more than 100 signatories
- 2015: Adoption of the UN SDGs and the Paris Climate Agreement
- 2020 and beyond: Sudden embracement of ESG metrics by global financial institutions following COVID, prompted by investor activism and regulatory changes

This timeline illustrates how significant finance has moved from specialized interest to common expectation.

2.3. Associated Theories

2.3.1. Stakeholder Theory

Advanced by R. Edward Freeman, this theory contends that the success of a firm relies on meeting the needs of all its stakeholders, not merely its shareholders (Bhatia & Wadhwani, 2022). Significant finance compliments this by placing greater weight on wider social and environmental outcomes as well as financial rewards (Serafeim, 2020).

2.3.2. Triple Bottom Line (TBL)

Developed by John Elkington, the TBL model gauges business success through three Ps: People, Planet, and Profit. Significant finance completely fits into this model by funding projects that create positive social and environmental impacts along with economic gain (Clark et al., 2015).

2.3.3. Modern Portfolio Theory (Redefined)

Whereas Modern Portfolio Theory (MPT) concentrates on return and risk, Substantial finance challenges it by introducing a third dimension—impact. Scholars advocate for an updated framework where risk, return, and sustainability coexist (SEBI, 2021; Ministry of Finance, 2022).

2.3.4. Theory of Moral Economy

This theory focuses on economic systems grounded in moral or ethical systems. Substantial finance is basically the application of moral economy to financial markets, moving from self-interest to common good (Sachs et al., 2021).

2.4. Global Trends in Sustainable Finance

Around the world, significant finance is on the rise. Based on the Global Sustainable Investment Alliance (GSIA), more than $35 trillion worth of assets were under management employing sustainable investment methods as of 2022—15% up from 2020 (CBI, 2022; OECD, 2020). Institutional investors such as BlackRock, Vanguard, and Goldman Sachs now factor in ESG metrics when conducting portfolio assessments (World Economic Forum, 2022).

Trends worth noting are:

- Surge of ESG Disclosure Requirements (e.g., EU's SFDR, India's BRSR, SEC's planned regulations)
- Boom in Green and Climate Bonds, particularly in the EU and Asia
- Growing Use of AI and Big Data in ESG ratings and sustainable portfolio building
- Incorporation of Climate Risk into central bank and financial regulator systems

Nations such as Germany, Japan, India, and Canada are actively developing national sustainable finance strategies, showing the shift of these practices from voluntary to regulated structures (G20 Sustainable Finance Working Group, 2021).

2.5. Literature Gaps Identified

Even with the growing literature on sustainable finance, there are some key gaps that still exist:

1. Definition Inconsistency: There is no standard definition of substantial finance, which results in inconsistent interpretation and application.
2. Insufficient Longitudinal Studies: Short-term effect or single case studies dominate the research; long-term effectiveness is hardly ever evaluated (Goyal & Joshi, 2020).
3. Underrepresentation of Emerging Economies: A large part of the literature is based on Europe and North America. Emerging markets, where the demand for sustainable finance is most pressing, are underrepresented.
4. Greenwashing Issues: There is limited empirical work on detecting and preventing greenwashing in financial reports and investment practices.
5. Data and Measurement Challenges: Standardized measures are required to assess the actual effect of ESG and sustainable finance initiatives (IFC, 2021; TERI, 2022)

These shortfalls provide scope for future studies and highlight the significance of sound academic discussion of the idea of significant finance.

3. Research Methodology

3.1. Research Design

This research follows a qualitative and exploratory design, focused on exploring and gaining in-depth insights into the evolving concept of substantial finance and its application towards promoting sustainable development (Creswell &Poth, 2018). Considering that the subject of study is multidisciplinary and involves interlacing finance, sustainability, economics, and ethics, the study employs a descriptive and analytical approach to critically evaluate existing literature, real-world financial instruments, and case-based evidence.

The study is non-experimental and utilizes secondary data analysis, which is suitable for researching trends, frameworks, and applications that have been seen and recorded in existing markets.

3.2. Data Collection Methods

The study utilizes secondary data as its main source, providing a broad, trustworthy foundation of insight. Data has been collected from the following:

- Research Articles and Academic Journals (e.g., Journal of Sustainable Finance & Investment, Harvard Business Review, Nature Sustainability)
- Whitepapers and Industry Reports (e.g., GSIA, World Bank, UN PRI, OECD)
- Corporate ESG Reports of leading companies and financial institutions
- Policy Guidance and Frameworks (e.g., EU Sustainable Finance Action Plan, SEBI BRSR norms, TCFD disclosures)
- Case Studies from authentic sources that present practical examples of significant finance (Tata Power, 2021; SEBI, 2021; UNEP FI, 2020).
- Reputed News and Financial Media (Bloomberg, Financial Times, The Economist, etc.)
- This allows for the study to be based on actual, current, and credible data, taking away all the possibilities of reliance on anecdotal evidence or guesswork.

3.3. Sample Selection

While this study does not collect any primary survey data or conduct interviews, it does utilize a purposeful sampling approach to choose the case studies and financial products for study review (Tata Power, 2021).

The following are the criteria used for selection of cases and products:

- Relevance to significant finance practices (e.g., ESG investing, impact finance)
- Evidence of impact on sustainable development
- Coverage in both developed and developing economies
- Public availability of transparent financial and sustainability reports.

Some case examples include institutions like BlackRock, HDFC Bank, IFC, Tesla, and the Government of Germany's Green Bonds program—selected to represent diversity in region, sector, and scale.

3.4. Analytical Tools and Techniques

With the qualitative research paradigm, the following analytical techniques are utilized:

- Thematic Analysis: Used to identify common patterns, ideas, and frameworks across literature and case studies.
- Comparative Analysis: Used to contrast various sustainable finance approaches across institutions or geographies.
- SWOT Analysis: Utilized in chosen case studies to evaluate strengths, weaknesses, opportunities, and threats in incorporating significant finance practices (Braun & Clarke, 2006).
- Framework Mapping: ESG and SDG alignment maps are employed to provide a visual connection between financial action and sustainability impact.

Although statistical modelling is not employed in this paper, stress is laid on clarity, critical thinking, and logical synthesis of the information presented.

3.5. Ethical Considerations

This research maintains high ethical standards in the use and presentation of data:

- Data Integrity: All sources are accurately referenced, and no data is falsified to suit any narrative.
- Avoidance of Plagiarism: Original analysis is done, and all secondary material is appropriately referenced according to academic citation conventions (American Psychological Association [APA], 2020).
- Objectivity: The research does not advocate for any particular financial institution, ideology, or political agenda.

- Respect for Confidentiality: Only public data is utilized—no confidential or proprietary data sets are accessed or revealed.

In addition, the research is based on the academic honesty, intellectual transparency, and responsible scholarship principles, hence acceptable for publication or institutional review.

4. Understanding Substantial Finance

4.1. Definition and Key Principles

Substantial Finance is not just a buzzword—it's the blueprint of the financial future. It is financial activities extending beyond profit-making and are positively involved in sustainable, inclusive, and ethical development (UNEP FI, 2020; Goyal & Joshi, 2020). Substantial finance is different from conventional finance, which operates mostly in terms of returns, as substantial finance works on the triple-axis of financial performance, environmental stewardship, and social equity (IFC, 2021; Serafeim, 2020).

At its essence, significant finance is driven by a number of guiding principles:

- Sustainability First: Decisions on finance are made considering long-term environmental and social impacts, rather than quarterly earnings.
- Transparency & Accountability: Disclosure of non-financial performance (e.g., carbon footprint, human rights impact) becomes as important as financial reporting (Clark, Feiner, &Viehs, 2015).
- Risk Recalibration: Sees climate change, inequality, and bad governance as material financial risks, and folds them into investment analysis.
- Alignment with Global Goals: Large finance has strong links with the UN Sustainable Development Goals (SDGs), investing capital in initiatives for clean energy, education, health, and climate action.
- In brief, large finance is a value-driven evolution of capital—an evolution where purpose and profit converge.

4.2. Key Instruments

Significant financing uses a set of cutting-edge financial instruments that balance economic returns with social and environmental effects. The three most common are listed below:

- Green Bonds

They are debt securities that raise funds for projects with obvious environmental advantages—such as clean energy, low-carbon transport, or climate-resilient infrastructure (Climate Bonds Initiative [CBI], 2022; SEBI, 2021).

Example: India's Government of India's ₹16,000 crore green bond initiative is dedicated to clean mobility and solar energy.

- ESG Funds

Environmental, Social, and Governance (ESG) funds judge companies on not just financial strength but on how ethically they run their businesses. Institutional and millennial investors Favor these funds (Morningstar, 2021).

Fact: ESG assets are expected to reach more than $50 trillion worldwide by 2025 (Bloomberg Intelligence, 2022).

- Impact Investing

Impact investments are undertaken with the aim of creating quantifiable social and/or environmental impact as well as a financial return. They are commonly employed in industries such as affordable housing, education, and healthcare (GIIN, 2020).

Real World: Acumen Fund and Omidyar Network invest in social startups that target poverty, sanitation, and access to education.

All of these tools are crucial to re-routing capital flows from exploitative to regenerative economic activity.

4.3. Role of Stakeholders

It takes a lot of finance not to be a one-player game. Its success relies on the cooperation of various actors, each contributing a specific role and responsibility.

- Government
  - Develops the policy framework, tax incentives, and regulatory guidelines (e.g., carbon pricing, green finance norms).
  - Issues sovereign green bonds and establishes ESG reporting standards (SEBI, 2021; Ministry of Finance, 2022).
- Corporates
  - Embed ESG in their operations and supply chains (Tata Power, 2021).
  - Publish sustainability reports, set carbon reduction goals, and invest impact into their business models.
- Investors (Retail & Institutional)
  - Rebalance their portfolios into ESG and impact-focused funds.
  - Employ active ownership to nudge companies toward improved governance and sustainability (McKinsey & Company, 2020; World Bank, 2022).

Absent stakeholder alignment, a lot of finance risks being merely window dressing or greenwashing. But synchronized, the impact is revolutionary—economically and morally.

4.4. Comparison with Traditional Finance

Table 1 highlights how substantial finance reshapes the financial DNA of decision-making—from transactional to transformational.

Table 1. Comparison of sustainable finance with traditional finance

Aspect	Traditional Finance	Substantial Finance
Primary Focus	Profit Maximization	Profit + People + Planet (Triple Bottom Line)
Risk Assessment	Market, credit, liquidity risks	Adds climate, social, and governance risks
Investment Horizon	Short- to medium-term	Long-term value creation
Success Metrics	ROI, EPS, Share Price	ROI + ESG Scores + SDG Alignment
Stakeholder View	Shareholder-Centric	Multi-Stakeholder (customers, society, environment)
Regulatory View	Compliance-focused	Proactive transparency and sustainability alignment

Source: EY, 2021; OECD, 2020.

5. Substantial Finance and Sustainable Development

5.1. Link between Finance and Sustainability

In the 21st century, finance isn't merely a matter of making money—it's a matter of making meaning. The linkage between finance and sustainability is irretrievable because the world has pressing issues like climate change, depletion of natural resources, poverty, and pandemics. The large finance takes on the role of a strategic catalyst that puts capital into not only what's profitable but into what's meaningful (World Economic Forum, 2022).

Conceptualize finance as the blood of the global economy—and sustainability its conscience. Without integrating the two, sustainable progress is unattainable.

Critical Crossings:

- Renewable energy investments minimize carbon pollution and green jobs.
- Water infrastructure financing enhances public health and food security.
- Healthcare impact investing increases access and innovation in underserved areas.

Essentially, money becomes a mission, and investment choices become ethical ones.

5.2. UN SDGS and Finance Alignment

The United Nations Sustainable Development Goals (SDGs)—17 worldwide goals to be completed by 2030—are a global call to action. They cover everything from poverty reduction to climate action, education, clean water, and gender equality (Schoenmaker & Schramade, 2019).

So, what about finance? Easy: no SDG can be realized without financial support.

Examples of Finance-SDG Alignment a shown in Table 2.

Table 2. SDG goals and their alignment

SDG Goal	Aligned Financial Action
SDG 7 Affordable Clean Energy	Green bonds to fund solar, wind, and hydro power projects
SDG 4 – Quality Education	Impact investing in ed-tech startups and affordable schooling
SDG 13 – Climate Action	ESG funds favouring low-carbon companies
SDG 6 – Clean Water and Sanitation	Public-private partnerships financing sanitation infrastructure

Source: Author Compilation.

5.3. Policy Support and Regulatory Frameworks

Regulators and governments worldwide are discovering that unless supportive policies exist, sustainable finance can't scale. Policies provide the tracks upon which the train of finance remains on course—towards sustainability.

Top Global Policy Shifts:

European Union (EU):

- Implemented the EU Taxonomy for Sustainable Activities, which identified what is green investment.
- Introduced the Sustainable Finance Disclosure Regulation (SFDR) to promote transparency in ESG investingUN Environment Programme, 2021.

India:

- SEBI has launched BRSR (Business Responsibility and Sustainability Reporting) for the top 1,000 listed companies.

- Issue of sovereign green bonds by the Reserve Bank of India to finance public sector climate initiatives.

United States:

- The SEC has put forward mandatory climate-related disclosures for listed companies.
- Government-backed incentives for ESG-aligned businesses and clean energy tax credits.

Policies create the trust, transparency, and stability that institutional capital needs to flow into sustainable projects.

5.4. International Case Studies

This section examines how various countries are putting massive finance into action on the ground—turning theory into practical change.

European Union – Leading by Law

- The EU is perhaps the world's leading authority in sustainable finance.
- Its Green Deal is set to make Europe the first climate-neutral continent by 2050.
- Large banks are now compelled to balance lending with ESG considerations under green stress testing frameworks.

Outcome: The EU alone released more €300 billion in green bonds during 2023, financing clean transport and renewable energy infrastructure.

India – Green Ambition, Emerging Action

- India has made significant strides by issuing sovereign green bonds of ₹16,000 crore in 2023.
- Banks such as HDFC Bank and SBI are incorporating ESG into their lending and risk models.
- Private equity firms are investing more in renewables, climate tech, and AgriTech startups.

- Example: Acumen India's investment in solar-powered irrigation for rural farmers.

USA – Market-Driven Momentum

- The U.S. sustainable investment market hit $17.1 trillion in 2022, fuelled by increasing investor demand.
- Green bonds are issued by tech giants such as Apple and Google, and they annually publish ESG reports.
- The Biden administration's Inflation Reduction Act provides hundreds of billions in tax credits for green infrastructure, EVs, and clean energy.
- Highlight: BlackRock's ESG ETFs and Vanguard's climate fund are revolutionizing American retail investment trends.

Major funding is not a luxury—a necessity in the current world scenario. Finance is a powerful tool for sustainable transformation when public policy, private money, and stakeholder behavior unite. It's through embracing SDGs, green financial instruments, or incorporating ESG in national policy that the world is gradually—but irresistibly—paying its way to a brighter future.

6. Case Study

6.1. Case: Tata Power's Green Bonds – Financing a Greener Future

Tata Power, India's largest integrated power company, is a standout in linking financial innovation with sustainability. It broke news in 2017 by issuing $320 million worth of Green Bonds on behalf of its subsidiary, Tata Power Renewable Energy Ltd. (TPREL), a major milestone in India's sustainable finance journey.

These bonds were not only listed globally (on the Singapore Stock Exchange) but also Climate Bonds Standard certified, drawing international investors seeking to finance climate-resilient infrastructure in emerging economies such as India.

This is a benchmark in the transition from conventional project financing towards purpose-driven capital allocation.

6.2. Application of Sustainable Finance Principles

Tata Power's Green Bond program is a classic example of how sound finance practices get infused into actual business strategy. Here's how:

- Use of Proceeds: The proceeds from the bond were specifically earmarked for renewable energy initiatives—namely solar and wind energy assets in India.
- Transparency & Accountability: Tata Power pledged yearly reporting on fund use and environmental disclosures in line with global green bond principles.
- Stakeholder Engagement: The issue drew institutional investors with ESG mandates, enhancing the company's international reputation and stakeholder confidence.
- Regulatory Compliance: The issue was in line with both India's green finance guidelines and international standards (ICMA Green Bond Principles).

This use case illustrates how profit and purpose can co-exist in the Indian financial system.

6.3. Measurable Impact

The results of Tata Power's green finance initiative have been tangible and transformative:

Environmental Impact

- Added over 600 MW of renewable capacity spread across states such as Maharashtra, Gujarat, and Karnataka.
- Led to an estimated 900,000 tonnes of CO_2 emissions avoided every year, which is equivalent to removing 200,000 cars from the road.

Financial Impact

- See significant foreign direct investment (FDI) from ESG-oriented funds.

- Improved Tata Power's credit rating and lowered cost of capital for future clean energy projects.

Social Impact

- Supported the creation of more than 3,000 green jobs during the maintenance and construction process.
- Enhanced energy access to remote rural areas through off-grid solar solutions underpinned by the same fund pool.

This case demonstrates how massive finance doesn't merely invest in sustainability—it provides it.

6.4. Lessons Learned

This case highlights the following key learnings for financial institutions, corporates, and policymakers:

1. Vision + Financial Innovation = Scalable Impact

Tata Power's green bond template demonstrates how embedding sustainability within the business core can unleash new capital sources, particularly from international investors who have ESG mandates (European Commission, 2021).

2. Transparency Creates Trust

Annual reporting, third-party assurance, and consistency with international standards were important in attaining investor trust.

3. Large Finance Is Replicable in Emerging Markets

India, which is normally regarded as a risk-taker market, was able to effectively draw in global green finance. This shatters the myth that ESG finance is feasible only in the developed world (SEC, 2022).

4. Policy Support Is Key

This was achieved through facilitative frameworks by SEBI and RBI, reflecting the significance of regulatory alignment.

Conclusion of Case Study

Tata Power's Green Bond odyssey is not merely a corporate finance tale—it's a shining example of how Indian businesses can "drive the global sustainable finance revolution" from the front. It shows that "with purposeful strategy, transparent metrics, and intelligent financing, sustainability is not only good ethics—it's good business."

Analysis and Discussion

The Tata Power Green Bond case study offers a rich lens through which we can examine the evolving landscape of substantial finance in India. This section dives deeper into the broader implications, industry-wide opportunities, and systemic challenges—while highlighting how technology is transforming sustainable finance from a concept into a reality. Wall Street Journal (WSJ), 2021

Key Trends from the Case Study

Table 3. Trends shaping sustainable finance

Trend	Description	Impact
Rise of ESG Investing	Global investors are allocating more capital to companies with strong ESG profiles.	Access to cheaper, long-term capital
Demand for Transparency	Stakeholders expect detailed ESG disclosures and impact reporting.	Companies improve governance & accountability
Clean Energy Push	Preference for renewable over conventional power projects.	Accelerates India's green energy goals
International Alignment	Adoption of global frameworks like ICMA Green Bond Principles.	Makes Indian issuances attractive to global capital

Source: Author Compilation.

The case study reveals several critical trends shaping substantial finance in India and globally in Table 3.

In essence, substantial finance is no longer niche—it's becoming mainstream.

Opportunities in the Sector

India is at the intersection of the climate crisis and economic development, and thus a rich terrain for sustainable finance. Some of the major opportunities are:

1. Renewable Energy Growth

India aims for 500 GW of renewable capacity by 2030.

Significant finance (such as green bonds) can unlock the ~$200B required to achieve this target.

2. Sustainable Agriculture

Finance can facilitate climate-resilient agriculture, organic farming, and Agri-tech startups Ministry of Finance, 2023.

Tools: Green microfinance, carbon credits for farmers.

3. Affordable Housing & Green Infrastructure

Green buildings and smart cities require rapid urbanization.

These can be financed by ESG-linked loans with improved terms.

Table 4. Opportunity landscape table

Sector	Sustainable Finance Tool	Potential Impact
Renewable Energy	Green Bonds, Solar Loans	Clean power, job creation
Agriculture	ESG-linked microfinance, Agri-ETFs	Climate adaptation, food security
Urban Infrastructure	Green REITs, Sustainability Loans	Resilient cities, low-carbon construction
MSME Financing	Social Impact Funds, Green Credit	Inclusive growth, local employment

Source: Author Compilation.

4. Financial Inclusion

FinTech's and MSMEs are impact invested by impact investing in these. This brings underbanked segments into the financial fold as shown in Table 4.

Barriers to Adoption

In spite of momentum, there are various barriers to the large-scale adoption of significant finance in India:

1. Lack of Awareness & Literacy

Numerous companies, particularly MSMEs, are not aware of ESG finance structures or opportunities.

2. Limited Green Financial Instruments

India has developed green bonds, but other instruments such as sustainability-linked loans, ESG derivatives, or carbon credits remain underdeveloped.

3. Regulatory Uncertainty

Unclear or inconsistent taxonomy and disclosure standards induce investor uncertainty.

4. Greenwashing Risks

Misleading presentation of sustainability practices by companies can attract money at the expense of trust.

Role of Technology and Innovation

Technology is a catalyst that enhances the effectiveness, transparency, and accessibility of substantial finance (refer Table 5).

Table 5. Key innovations driving sustainable finance

Tech	Application in Sustainable Finance
AI & ML	ESG risk analysis, fraud detection (greenwashing), real-time reporting
Blockchain	Transparent tracking of green bond proceeds and carbon credit exchanges
Cloud Platforms	Enable ESG data collection and reporting across supply chains
Big Data & IoT	Environmental impact tracking (e.g., energy, water, emissions)
Carbon Market Tech	Platforms for carbon credit trading and verification

Source: Author Compilation.

Real example:

Tata Power and other Indian utilities are deploying smart metering and IoT sensors to monitor the performance and emissions reduction of renewable projects—providing real-time data to investors.

Conclusion

The future of finance is not just about returns—it's about responsibility. The Tata Power case and surrounding ecosystem trends show that India has the ambition and ability to lead in substantial finance. However, success will depend on bridging awareness gaps, strengthening regulatory clarity, innovating financial tools, and leveraging technology.

If done right, substantial finance won't just fuel the economy—it will heal the planet.

Summary

By way of analysis of substantial finance as a force of transformation, the following major insights have emerged:

1. Substantial Finance is Taking Off

The convergence of financial instruments with sustainability objectives is now no longer optional but is increasingly going mainstream, particularly in large corporations and institutional investors.

2. India is a fertile ground for Sustainable Investments

With climate ambitions, government-supported programs, and growing awareness of ESG, India offers enormous opportunities in renewable energy, agriculture, green infrastructure, and inclusive finance.

3. Real-World Applications Drive Credibility

Successful case studies such as Tata Power's Green Bonds prove that significant finance can provide tangible environmental, social, and financial returns when deployed strategically.

4. Transparency, Governance, and Innovation are Critical

Success of major finance depends largely on strong ESG reporting, regulatory convergence, and using technology (such as AI, blockchain, and big data) to drive impact and accountability.

Surprising Insights

Throughout the course of this study, a few surprising but thought-provoking observations emerged:

1. Green Finance Is Pulling International Capital Quicker Than Anticipated

Against the perception that India is a risky market for ESG investment, international investors are becoming increasingly attracted to India's green efforts, owing to high-impact potential and government support.

2. ESG Ratings Are Not Standardized

Various ESG rating agencies apply different metrics, which creates inconsistencies and possible confusion for investors and companies alike.

3. Small Businesses Are Still Left Behind

MSMEs are missing out on a lot of finance potential with low ESG literacy, and limited presence of sustainable finance products, and no regulatory impetus for disclosure.

4. Tech Is Outpacing Policy

Innovations such as blockchain and carbon trading platforms are evolving fast, but regulatory systems are behind, creating uncertainty in adoption.

The results corroborate that large finance is not just a trend—it's a paradigm change in how we think about capital, accountability, and growth. Though challenges persist, the alignment of global trends, technological innovation, and environmental imperative makes this an opportune time for India to be at the forefront of sustainable finance innovation.

Recommendations

Building upon the findings and analysis, this chapter proposes strategic recommendations to bridge existing gaps and accelerate the adoption of substantial finance in India and beyond. The suggestions are categorized into three domains—policy-level interventions, corporate practices, and academic/research directions.

Policy Recommendations

For sustainable finance to thrive, a robust and supportive policy environment is essential. The following recommendations are proposed for regulators and public institutions:

1. Enhance ESG Disclosure Norms
   - Require uniform ESG reporting frameworks from listed as well as large unlisted companies.
   - Align with international standards such as TCFD (Task Force on Climate-related Financial Disclosures) and GRI (Global Reporting Initiative).
2. Create Green Taxonomy
   - Implement a clear classification system of green activities to remove confusion and greenwashing.
   - Make sure that this taxonomy is aligned with global best practices but customized for Indian developmental requirements.

3. Incentivize Sustainable Investment
   - Provide tax incentives or interest subsidies on social impact projects, renewable infrastructure, and green bonds.
   - Offer risk-sharing mechanisms or partial guarantees of credit to de-risk private investment in ESG industries.
4. Form a Central Sustainability Finance Task Force
   - Form a cross-functional task force comprising members of RBI, SEBI, Ministry of Finance, and industry specialists to monitor and coordinate sustainable finance efforts.

Recommendations for The Corporate Sector

Companies, particularly large corporate and financial institutions, are prime facilitators of significant finance. The practices below are encouraged:

1. Embed ESG into Core Strategy

Address ESG not as an item of compliance but as a strategic growth pillar, part of business planning, risk management, and performance review.

2. Enhance ESG Communication

Increase transparency through issuing comprehensive sustainability reports, case studies, and measurable impact metrics to create investor and public confidence.

3. Invest in Capacity Building

Educate internal staff, board members, and important stakeholders on principles of sustainable finance, tools of impact measurement, and international ESG practices.

4. Support Green Supply Chains

Promote vendors and suppliers toward green approaches through technical assistance, financial incentives, and ESG-connected procurement policies.

5. Harness Financial Innovation

Investigate and issue green bonds, sustainability-linked loans, and ESG mutual funds to access increasing investor demand and establish ESG credentials.

Future Research Directions

Significant finance is a new and developing discipline. Ongoing academic and industry research can reinforce its foundations and reveal new insights:

1. ESG Ratings and Standardization

Research ESG rating methodological differences and limitations, and recommend models of harmonization and reliability.

2. The Role of Significant Finance for MSMEs

Discuss ways by which green finance tools can become affordable and helpful for micro, small, and medium-sized enterprises (MSMEs).

3. Green Finance and Technology

Research the use of AI, blockchain, and fintech in sustainable finance—particularly for monitoring carbon credits, ESG compliance, and green bond certification.

4. Investor Behaviorand ESG Perception

Carry out behavioural finance research to reveal how individual and institutional investors see ESG considerations in making investment decisions.

5. Post-Investment Impact Assessment

Create models to monitor long-term financial and social returns of ESG-connected investments, particularly in emerging economies.

Successful execution of these suggestions can hasten the shift toward a sustainable financial system, generating value not only for investors and firms, but for society and the planet as well. As the global world transitions to a greener economy, India can emerge as a global frontrunner in the large finance movement—with appropriate policies, innovation, and concerted action.

References

Amel-Zadeh, A., & Serafeim, G. (2018). Why and how investors use ESG information: Evidence from a global survey. *Financial Analysts Journal,* 74 (3), 87–103. https://doi.org/10.2469/faj.v74.n3.2.

Bhatia, A., & Wadhwani, A. (2022). Role of ESG disclosures in investment decisions: An Indian perspective. *Journal of Sustainable Finance & Investment*, 12 (1), 45–58.

BlackRock. (2020). *Sustainability as BlackRock's New Standard for Investing.* https://www.blackrock.com.

Bocken, N. M. P., Short, S. W., Rana, P., & Evans, S. (2014). A literature and practice review to develop sustainable business model archetypes. *Journal of Cleaner Production*, 65, 42–56. https://doi.org/10.1016/j.jclepro.2013.11.039.

CBI (Climate Bonds Initiative). (2022). *Green Bonds Market Summary – 2021.* https://www.climatebonds.net.

CDP India. (2021). *Environmental Disclosure and Performance Insights Report*. https://www.cdp.net/en.

CFA Institute. (2022). *Guidance on Integrating ESG Factors Throughout the Investment* Process. https://www.cfainstitute.org.

Clark, G. L., Feiner, A., & Viehs, M. (2015). *From the stockholder to the stakeholder: How sustainability can drive financial outperformance.* University of Oxford, Smith School of Enterprise and the Environment. https://ssrn.com/abstract=2508281.

Deloitte. (2021). *Sustainable Finance: Creating Value for the Future.* https://www2.deloitte.com.

EY India. (2021). *ESG and sustainable finance: The future of financial services*. Ernst & Young. https://www.ey.com/en_in/esg.

G20 Sustainable Finance Working Group. (2021). *Sustainable Finance Roadmap.* https://g20sfwg.org/.

Global Reporting Initiative (GRI). (2022). *GRI Standards.* https://www.globalreporting.org.

Government of India. (2023). *India's Long-Term Low Emission Development Strategy* (LT-LEDS). Ministry of Environment, Forest and Climate Change.

Goyal, M., & Joshi, R. (2020). Role of sustainable finance in achieving SDGs: A study in Indian context. *International Journal of Management*, 11 (5), 1–10.

Impact Investors Council (India). (2021). *The India Impact Investing Story*. https://iiic.in/.

International Finance Corporation (IFC). (2021). *Green Bonds: Country Experiences, Barriers and Options*. World Bank Group. https://www.ifc.org/.

KPMG. (2020). *The time has come: The KPMG Survey of Sustainability Reporting 2020*. https://home.kpmg/xx/en/home/insights/2020/11/the-time-has-come-survey-of-sustainability-reporting.html.

Kumar, P., & Jha, S. (2022). ESG investment in India: Opportunities and challenges. *Asian Journal of Finance & Accounting*, 14 (2), 22–35.

McKinsey & Company. (2020). *Valuing ESG: A Global Perspective*. https://www.mckinsey.com.

Ministry of Finance (India). (2022). *National Monetisation Pipeline (NMP) and Green Infrastructure Development*. https://www.finmin.nic.in.

Morningstar. (2021). *How ESG Funds Performed During COVID-19*. https://www.morningstar.in.

MSCI. (2022). *ESG Ratings Methodology*. https://www.msci.com/our-solutions/esg-investing.

Narayan, S. (2021). ESG investments: Unlocking the trillion-dollar opportunity in India. *Mint*. https://www.livemint.com.

OECD. (2020). *Developing Sustainable Finance Definitions and Taxonomies*. OECD Publishing. https://www.oecd.org/environment/.

RBI (Reserve Bank of India). (2022). *Report of the Sustainable Finance Group*. https://rbi.org.in.

S&P Global. (2022). *The ESG Advantage: How Sustainability Drives Financial Performance*. https://www.spglobal.com.

Sachs, J. D., Schmidt-Traub, G., Kroll, C., Lafortune, G., & Fuller, G. (2021). *Sustainable Development Report 2021*. Cambridge University Press.

SEBI. (2021). *Business Responsibility and Sustainability Reporting (BRSR) Framework*. Securities and Exchange Board of India. https://www.sebi.gov.in.

Serafeim, G. (2020). Social-impact efforts that create real value. *Harvard Business Review*, 98 (5), 38–48.

Shiller, R. J. (2019). *Narrative Economics: How Stories Go Viral and Drive Major Economic Events*. Princeton University Press.

Statista. (2023). *ESG investment trends in India and Asia-Pacific*. https://www.statista.com.

Tata Power. (2021). *Green Bond Issuance and Sustainability Report*. https://www.tatapower.com.

TCFD. (2021). *Recommendations of the Task Force on Climate-related Financial Disclosures*. https://www.fsb-tcfd.org.

Tesla Inc. (2022). *Impact Report*. https://www.tesla.com/ns_videos/2022-tesla-impact-report.pdf.

The Energy and Resources Institute (TERI). (2022). *India's Green Finance Landscape*. https://www.teriin.org.

UNDP. (2022). *Financing the 2030 Agenda for Sustainable Development*. https://www.undp.org.

UNEP FI. (2020). Principles for Responsible Banking Progress Report. *United Nations Environment Programme Finance Initiative*. https://www.unepfi.org.

United Nations. (2015). *Transforming Our World: The 2030 Agenda for Sustainable Development.* https://sdgs.un.org.

World Bank. (2021). *Mobilizing Private Finance for Development.* https://www.worldbank.org.

World Economic Forum. (2022). *Global Risks Report 2022*. https://www.weforum.org.

Chapter 2

The Changing Role of Banks in the Financial System: Social Versus Conventional Banks and the Role of Banks in Framing the Public Policy of the Nation

Subhrodipto Basu Choudhury[1,*]
and Soma Garani[2,†]
[1]Department of Business Analytics, ISMS Sankalp Business School, Pune, Maharashtra, India
[2]Department of Fish Nutrition, WBUAFS, Kolkata, West Bengal, India

Abstract

The financial system is the backbone that regulates the transformation of economic policy across geography. Monetary and fiscal policies are usually targeted to regulate the economy of a country. Various factors are analysed from the background of economics. Macro-economic factors GDP, gender contribution, FDI (foreign direct investment), etc. are considered during the analysis. It needs to be studied intermittently so that preventive and appropriate measures can be taken to regulate the supply of money with the demand of individuals.
In this chapter, different types of banks are studied in terms of role, responsibility, and implementation of monetary policy as prescribed by the finance ministry of any nation. In the later part, the The role of technology in the banking system will also be deeply focused on to get a clear view of the banking system integrated with modern-day technology.

---

* Corresponding Author's Email: subhrodiptobasuchoudhury@gmail.com
† Corresponding Author's Email: somaofficial@gmail.com

In: Environmental, Social, and Governance (ESG) ...
Editor: Veena Grover
ISBN: 979-8-90134-138-4

Keywords: public policy, banking, economy, financial system

1. Introduction

The financial system is the backbone of an economy. Infrastructural development of any nation depends on its economic and financial health. As per UNO (United Nation Organisation) there are three pillars to study the economy of any nation. They are health, education and employment. To obtain these, the government of a nation formulates different strategies to implement public policy for the well-being of its citizen.

To study the overall economic health of a nation, research generally uses or creates different parameters of econometric indices like GDP, HDI (Human Development Index), CPI (Consumer Price Index), WPI (Wholesale Price Index), GDP deflator, and so on. These parameters assist them to identify the following:

a) Economic health
b) Wealth distribution trend
c) Health condition of its citizens
d) Health on fiscal policy
e) International trade relations
f) Employment opportunities
g) Banking role in finance

Banking is a process through which people can keep their monetary wealth in safe custody to ensure security and can withdraw it as and when required. People can deposit their money in different processes as provided to them prescribed by the financial system. There are mainly current account (CA) and savings accounts (SA). CA are generally used for business purposes whereas SA are used for individual purposes. Apart from this, banks provide other facilities to its customers listed below:

a) Cheque facility
b) Demand draft facility
c) ATM
d) Online banking system
e) Locker facility

In India, the banking system is governed and controlled by the RBI (Reserve Bank of India) estd. in 1934. RBI regulates different policies and parameters as per recommendation from the Ministry of Finance.

1.1. Public Policy

A key framework for resolving social problems and managing political choices is public policy. It includes a variety of measures and directives developed by public authorities to accomplish social objectives, impacting international relations, justice, and legislation. The following sections elaborate on the key aspects of public policy.

1.2. Components

Public policy is defined as a public action plan aimed at solving social problems (Cao, 2024).

Key components include public policy actors, resources, and models, which collectively shape the decision- making process (BEBEL, 2024).

2. Role in Legal and International Contexts

Public policy significantly impacts legal operations, guiding the formulation and implementation of laws while maintaining the authority of the legal system (Cao, 2024).

In international relations, public policy provides frameworks for cooperation and conflict resolution, addressing the complexities of globalization (Xu, 2024).

3. Challenges

Despite its benefits, public policy can sometimes undermine legal authority or distort legal functions, necessitating a careful balance (Cao, 2024).

Additionally, public policy faces challenges in effectively managing international conflicts due to varying national interests and cultural differences (Xu, 2024).

While public policy is essential for governance and societal progress, its potential to conflict with legal frameworks and its challenges in international contexts highlight the need for careful consideration in its formulation and implementation.

4. Banking Role to Measure Efficiency Public Policy

The banking sector plays a vital role in measuring the efficiency of public policy, particularly through the lens of policy efficiency and operational efficiency. In India, Public sector banks (PSBs), for instance, have been identified as key vehicles for implementing government policies, demonstrating higher policy efficiency compared to private sector banks (PVBs) (Kundu & Banerjee, 2021). This multifaceted role of banks can be analyzed through various efficiency metrics, which highlight their contributions to financial inclusion and economic development.

Policy Efficiency

- PSBs are essential for executing government initiatives like the Pradhan Mantri Jan Dhan Yojana (PMJDY) and Pradhan Mantri Mudra Yojana (PMMY), achieving a technical efficiency score ranging from 62.6% to 70.6%.
- The ability of PSBs to align with government policies underscores their importance beyond mere financial metrics.

Operational Efficiency

- While PVBs exhibit superior operational efficiency, PSBs have shown improvements in both operational and policy effectiveness over time (Kundu & Banerjee, 2021).
- The analysis of efficiency using Data Envelopment Analysis (DEA) reveals that older and larger PSBs tend to perform better in both paradigms (Kundu & Banerjee, 2021).

Implications for Policy Makers

- The findings suggest that focusing solely on operational efficiency may overlook the significant role of PSBs in social and policy contexts, indicating a need for reforms to enhance their effectiveness (Kundu & Banerjee, 2021).

Conversely, while PSBs are vital for policy implementation, their operational challenges in a competitive environment raise concerns about their long-term sustainability and efficiency, suggesting a potential requirement for structural improvements to maintain their effectiveness in public policy execution.

5. Macro-Economic Factors for Analyzing Economic Growth

Economic development is sensative to several macroeconomic factors that shape the overall economic environment. Key elements include inflation rates, government policies, foreign direct investment, and the entrepreneurial landscape. Understanding these factors is crucial for formulating effective economic strategies. The following sections outline the primary macroeconomic factors that contribute to economic growth.

Inflation and Economic Stability

- Low to moderate inflation is essential for fostering economic growth, as it encourages investment and consumer spending (Cervelló-Royo et al., 2024).
- High inflation can deter investment and create uncertainty, negatively impacting economic performance (Arifi, 2022).

Government Policies and Economic Freedom

- Government revenue and expenditure significantly influence economic growth; higher revenue can lead to increased public investment, while excessive expenditure may hinder growth (VINTILĂ, 2024).

- Economic freedom, including low tax burdens and regulatory frameworks, promotes entrepreneurship and innovation, which are vital for growth (Cervelló-Royo et al., 2024).

Foreign Direct Investment (FDI)

- FDI is an important player in economic growth, providing capital, technology, and expertise, which can enhance productivity and create jobs (Arifi, 2022).
- Trade openness, measured by the sum of exports and imports, also correlates positively with economic growth, facilitating market access and competition (VINTILĂ, 2024).

While these macroeconomic factors are generally seen as drivers of economic growth, it is important to consider that their effects can vary based on the specific economic context and the interplay between different variables. For instance, in some cases, high government expenditure may be necessary to stimulate growth in a recessionary environment, highlighting the complexity of macroeconomic dynamics.

6. International Trade Relations

International trade relations encompass the complex interactions between countries regarding the exchange of goods, services, and capital. These relations are influenced by various factors, including economic policies, political stability, and international agreements. The dynamics of international trade are critical for economic development, as they facilitate technological advancements and enhance competitiveness among nations. Below are key aspects of international trade relations.

Economic Transactions

- International trade is characterized by interstate economic transactions, which are essential for the global economy (Han, 2024).
- Trade allows countries to specialize, increasing productivity and overall production volume (Гусейнова et al., 2023).

Influence of Political Relations

- The relationship between international relations and trade is interdependent; political stability and the enforcement of laws significantly impact trade flows (Chen, 2022).
- Frictions can arise from geopolitical tensions, affecting trade agreements and economic cooperation (Chen, 2022).

Legal Framework

- International economic relations are governed by a complex legal framework that has evolved over time, influencing currency relations and trade laws (Muzyka-Stefanchuk & Yakymchuk, 2023).
- The development of international economic law has been crucial in regulating trade practices and ensuring fair competition among nations (Muzyka-Stefanchuk & Yakymchuk, 2023).

While international trade relations are often viewed as beneficial for economic growth, they can also lead to disparities and conflicts among nations, highlighting the need for balanced and fair-trade practices.

7. Tax Redemption and Fixation as per Demand and Supply

The economic implications of tax redemption, particularly through the implementation of Goods and Services Tax (GST), significantly influence the demand and supply of goods and services. By streamlining the tax structure, GST aims to eliminate cascading taxes, thereby enhancing productivity and economic growth. This transition affects both consumers and producers, leading to various outcomes in the market.

Impact on Demand

- Consumer Prices: GST is expected to lower prices due to the elimination of multiple indirect taxes, making goods and services more affordable (Jangra, 2017).
- Consumption Patterns: The uniform tax rate can shift consumer preferences towards goods with lower tax burdens, altering overall demand structures (Wen, 2006).

Impact on Supply

- Cost Reduction for Producers: By removing cascading taxes, GST reduces material costs for producers, potentially increasing supply (Kavitha, 2023).
- Investment Incentives: A simplified tax system encourages investment in production, as businesses face fewer tax-related uncertainties (Jangra, 2017).

While the GST framework aims to create a more efficient economic environment, it may also impose a burden on certain sectors, particularly small retailers who might struggle with compliance costs. This duality highlights the complexity of tax reforms and their varied impacts on different market participants.

8. Balance of Credit

The balance of credit in a country's economy is influenced by several key factors, including government debt levels, financial inclusion, regulatory frameworks, and the interplay between banks and governments. Understanding these factors allows policymakers to implement strategies that promote economic stability.

Key Factors Influencing Credit Balance

- Government Debt: High levels of public and private debt can create vulnerabilities, amplifying economic shocks and increasing recession risks (Sutherland et al., 2012).
- Regulatory Frameworks: Robust regulatory systems and transparency are essential for maintaining market stability and managing risks effectively (Zhao, 2024).
- Bank-Government Interaction: The relationship between banks and governments is crucial; sovereign creditworthiness underpins financial stability and asset pricing (Caruana & Avdjiev, 2012).

9. Policy Implications

Policymakers can utilize this information to:

- Implement micro-prudential regulations to manage debt levels.
- Foster financial inclusion through improved information management systems.
- Build fiscal and capital buffers during economic upturns to mitigate downturn impacts (Caruana & Avdjiev, 2012).

Conversely, excessive focus on debt reduction may hinder necessary investments in growth and innovation, potentially stalling economic progress. Balancing these priorities is essential for sustainable economic health.

10. Infrastructural Investment

Infrastructural investment in developing economies is driven by a combination of economic, social, and political factors. Understanding these drivers is crucial for maximizing the benefits of such investments and ensuring sustainable development. The following sections outline the key drivers identified in the literature.

Economic Growth and Development

- Transport Infrastructure: Investments in transport infrastructure significantly stimulate economic development by enhancing the movement of goods and people, which is essential for trade and economic activities (Kadyraliev et al., 2022).
- Government Expenditure: Increased government infrastructure spending is critical for fostering investment and economic growth, particularly in emerging markets like Nigeria (Azolibe et al., 2020).

Policy and Planning Considerations

- Efficiency and Accessibility: Effective infrastructure planning must prioritize the efficiency of expenditure and accessibility, ensuring that investments yield maximum returns and improve quality of life (Glaser, 2018).

- Public-Private Partnerships: In low-income developing countries, infrastructure is primarily funded through public sector initiatives, with private participation often facilitated via Public-Private Partnerships (PPPs) (Gurara et al., 2018).

Social and Environmental Factors

- Sustainability and Resilience: Infrastructure projects must consider local environmental attributes and aim for sustainability to avoid negative impacts on communities and ecosystems (Glaser, 2018).
- Indirect Benefits: Investments should also focus on maximizing indirect benefits, such as enhancing human capital and productivity, which are crucial for long-term development (Glaser, 2018).

While these drivers highlight the importance of strategic investment in infrastructure, it is also essential to recognize the challenges posed by poor policy decisions and the potential negative impacts on communities, which can undermine the intended benefits of such investments.

11. Role of Banking System in Finance

The banking system plays a vital part in the financial landscape, acting as a facilitator of economic growth and development. By assembling savings and sanctioned loans, banks contribute significantly to capital allocation, investment financing, and overall economic stability. This multifaceted role is evident across various contexts, including regional economies and specific sectors like green finance.

Capital Mobilization and Investment

- Banks aggregate deposits from households and businesses, creating a pool of capital for lending.
- They provide essential financing for investments in industries and agriculture, which are vital for national economic growth (Khairullah & Rosita, 2022).
- The banking sector's ability to channel funds into productive sectors enhances economic performance and stability.

Regional Economic Development

- In regional markets, banks facilitate financial transactions and allocate capital, supporting local businesses and infrastructure (Kosmurzaevich, 2024).
- They play an essential part in fostering economic resilience and inclusive prosperity within specific geographic areas (Kosmurzaevich, 2024).

Green Finance Initiative

- Banks are increasingly involved in promoting green finance, which supports environmentally friendly projects and infrastructure development (Sarkar & Latta, 2022).
- This shift towards sustainable banking practices is essential for achieving long-term economic growth without compromising environmental goals (Sarkar & Latta, 2022).

Although the banking system is essential to economic growth, it faces obstacles such as inadequate infrastructure and management problems, especially in emerging nations. These elements may make banking projects less successful in fostering long-term, steady growth.

12. Role of Banking System in Any Economy

The banking system plays a crucial role in the economic development of any country by facilitating financial transactions, mobilizing savings, and providing essential capital for investments. It acts as a bridge between investors and debtors, thereby fostering wealth creation and economic growth. The following sections outline the key functions and impressions of the banking system on the economy.

Financial Intermediation

- Banks collect deposits from households and businesses, which are then transformed into loans for investments, stimulating economic activity.

- They make it easier to allocate resources, guaranteeing that money is used for worthwhile endeavours, which is essential for economic growth (Hasan, 2024).

Economic Stability and Growth

- The banking system contributes to economic stability by managing liquidity and providing a safety net during financial crises (Shukla, 2024).
- In developing economies, banks play a more pronounced role in growth compared to alternative financial markets, which are less developed.

Regional Development

- Banks support local economies by financing infrastructure projects and small businesses, thus promoting regional economic development and resilience (Kosmurzaevich, 2024).
- They enhance cash flow and facilitate trade, which is particularly important in emerging markets like India (Singh et al., 2022).

Conversely, while the banking system is essential for economic growth, its effectiveness can be hindered by regulatory challenges and technological disruptions, which may affect its ability to acclimate to moving market dynamics (Shukla, 2024).

13. Benefits of Economics by Banking Sector

The banking sector has a major contribution in economic development by facilitating investment, redistributing capital, and enhancing financial stability. It serves as a conduit for savings and investments, which are essential for fostering economic growth. The following sections outline the key benefits of the banking sector in this context.

Financial Resource Allocation

- Banks mobilize savings from households and businesses, providing necessary capital for investments.

- They offer various deposit products, confirming a steady method of funds for lending, which is vital for economic activities.

Economic Growth Stimulation

- A strong banking sector correlates positively with long-term economic growth, particularly in developing countries (Saqib, 2016).
- The banking system's ability to channel funds to productive uses enhances national income and employment opportunities (Işil & Erik, 2017).

Support for Structural Development

- The banking sector aids in the structural transformation of economies by directing funds to sectors that yield the highest economic value (Işil & Erik, 2017).
- Even though it has difficulties, the banking sector is crucial to promoting overall economic development in places like South Sudan (AKUIEN, 2023).

Conversely, while the banking sector is pivotal for economic growth, its effectiveness can be hindered by political instability and inadequate regulatory frameworks, which may limit its potential impact on development.

14. Challenges to Determining the Economic Efficiency of the Banking Sector

The banking sector faces numerous challenges that can delay its efficiency. These challenges stem from both internal factors, such as governance and risk management, and external pressures, including competition and global economic trends. Understanding these challenges is essential for enhancing the sector's contribution to economic stability and growth.

Internal Challenges

- Non-Performing Loans (NPLs): High levels of NPLs significantly impact banks' profitability and capital adequacy, as seen in the Indian banking sector, where 7.5% was the gross NPA ratio in March 2021 (Santhosh, 2023).

- Governance Issues: Poor leadership and governance have historically led to financial crises, as noted in the Kenyan banking industry (Muriithi & Louw, 2017).
- Economic Capital Calculation: The lack of agreement on how to compute capital poses challenges for risk management and regulatory compliance (Lopez, 2010).

- External Challenges

- Competition from Fintech: The rise of fintech companies and digital payment platforms has intensified competition, forcing traditional banks to adapt rapidly (Santhosh, 2023).
- Global Economic Trends: Uncertain global financial conditions can lead to instability, affecting banks' operations and economic contributions (Muriithi & Louw, 2017).

Despite these challenges, some argue that the banking sector can adapt and innovate to overcome obstacles, potentially leading to a more resilient economic framework. However, the ongoing issues highlight the need for continuous reform and strategic planning to ensure long-term sustainability.

Conclusion

A Nation is built up with efficient and effective utilisation of its resources to address public issues and provide a better life of its citizens. It is obvious that not all problems are not addressed properly, but the aim is usually to resolve most problems. It is true that if citizens live their lives happily, they can contribute with utmost efficiency to the development of any nation. Banks are crucial in providing custody or security for their financial assets. Additionally, it regulates the economy's money flow in accordance with the rules set forth by federal banks such as the Reserve Bank of India (RBI). In addition, banks participate in the management of foreign exchange reserves and regulate various rates, such as the statutory liquidity ratio (SLR), the repo rate, and the reverse repo rate. Therefore, banks can be considered the foundation of any economy, independent of the contributions made by its population.

References

Akuien, A. D. (2023). The importance of Banking sector in the growth of Nation economy: A case study of Stanbic bank in South Sudan. *International Journal of Science and Business*, 28 (1), 1-20.

Amritha, N. P. (2018). Financial Innovations in Indian Banking Industry: An Evaluation of Innovativeness and Financial Performance of Selected Banks (Doctoral dissertation, Department of Commerce and Management Studies, University of Calicut, 2018.).

Arifi, E. A. (2022). Evaluating macroeconomic factors and their influence on economic growth: empirical evidence from Western Balkan economies. *Journal of Liberty and International Affairs*, 8 (2), 21-34.

Azolibe, C. B., Okonkwo, J. J., & Adigwe, P. K. (2020). Government infrastructure expenditure and investment drive in an emerging market economy: Evidence from Nigeria. *Emerging Economy Studies*, 6 (1), 61-85.

Caruana, J., & Avdjiev, S. (2012). Sovereign creditworthiness and financial stability: an international perspective. *Banque de France Financial Stability Review*, 16 (April), 71-85.

Cervelló-Royo, R., Devece, C., & Lull, J. J. (2024). Analysis of economic growth through the context conditions that allow entrepreneurship. *Review of Managerial Science*, 1-23.

Chen, Z. *Political Risks and Countermeasures of Chinese Enterprises' Investment in European Trade.*

Glaser, B. S., Kennedy, S., & Mitchell, D. (2018). *The new southbound policy: Deepening Taiwan's regional integration.* Rowman & Littlefield.

Gurara, D., Klyuev, V., Mwase, N., & Presbitero, A. F. (2018). Trends and challenges in infrastructure investment in developing countries. *International Development Policy| Revue internationale de politique de développement*, (10.1).

Han, X., Lukoianove, T., Zhao, S., & Liu, X. (2024). International relations in international business research: A review and research agenda. *Journal of Business Research*, 174, 114536.

Hasan, M. M. (2024). The Significance of a Financial System in the Economic Advancement of a Country. *Saudi J Econ Fin*, 8 (10), 324-331.

Işıl, G., & Erik, E. (2017). Analysis of the Effect of Developments in Banking Sector on the Economic Development: The Case of Turkey. In *New Challenges in Banking and Finance: 2nd International Conference on Banking and Finance Perspectives* (pp. 153-170). Springer International Publishing.

Jangra, A. (2017). Impact of goods & services tax (GST) on economic development. *Sai Om Journal of Commerce & Management: A Peer Reviewed International Journal*, 4, 18-22.

Kavitha, R., & Sree, T. B. (2023). Repercussion of Goods and Services Tax System: Empirical Evidence from Small and Medium Retailers. *Vision: Journal of Indian Taxation*, 10 (1), 25-35.

Khairullah, A. H., & Rosita, S. (2022). Theoretical Study of Indian Banking System. *Journal of Social Commerce*, 2 (1), 42-46.

Kosmurzaevich, B. S. (2024). The Banking System Is an Important Element of the Regional Market Economy. *International Journal of Advance Scientific Research*, 4 (05), 68-72.

Kundu, S., & Banerjee, A. (2022). Operational and policy efficiency: a comparison between public and private Indian banks. *International Journal of Productivity and Performance Management*, 71 (4), 1537- 1558.

Li, W. (2006). Impact of tax policy on transition of industry structure: analysis of demand ways. *Taxation and Economy*, 144 (1), 7-11.

Lopez, J. A. (2010). Challenges in economic capital modelling. *FRBSF Economic Letter,* 2010, 19.

Muriithi, S. M., & Louw, L. (2017). The Kenyan banking industry: Challenges and sustainability. *Managing knowledge and innovation for business sustainability in Africa*, 197-222.

Muzyka-Stefanchuk, O. A., & Yakymchuk, N. Y. (2023). International Monetary Legal Relations and International Economic Relations: Interconnection and Mutual Influence. *Analytical-Comparative Law*, (5), 648-653.

Saqib, N. (2016). Banking sector liberalization and economic growth: case study of Pakistan. *Journal of Business Economics and Management*, 17 (1), 125-139.

Sarkar, D., & Latta, A. (2022). Role of banking system in green finance in the context of India: An analysis. *Asian Journal of Management*, 13 (3), 227-234.

Shukla, R. (2024). Impact on Indian Commercial Banks. Knowledgeable Research: A Multidisciplinary *Peer-Reviewed Refereed Journal*, 3 (01), 28-36.

Singh, J. N., Saini, K., Tiwari, P., & Porwal, S. (2022, December). Role of banking system in economic development. In *2022 4th International Conference on Advances in Computing, Communication Control and Networking* (ICAC3N) (pp. 2163-2167). IEEE.

Sutherland, D., & Hoeller, P. (2012). *Debt and macroeconomic stability: An overview of the literature and some empirics.*

Vintilă, A. I. (2024). *Analysis of the Determinants of Economic Growth: An Empirical Study on the EU- 28 Countries.*

Zhao, C. (2024). Key Factors for Financial Market Stability and Policy Response. *Journal of World Economy*, 3 (3), 15-18.

Гусейнова, Ш. А., Будагов, Е. А., & Мамедова, Ж. Е. (2022). Modern Theory of International Trade. *Time Description of Economic Reforms*, (4), 67-72.

Chapter 3

The Integrated Approach of ESG, SDGs, and Sustainable Finance

Ambar Srivastava*
Deepika Singh†
and Ishita Dave‡
Department of Commerce, Christ University, Delhi NCR, India

Abstract

In recent years, sustainability has emerged as a popular buzzword. The practice of considering Environmental, Social and Governance (ESG) factors when making investment decisions in the financial industry is known as "sustainable finance" and it results in longer-term investments in sustainable projects and economic activities. Sustainable Development Goals (SDGs) also play a crucial role in the adoption of sustainable practices. Investing in companies and projects that use sustainable ESG practices is already becoming more popular and there is a rising need for finance experts with knowledge of this emerging but specialized area. Stakeholder demands and regulations with an environmental focus will increase pressure on organizations to set public climate-related goals. This study tries to find out the interrelationship between ESG, SDGs and Sustainable Finance. This study also explores popular sustainable finance products available to organizations and the challenges organizations face with sustainable financing.

* Corresponding Author's Email: amber.srivastava3@gmail.com
† Corresponding Author's Email: deepika.singh@bcomh.christuniversity.in
‡ Corresponding Author's Email: ishita.dave@bcomh.christuniversity.in

In: Environmental, Social, and Governance (ESG) …
Editor: Veena Grover
ISBN: 979-8-90134-138-4

Keywords: ESG, sustainable development goals (SDGs), sustainable finance, environmental, social, governance, challenges

1. Introduction

Modern society has witnessed growth in globalization which led to corporations adapting their role according to it. These corporations majorly have a massive role in the development of the economy but they also go beyond this objective of generating profit. While making the decisions, companies have now decided to consider a broader perspective including stakeholders, employees, their customers, communities and the environment. This alteration has led to the adaption of Environmental, Social and Governance (ESG) practices, Sustainable Development Goals (SDGs) and the use of Sustainable Finance. The economy and society's development come with a lot of opportunities but also faces many challenges. To combat these severe sustainability development problems in society, corporations have come up with ESG, SDG and sustainable finance as action plans for this sustainability.

ESG stands for a collection of principles or models that help the firm orient itself towards ethical impact and sustainability. The letters E, S and G stand for Environment, Social and Governance [1]. Investors are using ESG as a standard technique to analyze what is the company's future potential and what are its ethical considerations. In another study authors found that to have a better evaluation of the sustainable development of an enterprise, the basic factors of ESG are considered to be very essential [2]. Also, in the process of investment analysis and business decision making ESG is an important factor that has to be considered. ESG issues may have a positive or negative impact on the financial performance or solvency of an entity, sovereign or individual as per the report by the European Banking Authority [3].

When discussing development, SDGs are another important factor to take into account. United Nations established 17 goals in 2017 which taken together are called Sustainable Development Goals (SDGs) which was also the newest part that was added to their 2030 agenda. They focused on targeting a broad range of independent issues which varied from social equity and environment sustainability to poverty eradication and economic growth while following the theme of "Leaving No One Behind." Sustainable Development Goals (SDGs) target all kinds of measures and legislation generally aimed at reducing the adverse externalities of human activity concerning their scope of relational, ecological and social inclusion [4].

Corporations or Organizations incorporate these ESG and SDG principles while making business decisions, promoting economic development and creating investment strategies, which is also termed sustainable finance. Investors have shown a keen interest in sustainability which is derived from three main factors that are financial relevance, nonfinancial objectives and tastes. Financial relevance talks about the company's positive impact on society which would attract customers, and employees and also get them great business opportunities while following trends such as climate change, financial inclusion and avoiding the fines that arise from environmental interventions. Non-financial objectives give space to companies to increase their impact on society while making profit sacrifices. While taste involves overlooking the social or financial consequences where investors sometimes prefer 'green' shares over the 'brown' ones because of their personal values or ethical distributions [5].

In ESG, the environment aspect refers to the assessment that is done by the firms and the organization to protect the environment and reduce the level of harm that is arising from their business. The factors that are considered in this aspect are pollution, climate change, natural resources, environmental opportunities as well as garbage. The treatment of the employees in a firm and the communities they serve are evaluated by the social aspect. Areas that focus on this aspect are employee relations, working conditions, diversity within the organization, human rights, equity and justice for employees, inclusion, product responsibility and community health and safety. How the management of the business directs and controls their organizational powers is assessed through corporate governance. This is done by examining the board's operations, composition and strict policies, pay, lobbying, corruption, donations and even their goals and plans [6].

There have been various studies that have stated a strong relationship between ESG practices, Sustainable Development Goals and financial performance that usually includes a hike in profits, reduced risks and a better way to enhance capital. Sustainable finance is yet considered to be the newly emerging idea and paradigm in the field of finance. The finance that considers ESG factors when making any decisions related to the business is Sustainable Finance [4]. The fundamental component of ethical or socially conscious investing is the relationship between (i) corporate ESG and standards and investing strategies and (ii) how it affects the financial returns after adjusting the risk [6]. The incorporation of ESG and SDGs into a firm plays a very crucial role in handling and avoiding risks such as climate change, resource scarcity and inequality. ESG provides a framework for organizations to inculcate practices that will allow them to have a lower harm to the environment while promoting social equity and strong governance. It also directly addresses the challenges which are caused by resource depletion and global warming. Simultaneously, SDGs offer a structured agenda to the firms to achieve sustainability and progress in society. It also involves handling inequalities and taking the initiative to enhance resilience against risks that are caused by climate. These frameworks come and work together, guiding the firms to have sustainable financial practices, aligning investments with global sustainability objectives and fostering long-term economic stability.

This study is crucial because it addresses the growing demand and emphasis that is been laid on integrating this ESG principle and SDGs into the financial decision-making. This study will revolve around three main objectives i.e., discussing the interrelationship between ESG, SDGs and Sustainable Finance then moving to explore the popular sustainable financial products that are available to the organizations and finally discussing the issues or challenges organizations face in funding sustainable finance.

2. Literature Review

Sustainable finance has emerged as the new revolutionary way of solving global challenges by aligning financial infrastructure with the SDGs enunciated by the United Nations Sustainable Development Goals (UNSDGs). The domain emphasizes a dimension of Environmental, Social and Governance criteria in the economic sectors that foster accountability and responsible ethics. Governance has been identified as the heart of sustainable finance, thus having a defining influence on strategy and ensuring that frameworks to achieve long-term objectives are executed.

2.1. Governance Structures Towards Achieving SDGs

Governance frameworks matter in the embedding of sustainability into organizational practices and policies. Abdulrasool and Al-Shimmery [7] demonstrate how in West Asia, governance mechanisms have made investments compatible with SDGs while focusing attention on transparency and stakeholder engagement. Meuleman [8] finds that participatory governance, policy coherence and adaptive frameworks are important elements in achieving SDGs, particularly for public institutions. Gherghina [9] digs deeper into the specific role of corporate governance when enhancing social responsibility in finance activities. The same conclusion follows Bhatti [10], saying that strong institutions and also transparency in regulations are above all important steps to sustainable finance, especially considering transition economies. Gharbi and Jarboui [11] look at what influence governance has on company performance and how this can therefore be helpful for companies trying to meet ESG expectations and ultimately far-reaching sustainability requirements. It moves beyond just reporting on sustainability, transforming the reports into tools to measure and show improvement in SDG implementation. The report enhances the level of transparency, accountability and stakeholder confidence, hence creating a culture of sustainable practice [8, 11].

2.2. Initiatives and Tools for Sustainable Finance

Sustainable finance instruments include green bonds, social bonds and loans with sustainability connections. All these have now become an important source of financing for initiatives aligned with SDGs. Hundreds of studies have explored the development and importance of these financial instruments. According to Abdulrasool and Al-Shimmery [7], new financial instruments including in West Asia, provide a means of redressing developmental imbalances by channelling investments to sustainable projects. It elaborates on the role of green bonds in detail. Gharbi and Jarboui [11] believe that green bonds are instrumental in financing environmental projects, providing access to significant investment funds in renewable energy and infrastructure. According to Bhatti [10], Public-Private Partnerships (PPP) should be resource mobilization instruments for sustainable development and highlight successful collaborations in renewable energy and waste management as relevant factors. According to Gherghina [9], the advantages of integrating ESG in the financial products as improving its attraction on the market but simultaneously aligning corporate objectives toward a long-term sustainability orientation that ensures companies achieve both the financial and developmental ambitions aligned with global developmental priorities.

2.3. Challenges Associated with Alignment of Governance Towards Sustainable Finance Goals

Despite the innovations, there are still severe barriers to aligning governance properly with sustainable finance initiatives. Bhatti [10] pointed out the lack of standardized metrics as being one of the major ones. It makes it complicated for organizations to measure and report on their contributions towards SDGs consistently. In such transition economies, governance structure faces limited access to green financing and insufficient institutional capacity. Abdulrasool and Al-Shimmery [7] also highlighted resource constraints in West Asia, which will make the governance alignment with the sustainability objectives even more challenging. Gherghina [9] also comments on the balance between financial performance and ESG compliance of corporations and how governance models need to evolve to balance those competing demands appropriately. Gharbi and Jarboui [11], suggested aligning governance standards across multiple markets is challenging, especially in regions where regulatory regimes differ. A harmonized approach to sustainable financial development would need international cooperation to ensure that policies have temporal consistency and therefore, reduce the disparities.

2.4. The Impact of Climate-Related Risks on Financial Decisions

The real economy has been adversely affected by climate change which caused the reduction in the output of the firm, hiking the costs and challenging the sustainable growth. Previous studies have shown that misallocation of corporate resources could intensify these challenges. Li [12] highlights the negative impact of climate change on corporate ESG performance and the negative impact it has on the firms. Cities which have a resource base have shown a better adaption because of behavioural shifts that are caused by climate. The negative effect is countered by mature and large companies along with external pressure like public environmental concerns and analysts' attention. Resource allocation was used as a mitigation strategy in this study. Cohen [13] explored in the survey how corporate sustainability risk factors impact financial stability, marking a significant contribution. It analyzed S&P500 companies from 2019 to 2021 by using Altman's Z- score and examined the influence of ESG risks on the firm's survival chance. Their findings revealed that Environment (E) and Social (S) hurt financial stability while Governance (G) did not have a significant effect. Also, adding to this they stated how smaller firms are more prone to social risks.

2.5. Social Considerations Like Employee Welfare, Inclusivity and Labour Relations

Global challenges like climate change, social inequality and governance failure are tackled by corporations by integrating ESG principles with CSR strategies. But this integration faces some hurdles such as inconsistent reporting standards, poor data quality and conflicts between the short-term financial goals and long-term objectives. The research highlighted the need to harmonize the ESG reporting standards, robust stakeholder engagement and a shift towards sustainability as a strategic priority. Corporations can align with global sustainability goals and maximize their societal contributions by addressing these challenges [1]. Senadheera [14] analyzed 981 published articles for bibliometric analysis talking about the significant research trends that included the growing focus on ESG matters, particularly the environmental pillar and their links to corporate performance. The global attention was reflected towards ESG concepts like green investing and circular economy.

2.6. Existing Framework for Environmental, Social and Governance (ESG)

Zairis [15] stated how sustainable finance has emerged as a vital component of sustainable development, incorporating ESG considerations into investment decisions in the financial sector. ESG has an impact that can transform the financial systems. Morton [16] talked about the Sustainable Development Goals (SDGs) as a framework that was built upon the progress made by the Millennium Development Goals (MDGs). There is also recognition that sustainable development requires a change in how the relationship between the company and quality of life is being viewed and simultaneously suggesting that this shift will bring Social, Environmental and Economic benefits. Sciarelli [17] stated how the integration of Environmental, Social and Governance (ESG) principles into the investment strategy and how it supports this transition towards sustainable growth. Socially responsible investment has gained attention in recent years because of the shift towards sustainable development.

Concluding the literature review, we can say that, governance remains a critical driver of sustainable finance and the achievement of SDGs as evidenced by the literature. Challenges include inconsistent metrics such as for green bonds and the availability of resources to apply such innovative solutions including Public Private Partnerships (PPPs). To fill this gap, future research should develop all-encompassing governance models integrating ESG considerations with standardized mechanisms for sustainability reporting. Addressing these challenges will then let sustainable finance continually evolve as a powerful tool for the betterment of global development and environmental stewardship.

3. Objectives of the Study

1. Explore the interrelationship between ESG, SDGs and Sustainable Finance
2. Identify the popular sustainable finance products available to organizations.
3. Examine the challenges faced by organizations with sustainable financing.

4. Research Methodology

This study has used a qualitative research approach which allows the researcher to have a deeper knowledge of the complex relationship between Environmental, Social and Governance (ESG) factors, Sustainable Development Goals (SDGs) and Sustainable Finance. This approach is usually applied to explore the multidimensional and dynamic phenomena that cannot be easily quantified such as the correlation between ESG principles and sustainable financial practices. This approach involves studying previous case studies, expert opinions and theoretical framework to insights about the study that is being conducted. It also helps to have an insight into how companies and policymakers navigate through these sustainability challenges. This approach provides an in-depth and rich view of how current trends are working while considering ESG investing and SDG integration. This approach supports the interpretation of how companies perceive the importance of ESG factors and SDG that are usually influenced by diversity in social, political and economic contexts.

The secondary data that was used in this study was sourced from a variety of academic, industry and government publications to have a better and more in-depth understanding of the relationship between Environment, Social and Governance (ESG), SDGs and Sustainable Finance. The data was sourced from academic databases like Scopus, Springer, Taylor and Francis, Emerald and Wiley and other online library. These platforms offer a wide range of articles that are published by scholars and various book chapters are also available for research. Moreover, some of the data was sourced from government publications and industry reports. These documents provided up-to-date data that helped to align all the knowledge into practical application. By combining these diverse sources, the study integrates both theoretical perspectives from academics and useful insights that helped to provide a better understanding of the topic on this subject matter.

A total of 20 research papers were reviewed based on specific criteria to ensure that findings are accurate and reliable and also provide some relevance to the study. These papers were chosen based on how they directly contributed to the study of ESG factors, SDGs and Sustainable Finance. The literature that was reviewed provided us with insights into how there is intersection between these topics. Also to maintain the relevance in the study more current trends were studied and the findings of literature that were established on these trends were considered.

Despite such varying and comprehensive approaches adopted while selecting the literature, there still were several limitations. First of all, the study is entirely based on secondary data which means the findings of the research paper are based on previous studies that did not capture the most recent current trends which limits the knowledge and applicability of real-time scenarios. While choosing the methodology it is important to look into the limitations and recognize them.

5. Findings

5.1. Interrelationship Between ESG, SDGs and Sustainable Finance

In order to achieve the SDGs, companies are increasingly integrating ESG concepts into their corporate strategy. ESG and SDGs are similar in that they promote ethical corporate practices, sustainable long-term growth and responsible investment. Studies have proven that firms that take into account ESG metrics can effectively control risks and opportunities and are aligned with SDGs that foster global development goals.

Examples include companies that have become environment-friendly; thus, they contribute to "Climate Action (SDG 13)" through a reduction in carbon footprint, renewable sources of energy and conducting environmentally friendly operations. A company that focuses on social inclusion, equitable economic development and diversity within its operations and supply chain promotes "Reduced Inequalities (SDG 10)." There now financial instruments such as green bonds that have emerged as instrumental in facilitating these initiatives, especially in financing projects on "Clean Energy (SDG 7)" and "Sustainable Cities (SDG 11)" [7, 10]. In doing so, it not only enables transition into a low-carbon economy but also opens up local communities to the benefits of sustainable development projects.

This sense has greatly depended on effective governance so that the operations of the business can be in harmony with SDG objectives. Good governance practice promotes transparency, accountability and ethical corporate practices necessary to track and fulfil the objectives of SDGs. Through the implementation of ESG within governance frameworks, organizations can monitor their progress towards achieving the goals of the SDGs and then alter their plans in suitable measures toward the effective accomplishment of these objectives [8].

There are certain overlapping areas between ESG and SDGs. The most significant overlaps are in the environmental domain. Many ESG initiatives share the goal of reducing environmental impact and parallel with goals in renewable energy, consumption and change for climate mitigation purposes. For instance, on climate change mitigation, ESG initiatives point directly to SDG 13 (Climate Action). The environmental aspects of ESG principles are found in clean energy (SDG 7) initiatives.

Social components of ESG include human rights safeguards, labour regulations, and community involvement, which also support SDG 3 and SDG

10 - social justice, health and well-being. Strong institutions and effective governance are an important part of the Sustainable Development Goals ensuring that businesses behave morally and responsibly (SDG 16).

All of these connections mean that ESG frameworks are not independent but interrelated with broader social goals. From the synergies generated by this integration, the adoption of ESG goes on to speed up the development of the SDGs and becomes an important weapon for companies that want to join other initiatives around the globe toward sustainability.

5.2. Popular Sustainable Finance Products

A few sustainable finance products have come forward as crucial tools for companies wanting to link their financial strategies to environmental and social goals. The most widely used ones are:

1. Green Bonds: These bonds are specifically tailored to invest in projects that align with environmental sustainability projects such as renewable energy installations, energy-efficient buildings and clean water initiatives. Green bonds have played an important role in financing those projects that fit within the scope of SDGs like Clean Water and Sanitation (SDG 6), Affordable and Clean Energy (SDG 7), and Climate Action (SDG 13). They have seen much progress, especially regarding the action on climate change and the degradation of the environment [9].
2. Social Bonds: Social ties focus on projects that have social impacts. Its key concerns are poverty reduction, health, education and affordable housing. These connections are in line with SDGs such as Decent Work and Economic Growth (SDG 8) and Reduced Inequalities (SDG 10) because they try to reduce social inequalities. Social relationships are increasingly becoming common globally, especially as governments and businesses focus on developing social infrastructure.
3. Sustainability-Linked Loans (SLLs): Sustainability-Linked Loans, abbreviated as SLLs refer to loans that are conditioned upon a borrower's ESG performance. They provide businesses with financial incentives to achieve certain levels of sustainability. A firm will enjoy a reduced rate of interest if it improves its ESG standards. In contrast, costs will escalate if the sustainability targets are not achieved. Due

to their flexibility, SLLs are the most attractive to businesses that intend to integrate sustainability into their business plans. These loans are being adopted at a growing rate by companies and they report improved long-term financial performance as well as increased stakeholder confidence [7].

Sustainable finance products have gained increased adoption most especially in emerging markets. The issuance of green and social bonds has grown remarkably well because they provide a means for attracting both impact-driven investors and financial return seekers. For example, companies operating in developing countries have now started issuing green bonds as a step toward funding renewable energy projects, hence contributing to the success of achieving global sustainability. In other words, there is an increasing trend of financial institutions in emerging economies recognizing the rising demand for these products as they respond to both local development priorities and global sustainability frameworks. Firms are also taking up the SLLs to enhance their ESG performance.

This trend is seen quite abundantly among large enterprises having access to the capital markets and the required experience needed in structuring such a complicated instrument. The use of SLLs is said to correlate with higher stakeholder confidence and better financial results; companies that have succeeded in achieving their sustainable development goals tend to carry even more minor borrowing costs, a bonus motivator for the purpose [8].

5.3. Challenges Faced by Organizations with Sustainable Financing

Organizational funding strategies should be aligned with global sustainability goals. Sustainable finance holds great promises in supporting sustainability and realizing United Nations' Sustainable Development Goals. However, it is shrouded with various challenges that are categorized as regulatory and compliance, greenwashing and financial, each posing different problems that require joint effort to solve. Despite the growing demand for sustainable finance products, these are still out of reach for many companies in smaller markets or emerging economies. The key reasons for this include:

5.3.1. Challenges Under Regulatory and Compliance

The regulatory environment concerning sustainable financing is intrinsically complex and involves different frameworks and requirements in jurisdictions.

This creates a condition of fragmentation with no universally defined standards for ESG and SDG reporting that in turn causes major inefficiencies.

1. Global Disparities: Separate reporting structures of different nations and regions make it complicated for cross-border operating entities to ensure compliance in an integrated manner. According to Meuleman [8], this lack of consistency creates uncertainty and inefficiencies in operations which impair the effective comparison of firms.
2. SME Burden: SMEs are most vulnerable essentially because they lack resources most of the time required to deliver strict reporting and compliance requirements. The burdensome bureaucratic obstacles and related costs might deter these organizations from engaging in sustainable finance.
3. Regulatory Adaptation Lag Overall: Regulatory frameworks are generally lagging behind the pace of rapidly changing sustainability parameters. This would be an example of inadequacy in adaptive frameworks towards new risks such as climate adaptation to ensure proper compliance initiatives.

This would call for a coordinated global framework for reporting ESG and SDG. Harmonization would facilitate transparency and comparability to inform investor decisions. It further involves that the regulatory body will also provide technical and financial capacity building for SMEs to fully prepare them in compliance.

5.3.2. Greenwashing Concerns

This extremely important challenge reflects the power of greenwashing-an untrue claim for the sake of sustainability. Greenwashing occurs when companies exaggerate their sustainability credentials or lie about sustainability credentials. Therefore, stakeholders lose confidence in sustainable finance.

1. Trust Deficit Greenwashing hurts stakeholder trust, allowing a misleading sustainability agenda to be a momentum grabber for every sustainability initiative. As Bhatti [10] put it, "It is damaging not just the individual institution but the credibility of the sustainable finance model more broadly."
2. The motivation for Misrepresentation: The high demand for sustainable product offerings creates this dilemma where companies desperate to access more funds and popularity could exaggerate about

work done. It now clouds the difference between sincere efforts and artificial steps in pursuit of a 'green reputation.'

3. Impact on Customers: Greenwashing would make misguided customers who adopt businesses that are not utilizing those 'green standards' which effectively results in resources being sucked dry off these 'unsustainable ventures.'

Measures should include strict verification processes that prevent greenwashing by other organizations. ESG claims of the regulatory body will get higher credibility because of independent auditing and certification. This very visible fact makes greenwashing difficult for companies to do.

5.3.3. Financial Restrictions

1. Monetary Barriers: Expensive setup and launch phases that are bound to limit participation, mainly among small businesses and firms in developing countries are what creating sustainable finance products would incur high certification costs. Third-party verification and detailed documentation on green and social bond issuance contribute to increased costs upfront.
2. Capital Access Concerns: Capital access in developing markets is expensive. As a result, capital access issues hinder the uptake of sustainable finance products. In these markets, investors perceive ESG-compliant ventures as riskier. Consequently, the commitment of capital is limited.
3. Market Shyness: There are no clear-cut regulations in some regions and no ESG metrics are defined. These factors make investors worry about investing in those regions. Thus, the growth of sustainable financing ventures is restrained. Such governments and finance institutions shall prepare particular incentives that specifically reduce or eliminate financial barriers. For example, these include subsidies in the form of certified expense offset by tax incentives for issuances of green bonds as well as public-private cooperation in reducing investment risks as perceived in developing markets. Therefore, there would be green finance facilitated by concessional loans that could support companies with very inadequate capital.
4. Limited Awareness and Expertise: Most organizations do not have the internal capacity to design sustainable finance products including green bonds or SLLs. According to Bhatti [10], the major barrier is

the lack of knowledge about how to align financial products with ESG criteria and SDG objectives. This lack of understanding prevents organizations from exploring these options which could otherwise help them enhance their environmental and social impact.

5. Higher Inorganic Costs: The most often associated costs with sustainable finance are the high inorganic costs involved. For instance, setting and issuing green bonds involve hefty front-loaded charges. This makes sustainable financing somewhat inaccessible to smaller enterprises that need capital inflows. Regulatory complexities require external certification and verification of the reports in question, further adding to the monetary burden [9]. As a result, SMEs might find that they are not invited or included in such offers.

Nevertheless, the adoption of sustainable finance products is likely to remain in growth as more companies appreciate the long-term benefits of sustainability-linked finance. Increased awareness and innovations of financial products may lead to more availability of these instruments, so more access might be possible for smaller firms into global sustainability efforts.

6. The Way Forward

Enabling Environment-Organizational financing should be aligned with sustainability goals by adopting a holistic approach that together deals with this challenge. Some strategic recommendations are as follows:

1. Strengthen Global Collaboration: For this purpose, governments, international organizations and regulatory bodies need to come together and formulate universal frameworks of ESG and SDG reporting that can be further supported through initiative builders like the International Sustainability Standards Board and the United Nations.
2. Technological Innovation Upgrade: For example, technology including blockchain and AI can be exploited to enhance the transparency and trackability in sustainable finance. For example, blockchain may be used to develop an immutable register of sustainability claims and hence the chances of greenwashing are reduced.

3. Capacity Building: Capacity Building programs must be developed as training programs and workshops that enlighten organizations, particularly SMEs about best practices in sustainable financing. This will offer the organization the ability to implement sustainable practices efficiently. Governments and development banks must innovate new financial instruments such as low-interest or performance-based incentives and sustainability-linked loans to encourage the issuance of green bonds.
4. Monitoring and Enforcement: The regulatory agencies must develop a holistic mechanism to monitor adherence and punish the practice of greenwashing. Audits must be periodic and enforcement of disclosure requirements more stringent that would deter the unethical act.
5. Public awareness about the need for sustainable finance would bring demand-side pressure on organizations to meet sustainability standards and further ethical practices.

Conclusion

The incorporation of the Environmental, Social and Governance (ESG) principle into Sustainable Development Goals (SDGs) using mechanisms of Sustainable Finance would form a critical response to contemporary challenges facing the world at large. This would within the integration, translate operational and financial excellence that means organizations contribute to a more sustainable future. Adopting sustainable finance instruments holds potentialities for accountability, transparency and innovation. However, the barriers include high implementation costs, inconsistent regulatory frameworks and the problem of greenwashing which needs to be overcome to achieve optimum impact.

The non-adoption of ESG principles and SDGs poses an enormous risk to organizations. A few impacts of non-alignment to the global sustainability agenda are reputation, investor confidence, fines imposed by the regulatory body and instability in finance. The markets becoming pro-businesses that know and act on ESG consideration can make slow-moving companies quickly become one that their competitors pass ahead destroying trust among stakeholders.

For instance, these problems would only be solved by standards for reporting ESG and financial incentives through advanced technology, capacity building and more interaction with stakeholders. The ideas presented above would not only transcend the current challenges but also fuel the adoption of sustainable finance in various sectors and industries.

Implications

Implications for Companies

1. It has now become a strategic imperative to integrate ESG principles as part of the corporate strategy in order to preserve competitiveness and resilience in an ever-changing marketplace.
2. Operational Excellence: Sustainability helps companies achieve operational efficiencies, reduce costs and make more money in the longer term.
3. Brand and stakeholder trust: ESG transparency builds brand value, enhances investor confidence and constructs a supportive relationship with consumers and communities.

Implications for Policymakers and Regulators

1. Standardization Efforts: Developing universal ESG and SDG compliance frameworks is critical to reducing inconsistencies and enabling fair comparison across markets.
2. Support SMEs: Financial and regulatory support for SMEs can democratize access to sustainable finance. In that sense, it means ensuring inclusivity in global sustainability efforts.
3. Improved monitoring and enforcement of sustainable claims may reduce fraudulent practices, thus enhancing trust in the offerings of sustainable finance.

Implications for the Finance Sector

1. Innovative Solutions: Financial institutions can create accessible and cost-effective sustainable finance products that suit different business needs.

2. Investor Confidence: Strong reliable ESG metrics and reporting processes will attract investors and channel more capital to such initiatives.

Prospective Considerations

ESG, SDGs and Sustainable Finance interplay can now help businesses contribute to the realization of global sustainability and continue to grow and stay relevant. The next phase is expected to witness significant leaps in technology and collaborative approaches among stakeholders that would allow for further fine-tuning of strategies to bridge current gaps. Research avenues open up by the exploration of quantitative implications of ESG practices on financial performance, development in the sustainability regulations framework and technological innovations in ESG compliance.

Therefore, it requires intense combined efforts from businesses, policymakers and financial institutions to create a supportive framework for sustainable finance. Barriers to be addressed, alignment of strategies with global sustainability goals and unlocking transformative opportunities can all contribute to a better society, the environment and the economy at large. Sustainable finance is not only a mechanism for achieving global objectives; it's also a strategic pathway toward a resilient and equitable future.

References

[1] Shapsugova, M. 2023. "ESG principles and social responsibility." *E3S Web of Conferences*. 420. https://doi.org/10.1051/e3sconf/202342006040.

[2] Li, T., Wang, K., Sueyoshi, T., and Wang, D. D. 2021. "ESG: Research progress and future prospects." *Sustainability,* 13 (21): 11663. https://doi.org/10.3390/su132111663.

[3] EBA publishes its report on the management and supervision of ESG risks for credit institutions and investment firms. (n.d.). *European Banking Authority* 2021. Retrieved from https://eba.europa.eu/publications-and-media/press-releases/eba-publishes-its-report-management-and-supervision-esg-risks.

[4] Ziolo, M., Bak, I., and Cheba, K. 2021. "The role of sustainable finance in achieving Sustainable Development Goals: does it work?." *Technological and Economic Development of Economy*, *27* (1): 45-70. https://doi.org/10.3846/tede.2020.13863.

[5] Edmans, A., and Kacperczyk, M. 2022. "Sustainable finance." *Review of Finance, 26* (6): 1309-1313. https://doi.org/10.1093/rof/rfac069.

[6] Lee, M. T., and Suh, I. 2022. "Understanding the effects of Environment, Social, and Governance conduct on financial performance: Arguments for a process and integrated modelling approach." *Sustainable Technology and Entrepreneurship,* 1 (1): 100004. https://doi.org/10.1016/j.stae.2022.100004.

[7] Abdulrasool, H. D., and Al-Shimmery, K. R. A. 2024. "Sustainable finance for implementing the Sustainable Development Goals in West Asia." In *The Emerald Handbook of Ethical Finance and Corporate Social Responsibility:* 1-20. https://doi.org/10.1108/9781804554074-003.

[8] Meuleman, L. 2021. "Public administration and governance for the SDGs: Navigating between change and stability." *Sustainability, 13* (11): 5914. https://doi.org/10.3390/su13115914.

[9] Gherghina, S. C. 2023. "Corporate finance, governance, and social responsibility." *Journal of Risk and Financial Management, 16* (6): 297. https://doi.org/10.3390/jrfm16060297.

[10] Bhatti, M., Shaikh, S., and Baladi, N. 2023. "Challenges of sustainable finance in transition economies." In *Entrepreneurship and Green Finance Practices:* 1-25. https://doi.org/10.1108/9781804556795-002.

[11] Gharbi, M., and Jarboui, A. 2024. "The impact of corporate social responsibility on firm financial performance: Does corporate governance matter?" *International Journal of Law and Management.* https://www.emerald.com/insight/content/doi/10.1108/00251740810863870.

[12] Li, Q., Tang, W., and Li, Z. 2024. "ESG systems and financial performance in industries with significant environmental impact: a comprehensive analysis." *Frontiers in Sustainability.* 5:1454822. https://doi.org/10.3389/frsus.2024.1454822.

[13] Cohen, G. 2022. "ESG risks and corporate survival." *Environment Systems & Decisions, 43* (1): 16-21. https://doi.org/10.1007/s10669-022-09886-8.

[14] Senadheera, S. S., Gregory, R., Rinklebe, J., Farrukh, M., Rhee, J. H., and Ok, Y. S. 2022. "The development of research on environmental, social, and governance (ESG): A bibliometric analysis." *Sustainable Environment: 8* (1). https://doi.org/10.1080/27658511.2022.2125869.

[15] Zairis, G., Liargovas, P., and Apostolopoulos, N. (2024). "Sustainable finance and ESG importance: A systematic literature review and research agenda." *Sustainability,* 16 (7): 2878. https://doi.org/10.3390/su16072878.

[16] Morton, S., Pencheon, D., and Squires, N. 2017. "Sustainable Development Goals (SDGs), and their implementation." *British Medical Bulletin:* 1-10. https://doi.org/10.1093/bmb/ldx031.

[17] Sciarelli, M., Cosimato, S., Landi, G., and Iandolo, F. 2021. "Socially responsible investment strategies for the transition towards sustainable development: The importance of integrating and communicating ESG." *The TQM Journal,* 33 (7): 39-56. https://doi.org/10.1108/tqm-08-2020-0180.

Chapter 4

Integrating ESG and SDG Frameworks: A New Paradigm for Corporate Sustainability

Jose M. Jomon[1,*]
and Rachel Mathews Jyothis[2,†]
[1]Sahrdaya Institute of Management Studies Thrissur, Kerala, India
[2]Ahalia School of Management, Palakkad, Kerala, India

Abstract

In today's fast-changing VUCA (volatility, uncertainty, complexity, and ambiguity) world, a myriad of stakeholders such as governments, investors, consumers, and society at large, are putting an extraordinary amount of pressure on businesses to adopt sustainable practices. This pressure is largely driven by a growing awareness of (and actions related to) environmental abuse, social injustice, and lack of adequate governance, which has had a significant negative effect on society and business over the long term. Two important frameworks have emerged to help with sustainable development associated with the UN Sustainable Development Goals (SDGs) and Environmental Social Governance (ESG). The following analysis aims to demonstrate how these two frameworks which are typically discussed separately can leverage some synergy to develop an integrated model for corporate sustainability. The SDGs outline 17 universal goals to be achieved by 2030, including the eradication of poverty, protection of the planet, and prosperity for all. ESG criteria are increasingly being used to gauge the sustainability and wider effects of a business from the investor's perspective. SDGs are

* Corresponding Author's Email: jomonjose83@gmail.com
† Corresponding Author's Email: jyothisrachel@gmail.com

In: Environmental, Social, and Governance (ESG) …
Editor: Veena Grover
ISBN: 979-8-90134-138-4

broad, high-level goals, and ESG measures provide more pragmatic levels of analysis.
This permits organizations to link operational activities with international development priorities while also providing a means to track and report progress with a marketing appeal to investors. For instance, activities related to climate action (SDG 13) will naturally correspond to the "Environmental" aspect of ESG, while initiatives to promote decent work (SDG 8) will contribute to the "Social" component. However, it is not always easy to harmonize the two. There tends to be a conflict between an organization's long-term sustainable development objectives and immediate pressures for performance. Additionally, there is also some ambiguity around historical metrics and the transformation of defined roles and gaps in the reporting structures. Taking this into consideration and notwithstanding these imperfections - the threat of having a strategic advantage through harmonization is still quite high. Corporations should stand to gain considerable benefits through the alignment of ESG indicators with relevant SDGs, as they will be better positioned to identify areas of risk, allocate resources, and connect with stakeholders in more meaningful ways, and vice-versa. This theoretical assessment aims to prepare analysis on the harmonizing dimension of ESG and SDGs while highlighting synergies and points of divergence. In addition, strategic recommendations are provided for those organizations variable in the act of advancing sustainability towards more responsible and anticipatory governance. Once coordinated effectively, this integration of ESG and SDGs can fundamentally redefine corporate purpose and create long-term value for businesses and society alike.

Keywords: ESG, SDG, corporate sustainability, sustainability frameworks, stakeholder engagement, sustainable development

1. Introduction

The business realm is gradually, yet determinately, beginning to understand the role of Sustainable Development Goals (SDGs) within their Environmental, Social and Corporate Governance (ESG) policies. These frameworks are being integrated into workflows as a mechanism for efficiency purposes. Competing and growing within various industries is contingent on these ideas being integrated. Ultimately, the decisions a firm makes stem from a strategic vision. The evolution of knowledge and understanding of phenomena paired with socio-economic matters has produced the premise that firms owe packets beyond what is compliant to the state and regulators and includes investors, consumers, and society on a broader scale (Khaled et al., 2021; Radu et al., 2023). The shift of awareness is what has invoked the discussions geared to creating frameworks around sustainability to enumerate public responsibilities and behavior for firms (Dhivedi, 2023). The most prominent documents in this regard are the Environmental, Social and Governance (ESG) criteria and the Sustainable Development Goals (SDG) formed by the United Nations (Delgado-Ceballos et al., 2022; Sarkar et al., 2023).

In different terms: as a choice. Growing knowledge about the material and public challenges has driven trades to be seen as liable—not only to governments and supervisory parties but also to financiers, customers, and societies (Khaled et al., 2021; Radu et al., 2023). This transition has also served as a catalyst for discussing the adoption of principles that govern the sustainability of trade (Dhivedi, 2023) and the accountability and moral prudence of trade. Two of them that stand out in this area among the above-mentioned are the Environmental, Social, and Governance (ESG) tests and the Sustainable Development Goals (SDGs) of the United Nations (Delgado-Ceballos et al., 2022; Sarkar et al., 2023). While ESG focuses on ethical and trustworthy movement of trade, trying to address environmental, public, and government issues, SDGs set up a fuller global agenda aimed at resolving worldwide challenges by 2030 (Sokolova & Teymurov, 2022; Consolandi et al., 2020; De Silva Lokuwaduge et al., 2022). Even though the two frameworks, ESG and SDG, have been separately used traditionally, there is a growing recognition that trading upon the blending of these frameworks enhances allied sustainability approaches and aligns trade goals accompanying worldwide preferences (Khaled et al., 2021; Alsayegh et al., 2020). An integrated approach further allows associations to set corporate-specific goals and improve the overall aims laid down by SDGs (Markopoulos & Ramonda, 2022; Aldowaish et al., 2022). This change enhances an organization's standing and competitive prestige, increasing the overall value approach through righteous practices (Jonsdottir et al., 2021). Thus, the article explores the theoretical integration of ESG and SDG frameworks, redrafting it as a paradigm for integrated sustainability. In doing so, it attempts to examine the correlation, advantages, and processes directed in integrated sustainability, projecting the sight of associations on utilizing dual paradigms to enrich sustainability sway while flowing allegiance to the demands of other stakeholders. The paper also highlights the challenges of integrating these paradigms and illustrates with some case studies that embody revered, multifaceted practicalities. With this rationale, the article seeks to contribute to the rising concern about linked sustainability by providing practical suggestions for solutions pursuing to adopt an integrated ESG-SDG approach (Khaled et al., 2021; Aldowaish et al., 2022; Sætra, 2021). Through the article, connected to this sense of reasoning, further hopes to contribute to the rising concern about integrated sustainability with concrete recommendations for the solutions aspiring to clear an integrated ESG-SDG approach.

2. Understanding ESG And SDG Frameworks

The Basically Different but Twin Fronts of Sustainable Practices within Corporations: An Understanding of the ESG and SDG Frameworks.

This paper presents insights on ESG and the SDGs from theoretical and practical considerations. While the two together foundations push businesses toward incidental and public accountability, they still have unique features, objectives, and uses that inform the ways or means in which businesses respond to the issues of sustainability (Delgado-Ceballos et al., 2022; Dwivedi, 2023; Sokolova & Teymurov, 2022; De Silva Lokuwaduge et al., 2022).

1.1. The ESG Framework

The ESG foundation has been widely accepted by companies and investors as a means of assessing their allied commitment and contribution to sustainable and righteous practices (Kim & Li, 2021; Alsayegh et al., 2020).

The three main components are:

- Environmental: This pillar considers the association's impact on the natural environment, taking into account energy consumption, waste disposal, pollution control, carbon footprint, and resource conservation. Companies undertaking environmental practices are dedicated to sustaining their reputation for the benefit of lessening their environmental impact in order to meet regulations and to collaborate with some other environmentally sensitive partners (Jin & Lei, 2023; Freiberg et al., 2019).
- Social: With respect to the social dimension, it looks at an association in terms of its relationships with its employees, customers, suppliers,

and the communities within which it operates. Important basic components are workers' rights, diversity and inclusion, health and safety standards, community engagement, and consumer protection. Strong public practices allow for employees to develop trust at the same time as drawing in talent and increasing customer satisfaction (Wang et al., 2023; Amaral et al., 2023).

- Governance: This dimension includes the assessment of ethical practices and clear management processes in any kind of business. It includes issues with respect to diversity among the board, payments made to the executives, shareholder rights, internal controls, and transparency in financial reporting. Good governance allows for a business to operate fairly and reduces risks associated with corruption while providing support for investors' trust (Ma et al., 2022; Shapsugova, 2023). The ESG framework acts as a significant motivator driving responsible corporate practices, urging corporations to enhance their ESG ratings so that they can grab various investments and meet colleague expectations (Kim & Li, 2021; Jin & Lei, 2023).

1.2. The SDG Framework

The Sustainable Development Goals (SDGs), started by the United Nations in 2015, offer an entire blueprint for calling all-encompassing sustainability challenges by 2030 (Markopoulos & Ramonda, 2022; Del Río Castro et al., 2020; Filho et al., 2018). Comprising 17 goals and 169 targets, the SDGs tackle fault-finding districts, containing:

- Poverty and Hunger: Aiming to eradicate want and hungriness, these aims supply instructions for basic human needs and financial impartiality.
- Health and Education: The SDGs stress a worldwide health approach and feature instruction as a fundamental right essential for pertaining to society's progress.
- Gender Equality and Clean Water: Goals around masculine balance and approach to clean water focus on the importance of impartiality and source chance for tenable development.

- Climate Action and Economic Growth: The SDGs advocate for environmental operation and all-embracing business-related progress, pushing for tenable industrialized practices and support administration (Filho et al., 2018; Eisenmenger et al., 2020).

The SDGs ensure all-encompassing collaboration among governments, trades, and civic organizations to build a tenable future for all. Unlike ESG, which focuses on association-distinguishing diversification, the SDGs supply a universal foundation for associations to join their movements with all-encompassing sustainability works (Del Río Castro et al., 2020; Filho et al., 2018; Eisenmenger et al., 2020; Griggs et al., 2014; Allen et al., 2018).

The SDG framework is the general blueprinted endeavor of the lone United Nations to attain maximum sustainability challenges by the year 2030. The SDGs include 17 goals and 169 targets; the most crucial areas they target are poverty and hunger, health and education, gender balance and clean water, climate action, and economic growth. The SDGs focus on poverty clairvoyance, parody key on calamity, diffusion of world-child disease, and rights as entitlements to melders in contention-based world-developing and maybe sustainable futures (Filho et al., 2018). The SDGs strive for overall cooperation among governments, businesses, and civil society in order to create positive futures for all people. While the ESG prattles much on companies defining the ES from day one, the SDGs provide a historical default one where sergeants can take heads and pour mouths into the very center of sustainable systems under which they stand (Del Río Castro et al., 2020; Filho et al., 2018; Eisenmenger et al., 2020; Griggs et al., 2014; Allen et al., 2018).

1.3. Comparing ESG and SDG Frameworks

A comparison of ESG and SDGs shows both frameworks are committed to sustainable practices, but there are differences in their scope, nature, and concentration:

- Scope and Application: ESG is almost entirely a corporate form used by financiers and stakeholders to assess association/test aspects of a firm regarding its sustainability and ethical standing, whereas the SDGs are a universal foundation for the sustainability of the planet designed to address cumulative challenges (Sætra, 2021).

- Goals and Metrics: ESG will continuously mean environmental, social, and governance tests directly linked to a company's actions, whereas SDGs deliver a set of wider targets (Soni, 2023).
- Integration and Synergies: With the incorporation above of the SDG objectives under the general guideline on the ESG plan, the companies can truly get involved in sustainable and responsible efforts set by means of common platforms. This approach not only enhances shared accountability but also carves its way to addressing critical and common challenges in sustaining a multifaceted growth continuum (Markopoulos & Ramonda, 2022).

1.4. Synergies Between ESG and SDG Frameworks

An integrated approach—heavy in its advocates—combining both ESG and SDG frameworks endorses better company accountability, contributing to that kind of accomplishment: a larger friendly impact via the front row of receiving questions on pressing issues worldwide (Khaled et al., 2021; Consolandi et al., 2020; Markopoulos & Ramonda, 2022; Sætra, 2021; Soni, 2023).

2. Rationale for Integrating ESG and SDG Frameworks

2.1. Intersections Between ESG and SDGs

Complementarities while indeed two disconnected processes, ESG and SDG frameworks send unique sustainability messages that can actually be consolidated into a common business charter. Simply put, ESG stakeholder assessments consider internal corporate practices and commitments towards environmental, social, and governmental issues that directly correlate with several SDGs (Mamedova, 2023). For example, initiatives that address the *environmental* aspect of ESG, such as reducing carbon emissions and waste, contribute to SDG 13, Climate Action, and SDG 15, Life on Land and Water. Similarly, the *social* aspect of ESG, touching on labor standards, diversity, and community engagement, matches up with SDG 8, Decent Work and Economic Growth, and SDG 10, Reduced Inequalities. Governance practices that emphasize transparency, ethics, and mature administration support SDG 16, Peace, Justice, and Strong Institutions (Khaled et al., 2021). This pattern of double fit then allows companies to strategically align their internal sustainability efforts with higher-level global goals, catalyzing alchemy that reinforces both corporate and societal impacts (Markopoulos & Ramonda, 2022; Soni, 2023; De Silva Lokuwaduge & Heenetigala, 2016; Escrig-Olmedo et al., 2019).

2.2. Drivers of Integration

Associations are driven by several factors to harmonize ESG and SDG into one model of sustainability:

- Regulatory Pressures: Around the world, governments and supervisory bodies are initiating stricter rules about incidental impact, public responsibility, and allied governance. Embracing an integrated ESG–SDG approach helps associations adhere to evolving regulations with enthusiastic adjustment, showing alignment with strategic means (Khaled et al., 2021).
- Stakeholder Expectations: Nowadays, consumers, employees, and local communities are far more alert to new trends in corporate sustainability and more likely to expect companies to uphold virtuous societal aims. Integrating ESG with SDGs enables organizations to align with these heightened aspirations and construct stronger commitments with their stakeholders (Aldowaish et al., 2022).
- Investor Demands: Investors expect that economic performance should not trump all other considerations and look favorably upon associations with strong sustainability affairs. Integrating ESG and SDG frameworks within the business model offers a valuable asset, aligning organizations with global sustainability goals (Markopoulos & Ramonda, 2022).
- Reputation Monitor: Companies that fully align their strategies with both ESG and SDG principles demonstrate deep respect for ethical and responsible business, thereby enhancing brand reputation. This unification signals a genuine pledge to societal causes and commands trust and credibility among customers and partners (Sætra, 2021; De Silva Lokuwaduge & Heenetigala, 2016; Escrig-Olmedo et al., 2019).

2.3. Integration Benefits for Business

The integration of ESG and SDGs provides multiple strategic benefits to companies, enhancing corporate resilience, relevancy, and social impact.

- Better Risk Management: By addressing a broader range of sustainability drivers, companies are better positioned to manage long-term risks from unforeseen challenges, regulatory changes, and societal issues. This integrated approach enables comprehensive risk assessments and mitigation strategies (Aldowaish et al., 2022).
- Enhanced Reputation: Companies that transparently align both ESG criteria and SDG goals are more capable of building a reputation as responsible and ethical businesses. This improved reputation fosters customer loyalty, boosts employee morale, and provides a competitive edge (Sætra, 2021).
- Improved Investor and Client Loyalty: This integrated sustainability model appeals to socially conscious investors and consumers who prioritize sustainability practices. It enhances investor confidence and nurtures a loyal customer base that values shared commitment to systemic positive change (Kim & Li, 2021).

Companies can ensure widespread sustainability by creating a unified strategy through ESG and SDG integration, aligning with global initiatives to build resilience, stakeholder trust, and long-term value (Khaled et al., 2021; Kim & Li, 2021; Wang et al., 2023).

3. Strategic Approaches to Integrating ESG and SDGS

3.1. Mapping ESG Metrics to SDGs

Through the joining of specific ESG best practices along with accepted SDGs, companies can form a compact sustainability strategy. This mapping process allows businesses to bridge efforts between the immediate and global. Through these processes and practices, both best practices and societal goals are attained (Markopoulos & Ramonda, 2022). A good example is when a company that is focused on reducing greenhouse gas emissions as part of the ESG environmental component connects this effort to SDG 13 (Climate

Action). Similarly, a company that emphasizes diversity and inclusion within its workforce—under the social component of ESG—links this to SDG 5 (Gender Equality) and SDG 10 (Reduced Inequalities). By strategically connecting ESG metrics to the SDGs, companies can not only identify the areas where their practices overlap with global priorities but also expand their positive impact (Khaled et al., 2021; Radu et al., 2023; Consolandi et al., 2020; Delgado-Ceballos et al., 2022).

3.2. Establishing Key Performance Indicators (KPIs)

Key Performance Indicators (KPIs) define corporate integration in ESG–SDG strategies. Setting measurable KPIs is crucial for evaluating the effectiveness of integrated ESG initiatives. Companies can thus quantify their achievements with respect to agreed-upon benchmarks, ensuring transparency and accountability (Horan, 2020; Hristov & Chirico, 2019). For instance, a technology company might set a target to reduce carbon emissions by 30 percent within five years; this goal would support both ESG environmental objectives and contribute to SDG 13 (Climate Action). A retail organization might consider KPIs related to fair labor practices, enabling fulfillment of ESG's social criteria and compliance with SDG 8 (Decent Work and Economic Growth) (Biggeri et al., 2019). By establishing and monitoring KPIs, companies can continually evaluate their progress and make data-driven adjustments to achieve their ESG and SDG objectives (Horan, 2020; Biggeri et al., 2019; Adams & Frost, 2008).

3.3. Stakeholder Engagement and Communication

Engaging stakeholders—including investors, customers, employees, and communities—is a pivotal process for the success of integrated ESG–SDG strategies. Effective communication of sustainability objectives, goals, and progress builds transparency and trust while fostering sustained stakeholder support for new corporate initiatives (Jun & Kim, 2021; Jónsdóttir et al., 2021). For example, investors have shown increasing interest in companies that incorporate sustainability into their projections and align with global goals (Bulmer & Yáñez-Araque, 2023). Enhancing customer loyalty toward a global brand can also be achieved by communicating the benefits of integrated ESG–SDG efforts, in line with the growing consumer preference for brands committed to social and environmental responsibility (Kulova & Nikolova-Alexieva, 2023). For employees, involving them in sustainability processes increases internal support for organizational initiatives (Aldowaish et al., 2022).

By maintaining transparency about progress, challenges, and achievements, companies can reinforce stakeholder confidence and create a shared commitment to sustainability (Jun & Kim, 2021; De Silva Lokuwaduge & Heenetigala, 2016; Bulmer & Yáñez-Araque, 2023). Through mapping metrics, setting KPIs, and engaging stakeholders, companies can align their ESG and SDG efforts, demonstrating a clear and credible commitment to sustainable growth and responsible business practices (De Silva Lokuwaduge & Heenetigala, 2016; Kulova & Nikolova-Alexieva, 2023).

4. Challenges and Limitations of Integration

4.1. Integrating the ESG and SDG Frameworks

Integrating the ESG and SDG frameworks presents significant challenges due to their differing aims, benchmarks, and methods of assessment. While ESG is a company-specific set of metrics focused on environmental, social, and governance areas, the SDGs address a broader spectrum of global challenges aimed at achieving sustainable development by 2030 (Beyne, 2020). Because of the varying scales and scopes of these frameworks, businesses often struggle to combine them on an even basis. Taking the goals set forth by ESG and attempting to align them with all 17 SDGs may create conflicts—some goals may require more resources than others, while others are less actionable within a business setting (Horan, 2020; Sciarelli et al., 2021). This complexity means that businesses must carefully prioritize and balance their sustainability goals to prevent fragmentation or conflicts among them (Khaled et al., 2021; Aldowaish et al., 2022; Delgado-Ceballos et al., 2022; Liang et al., 2022).

4.2. Difficulty in Data Collection and Measurement

One of the key hindrances in implementing an integrated ESG–SDG strategy is the challenge of obtaining accurate data and measurement capabilities. It is often difficult to collect relevant information from various operational areas, suppliers, and external partners about ESG and SDG performance (Zaccone & Pedrini, 2020; Horan, 2020). Many companies lack standardized indicators for comparing data, which prevents them from showcasing progress and ensuring accountability (Young-Ferris & Roberts, 2021). Transparency is also a major concern, as inconsistent data reporting and a lack of visible benchmarks hinder stakeholders' understanding of a company's actual impact. Establishing robust systems for consistent data collection and measurement is feasible but demands substantial capital investments and long-term commitments to transparency (Young-Ferris & Roberts, 2021; Aldowaish et al., 2022; Henriksson et al., 2019).

4.3. Balancing Short-Term and Long-Term Goals

When integrating ESG and SDG frameworks, a major tension arises between short-term financial performance and long-term sustainability outcomes. Meeting SDG targets generally demands high upfront investments, often leading to reduced immediate profitability (Muhmad & Muhamad, 2020). Similarly, maintaining high ESG standards—such as cutting emissions or improving employee benefits—may increase operational costs in the short run. Therefore, management must balance these short-term challenges with the long-term benefits of sustainable practices, including enhanced reputation, risk mitigation, and strengthened stakeholder loyalty and trust (Yang & Li, 2023).

This balance is often difficult to achieve, as shareholders frequently pressure companies to prioritize short-term financial returns, leading to compromises in sustainability commitments (Aldowaish et al., 2022; Yang & Li, 2023). Nonetheless, overcoming such challenges requires strategic planning, investment in data infrastructure, and alignment of corporate and societal goals. By addressing these barriers, companies can move toward a more integrated sustainability approach that aligns corporate priorities with global imperatives (Khaled et al., 2021; Zhao et al., 2018).

5. Case Studies of Successful Integration

5.1. Examples of Companies Leading in ESG–SDG Integration

Several companies have established in them the capacity to effectively amalgamate the ESG and SDG frameworks, showing that the corporate strategic alignment with priorities set globally is capable of great results. A few include:

- Unilever: In aligning its ESG strategy with specific SDGs, Unilever involves objectives focusing on sustainability goals such as reducing greenhouse gas emissions (SDG 13: Climate Action) and improving global hygiene and sanitation (SDG 6: Clean Water and Sanitation). Unilever's "Sustainable Living Plan" connects ESG goals with measurable KPIs and empowers the company to fuse sustainability into its brand image, guarantee higher operational efficiency, and build lasting trust among stakeholders. With such an approach, Unilever learns about how important it is to fix specific targets, embrace transparency in reporting, and sync sustainability with business growth (Aldowaish et al., 2022; Delabre et al., 2019).
- IKEA: IKEA has taken an aggressive stance toward aligning its ESG practices with SDG goals concerning renewable energy (SDG 7: Affordable and Clean Energy) and sustainable consumption (SDG 12: Responsible Consumption and Production). It sets ambitious goals for the use of renewable materials and the eventual ban on the use of single-use plastic in its products. The focus now on integrating SDGs into a business model reinforces IKEA's profile as a responsible retailer and seeks the appeal of green consumers. This case exemplifies goal-oriented strategies and the leverage of sustainability in customer loyalty (Puriwat & Tripopsakul, 2023; Lee & Rhee, 2023).
- Microsoft: Microsoft leads the pack in joining its ESG initiatives with the SDGs, particularly SDG 9 (Industry, Innovation, and Infrastructure) and SDG 13 (Climate Action). The commitment to becoming carbon negative by 2030 directly advances the sustainability and governance framework it purports to stand for. Because of how it has applied leading technological advancement to lessen its carbon footprint and sustain its innovation, Microsoft

underscores competency in that core approach. This case study underscores how companies can integrate ESG–SDG frameworks by aligning their sustainability goals with their technological strengths and innovation capabilities (Dantas et al., 2020; Del Río Castro et al., 2020).

5.2. Insights and Best Practices

These case studies provide valuable insights into best practices for ESG–SDG integration:

1. Define Clear and Measurable Goals: Companies should set specific, measurable targets for their ESG and SDG initiatives, as demonstrated by Unilever and Microsoft. These clear goals enable transparency and accountability, allowing stakeholders to track progress and support corporate sustainability efforts (Aldowaish et al., 2022).
2. Align Core Competencies with Sustainability Goals: Microsoft's success highlights the importance of aligning a company's strengths, such as technology or innovation, with its sustainability objectives. Leveraging core competencies makes it easier to achieve ESG–SDG targets and enhances brand value (Khaled et al., 2021).
3. Foster Stakeholder Engagement: Engaging stakeholders, from customers to investors, is essential. IKEA's commitment to sustainable products and packaging resonates with its eco-conscious customer base, showing that stakeholder alignment can drive both profitability and social impact (Mamedova, 2023).
4. Prioritize Long-Term Vision Over Short-Term Gains: Companies that successfully integrate ESG and SDG frameworks, like Unilever and Microsoft, balance long-term sustainability with short-term operational demands. This approach helps in building resilience and creating sustained value for the business and its stakeholders (Wang et al., 2023).

By following these best practices, companies can create robust strategies for integrating ESG and SDG frameworks, enabling them to achieve sustainability goals while strengthening their competitive advantage in the marketplace (Kim & Li, 2021; Henriksson et al., 2019).

This case study opened up several important practices and their worth towards ESG–SDG integration.

1. Establish Clear Goals that are Measurable. Companies (e.g., Unilever, Microsoft) need to develop specific goals around their SDG and ESG action that are measurable. These clear goals facilitate an open flow of information, allowing for corporate accounting to be made available to interested parties, enabling them to monitor progress, contribute to and even assist in the corporate sustainable development process (Aldowaish et al., 2022).
2. Correlate Core Competencies with Sustainability Goals. This brings up another key point: The successes of Microsoft highlight that a company must match its inherent capabilities, technological or otherwise, to its sustainability goal or societal impact. Doing business with core competencies makes it easier for a business to enter areas of ESG–SDG realization and increases brand value (Khaled et al., 2020).
3. Engage Stakeholders. And so bringing stakeholders along is going to be critically important, whether those are consumers or investors. To tap a sustainable pricing system, the IKEA philosophy suits its environmentally suggestive customer base; stakeholder coherence can generate profitability and social advantage (Mamedova, 2023).
4. Foresight Over Immediate Results. Companies that have successfully crystallised into an active ESG and SDG system, like Unilever or Microsoft, understand the way to balance some of their short-term operational imperatives with a sustainable wider narrative. At a broad level, it defines a support model and over a period creates a mound of value for the business and stakeholders (Wang et al., 2023).
5. Long-Term Vision Rather Than Short-Term Gains. Companies who have successfully laid a path to integrate into an active ESG and SDG system such as Unilever and Microsoft know how to set some of their short-term operational demands against the longer-term goals of sustainability. This basically defines a model of support and helps business and stakeholders to have a pile of value over a period (Wang et al., 2023).

6. Future Directions for ESG and SDG Integration

6.1. Outlook on Growth and Innovations

Towards the future of responsible practices in business, there exists a probable panorama composed of further emerging trends, although quite advanced regarding ESG–SDG integration. By technological innovations, we mean AI, big data, and IoT, which have become pivotal for companies aspiring to enhance sustainability investments (Saxena et al., 2022). For example, AI might help such analysts monitor carbon emissions in real time on environmental data; this provides better accuracy and transparency of ESG reporting (Di Vaio et al., 2020). Big analytics enables one to employ social and governance metrics through pooled insights to foresee and steer their SDG-related initiatives better, as substantiated by Wu et al., (2022). The basic structure of these technologies contributes to reducing the effort required in collecting and processing data, while it becomes possible to meet the integrated goals of spending plans such as ESG (and planned tax and reporting costs) more precisely (Sætra, 2021).

6.2. Policy Implications and Global Standards

With the increased desire for ensuring standardized reporting frameworks in service of ESG–SDG integration, settled by quite many a stakeholder insisting on transparent and comparable data on corporate sustainability efforts, it becomes imperative to look towards policy developments, which may focus on either constructing singular standards, whereby companies can respect them in a single manner for both ESG and SDG, through regulatory initiatives or via international accords (Stefanescu, 2021). The ongoing momentum toward harmonious global standards for sustainability reporting is signified by the recent move of the International Sustainability Standards Board (ISSB) and underlines the urgency of such movement (Abeysekera, 2022). At an appropriate time, such policies will be a benchmark for corporate accountability to enhance the company's ability to access validated and credible information that will serve their broad stakeholders; these developments are largely beneficial to stakeholders (Sætra, 2021).

7. Further Studies on ESG-SDG Integration and Development Potential

In the field of integrating ESG and SDGs, there is immense potential for more industry-oriented models to be built on unique predicaments and opportunities, of which we envisage there are endless prospects. Further explorations are needed in an attempt to assess the long-term financial impacts of integration as a new manifestation of sustainability, chiefly focusing on whether or not it can be established that such approaches generate definitive returns on investments (Bhattacharya & Bhattacharya, 2023). Furthermore, research could also look into the relation between ESG–SDG integration and corporate innovation, especially how these integrated approaches might instigate new products, services, and business models that benefit the firm and society alike. Their findings on these subjects can only serve to reinforce a comprehensive understanding as a guide to companies faced with these challenges of integrating ESG and SDG goals such that optimal contributions are made on the economic and corporate front (Aldowaish et al., 2022; Broadstock et al., 2019; Behl et al., 2021).

Conclusion

In conclusion, the application of an integrative ESG–SDG framework is truly revolutionary: corporate sustainability is achieved by means of strategy formulation that is aligned with the global development agenda. This alignment guarantees resilience and long-term value creation for companies but also addresses some of the major environmental and social problems (Khaled et al., 2021; Mamedova, 2023). The established relationship between the ESG and SDG goals offers companies a way to comply with regulations, develop good relations with stakeholders, and add a significant contribution to our society and the planet. However, challenges exist: measuring data, alignment complexity, short-term versus long-term goals, and the like. But adopting this integrated approach opens companies to enhanced reputation, better risk management, and increased loyalty from investors and consumers alike (Aldowaish et al., 2022; Sokolova & Teymurov, 2022).

As sustainability becomes the norm, companies are motivated to use ESG–SDG integration as a means to make a difference in the world. Deploying new technology, engaging stakeholders in dialogue, and accepting standardized reporting practices enable businesses to accomplish whatever sustainability goals they set and therefore contribute toward a more sustainable and equitable world (Sætra, 2021). This undertaking to integrate the ESG and SDG frameworks will not only realize corporate objectives but will also bolster a coordinated global effort toward sustainable development, thus granting businesses a leading edge in what is largely perceived as rapid change (Alsayegh et al., 2020; Jonsdottir et al., 2021; Zhang et al., 2023).

References

Abeysekera, I. (2022). A framework for sustainability reporting. *Sustainability Accounting, Management and Policy Journal*. https://doi.org/10.1108/sampj-08-2021-0316.

Adams, C., & Abhayawansa, S. (2021). Connecting the COVID-19 pandemic, environmental, social and governance (ESG) investing and calls for 'harmonisation' of sustainability reporting. *Critical Perspectives on Accounting*, *82*, Article 102309. https://doi.org/10.1016/j.cpa.2021.102309.

Adams, C., & Frost, G. (2008). Integrating sustainability reporting into management practices. *Accounting Forum*, *32* (4), 288–302. https://doi.org/10.1016/j.accfor.2008.05.002.

Aldowaish, A., Kokuryo, J., Almazyad, O., & Goi, H. (2022). Environmental, social, and governance integration into the business model: Literature review and research agenda. *Sustainability*, *14* (5), Article 2959. https://doi.org/10.3390/su14052959.

Allen, C., Metternicht, G., & Wiedmann, T. (2018). Initial progress in implementing the Sustainable Development Goals (SDGs): A review of evidence from countries. *Sustainability Science*, *13* (6), 1453–1467. https://doi.org/10.1007/s11625-018-0572-3.

Alsayegh, M., Rahman, R., & Homayoun, S. (2020). Corporate economic, environmental, and social sustainability performance transformation through ESG disclosure. *Sustainability*, *12* (9), Article 3910. https://doi.org/10.3390/su12093910.

Amaral, M., Willerding, I., & Lapolli, É. (2023). ESG and sustainability: The impact of the pillar social. *Concilium*. https://doi.org/10.53660/clm-1643-23j43.

Behl, A., Kumari, P., Makhija, H., & Sharma, D. (2021). Exploring the relationship of ESG score and firm value using cross-lagged panel analyses: Case of the Indian energy sector. *Annals of Operations Research*, *313* (1), 231–256. https://doi.org/10.1007/s10479-021-04189-8.

Beyne, J. (2020). Designing and implementing sustainability: An integrative framework for implementing the Sustainable Development Goals. *European Journal of Sustainable Development*, *9* (3), 1. https://doi.org/10.14207/ejsd.2020.v9n3p1.

Bhattacharya, A., & Bhattacharya, S. (2023). Integrating ESG pillars for business model innovation in the biopharmaceutical industry. *Australasian Accounting, Business and Finance Journal*, *17* (1), 159–176. https://doi.org/10.14453/aabfj.v17i1.12.

Biggeri, M., Clark, D., Ferrannini, A., & Mauro, V. (2019). Tracking the SDGs in an 'integrated' manner: A proposal for a new index to capture synergies and trade-offs between and within goals. *World Development, 122*, 628–647. https://doi.org/10.1016/j.worlddev.2019.05.022.

Broadstock, D., Matousek, R., Meyer, M., & Tzeremes, N. (2020). Does corporate social responsibility impact firms' innovation capacity? The indirect link between environmental & social governance implementation and innovation performance. *Journal of Business Research, 119*, 99–110. https://doi.org/10.1016/j.jbusres.2019.07.014.

Bulmer, E., & Yáñez-Araque, B. (2023). Tackling climate change through multi-stakeholder partnerships: Promoting SDG 17 to combat climate change. *Energies, 16* (9), Article 3777. https://doi.org/10.3390/en16093777.

Castro, G., Fernández, M., & Colsa, Á. (2021). Unleashing the convergence amid digitalization and sustainability towards pursuing the Sustainable Development Goals (SDGs): A holistic review. *Journal of Cleaner Production, 280* (Pt 2), Article 122204. https://doi.org/10.1016/j.jclepro.2020.122204.

Consolandi, C., Phadke, H., Hawley, J., & Eccles, R. (2018). Material ESG outcomes and SDG externalities: Evaluating the health care sector's contribution to the SDGs. *Organization & Environment, 33* (4), 511–533. https://doi.org/10.1177/1086026619899795.

Dantas, T., de-Souza, E., Destro, I., Hammes, G., Rodriguez, C., & Soares, S. (2021). How the combination of circular economy and Industry 4.0 can contribute towards achieving the Sustainable Development Goals. *Sustainable Production and Consumption, 26*, 213–227. https://doi.org/10.1016/j.spc.2020.10.005.

Delabre, I., Alexander, A., & Rodrigues, C. (2019). Strategies for tropical forest protection and sustainable supply chains: Challenges and opportunities for alignment with the UN sustainable development goals. *Sustainability Science, 15* (6), 1637–1651. https://doi.org/10.1007/s11625-019-00747-z.

Delgado-Ceballos, J., Ortiz-de-Mandojana, N., Antolín-López, R., & Montiel, I. (2022). Connecting the Sustainable Development Goals to firm-level sustainability and ESG factors: The need for double materiality. *Business Research Quarterly, 26* (1), 2–10. https://doi.org/10.1177/23409444221140919.

Dwivedi, P. (2023). Role of environmental, social and governance (ESG) in achieving Sustainable Development Goals: A brief review. *Public Health Open Access*. https://doi.org/10.23880/phoa-16000259.

Eisenmenger, N., Pichler, M., Krenmayr, N., Noll, D., Plank, B., Schalmann, E., Wandl, M., & Gingrich, S. (2020). The Sustainable Development Goals prioritize economic growth over sustainable resource use: A critical reflection on the SDGs from a socio-ecological perspective. *Sustainability Science, 15* (4), 1101–1110. https://doi.org/10.1007/s11625-020-00813-x.

ElAlfy, A., Weber, O., & Geobey, S. (2021). The Sustainable Development Goals (SDGs): A rising tide lifts all boats? Global reporting implications in a post SDGs world. *Journal of Applied Accounting Research*. https://doi.org/10.1108/JAAR-06-2020-0116.

Escrig-Olmedo, E., Fernández-Izquierdo, M., Ferrero-Ferrero, I., Rivera-Lirio, J., & Muñoz-Torres, M. (2019). Rating the raters: Evaluating how ESG rating agencies integrate sustainability principles. *Sustainability*, *11* (3), Article 915. https://doi.org/10.3390/su11030915

Filho, W., Tripathi, S., Guerra, J., Giné-Garriga, R., Lovren, V., & Willats, J. (2018). Using the sustainable development goals towards a better understanding of sustainability challenges. *International Journal of Sustainable Development & World Ecology*, *26* (2), 179–190. https://doi.org/10.1080/13504509.2018.1505674.

Freiberg, D., Rogers, J., & Serafeim, G. (2020). How ESG issues become financially material to corporations and their investors. *ERPN: Regulation (Topic)*. https://doi.org/10.2139/ssrn.3482546.

Griggs, D., Smith, M., Rockström, J., Öhman, M., Gaffney, O., Glaser, G., Kanie, N., Noble, I., Steffen, W., & Shyamsundar, P. (2014). An integrated framework for sustainable development goals. *Ecology and Society*, *19* (4), Article 49. https://doi.org/10.5751/ES-07082-190449.

Henriksson, R., Livnat, J., Pfeifer, P., & Stumpp, M. (2019). Integrating ESG in portfolio construction. *Journal of Portfolio Management*, *45* (4), 67–81. https://doi.org/10.3905/jpm.2019.45.4.067.

Horan, D. (2020). National baselines for integrated implementation of an environmental Sustainable Development Goal assessed in a new integrated SDG index. *Sustainability*, *12* (17), Article 6955. https://doi.org/10.3390/su12176955.

Hristov, I., & Chirico, A. (2019). The role of sustainability key performance indicators (KPIs) in implementing sustainable strategies. *Sustainability*, *11* (20), Article 5742. https://doi.org/10.3390/su11205742.

Jin, X., & Lei, X. (2023). A study on the mechanism of ESG's impact on corporate value under the concept of sustainable development. *Sustainability*, *15* (11), Article 8442. https://doi.org/10.3390/su15118442.

Jonsdottir, G., Sigurjonsson, T., Alavi, A., & Mitchell, J. (2021). Applying responsible ownership to advance SDGs and the ESG framework, resulting in the issuance of green bonds. *Sustainability*, *13* (13), Article 7331. https://doi.org/10.3390/su13137331.

Jun, H., & Kim, M. (2021). From stakeholder communication to engagement for the Sustainable Development Goals (SDGs): A case study of LG Electronics. *Sustainability*, *13* (15), Article 8624. https://doi.org/10.3390/su13158624.

Khaled, R., Ali, H., & Mohamed, E. (2021). The Sustainable Development Goals and corporate sustainability performance: Mapping, extent and determinants. *Journal of Cleaner Production*, *311*, Article 127599. https://doi.org/10.1016/j.jclepro.2021.127599.

Kim, S., & Li, Z. (2021). Understanding the impact of ESG practices in corporate finance. *Sustainability*, *13* (7), Article 3746. https://doi.org/10.3390/su13073746.

Kulova, I., & Nikolova-Alexieva, V. (2023). ESG strategy: Pivotal in cultivating stakeholder trust and ensuring customer loyalty. *E3S Web of Conferences*. https://doi.org/10.1051/e3sconf/202346203035.

Lee, H., & Rhee, T. (2023). How does corporate ESG management affect consumers' brand choice? *Sustainability*, *15* (8), Article 6795. https://doi.org/10.3390/su15086795.

Liang, Y., Lee, M., & Jung, J. (2022). Dynamic capabilities and an ESG strategy for sustainable management performance. *Frontiers in Psychology, 13*, Article 887776. https://doi.org/10.3389/fpsyg.2022.887776.

Lokuwaduge, C., & Heenetigala, K. (2017). Integrating environmental, social and governance (ESG) disclosure for sustainable development: An Australian study. *Business Strategy and the Environment, 26* (4), 438–450. https://doi.org/10.1002/bse.1927.

Lokuwaduge, C., Smark, C., & Mir, M. (2022). The surge of environmental social and governance reporting and Sustainable Development Goals: Some normative thoughts. *Australasian Business, Accounting and Finance Journal, 16* (2), Article 2. https://doi.org/10.14453/aabfj.v16i2.2.

Ma, J., Gao, D., & Sun, J. (2022). Does ESG performance promote total factor productivity? Evidence from China. *Frontiers in Ecology and Evolution, 10*, Article 1063736. https://doi.org/10.3389/fevo.2022.1063736.

Mamedova, S. (2023). Integration of sustainable development principles into the corporate strategy of state-owned companies: Development of an effective system for disclosing ESG factors in reporting. *Auditor*. https://doi.org/10.12737/1998-0701-2023-9-11-25-28.

Markopoulos, E., & Ramonda, M. (2022). An ESG-SDGs alignment and execution model based on the Ocean Strategies transition in emerging markets. *Creativity, Innovation and Entrepreneurship*. https://doi.org/10.54941/ahfe1001511.

Muhmad, S., & Muhamad, R. (2020). Sustainable business practices and financial performance during pre- and post-SDG adoption periods: A systematic review. *Journal of Sustainable Finance & Investment, 11* (4), 291–309. https://doi.org/10.1080/20430795.2020.1727724.

Puriwat, W., & Tripopsakul, S. (2023). Sustainability matters: Unravelling the power of ESG in fostering brand love and loyalty across generations and product involvements. *Sustainability, 15* (15), Article 11578. https://doi.org/10.3390/su151511578.

Radu, O., Dragomir, V., & Ionescu-Feleagă, L. (2023). The link between corporate ESG performance and the UN Sustainable Development Goals. *Proceedings of the International Conference on Business Excellence, 17* (1), 776–790. https://doi.org/10.2478/picbe-2023-0072.

Sætra, H. (2021). A framework for evaluating and disclosing the ESG related impacts of AI with the SDGs. *Sustainability, 13* (15), Article 8503. https://doi.org/10.3390/su13158503.

Sarkar, S., Nair, M., & Datta, A. (2023). Role of environmental, social, and governance in achieving the UN Sustainable Development Goals: A special focus on India. *Environmental Progress & Sustainable Energy, 42* (5), e14204. https://doi.org/10.1002/ep.14204.

Saxena, A., Singh, R., Gehlot, A., Akram, S., Twala, B., Singh, A., Montero, E., & Priyadarshi, N. (2022). Technologies empowered environmental, social, and governance (ESG): An Industry 4.0 landscape. *Sustainability, 15* (1), Article 309. https://doi.org/10.3390/su15010309.

Sciarelli, M., Cosimato, S., Landi, G., & Iandolo, F. (2021). Socially responsible investment strategies for the transition towards sustainable development: The importance of integrating and communicating ESG. *The TQM Journal*. https://doi.org/10.1108/tqm-08-2020-0180.

Shapsugova, M. (2023). ESG principles and social responsibility. *E3S Web of Conferences*. https://doi.org/10.1051/e3sconf/202342006040.

Sokolova, N., & Teymurov, E. (2022). Correlation of Sustainable Development Goals and ESG principles. *Courier of Kutafin Moscow State Law University (MSAL)*. https://doi.org/10.17803/2311-5998.2021.88.12.171-183.

Soni, T. (2023). Demystifying the relationship between ESG and SDG performance: Study of emerging economies. *Investment Management and Financial Innovations*, *20* (3), 1–12. https://doi.org/10.21511/imfi.20 (3).2023.01.

Ştefănescu, C. (2021). Linking sustainability reporting frameworks and sustainable development goals. *Accounting Research Journal*. https://doi.org/10.1108/arj-07-2020-0196.

Vaio, A., Palladino, R., Hassan, R., & Escobar, O. (2020). Artificial intelligence and business models in the sustainable development goals perspective: A systematic literature review. *Journal of Business Research*, *121*, 283–314. https://doi.org/10.1016/j.jbusres.2020.08.019.

Wang, K., Yu, S., Mei, M., Yang, X., Peng, G., & Lv, B. (2023). ESG performance and corporate resilience: An empirical analysis based on the capital allocation efficiency perspective. *Sustainability*, *15* (23), Article 16145. https://doi.org/10.3390/su152316145.

Wu, S., Shirkey, G., Celik, I., Shao, C., & Chen, J. (2022). A review on the adoption of AI, BC, and IoT in sustainability research. *Sustainability*, *14* (13), Article 7851. https://doi.org/10.3390/su14137851.

Yang, F., & Li, X. (2023). Corporate financialization, ESG performance and sustainability development: Evidence from Chinese-listed companies. *Sustainability*, *15* (4), Article 2978. https://doi.org/10.3390/su15042978.

Young-Ferris, A., & Roberts, J. (2021). 'Looking for something that isn't there': A case study of an early attempt at ESG integration in investment decision making. *European Accounting Review*, *32* (3), 717–744. https://doi.org/10.1080/09638180.2021.2000458.

Zaccone, M., & Pedrini, M. (2020). ESG factor integration into private equity. *Sustainability*, *12* (14), Article 5725. https://doi.org/10.3390/su12145725.

Zhang, K., Kassim, A., & Guo, Y. (2023). Research on corporate sustainability from an ESG perspective. *Frontiers in Business, Economics and Management*. https://doi.org/10.54097/fbem.v8i2.7147.

Zhao, C., Guo, Y., Yuan, J., Wu, M., Li, D., Zhou, Y., & Kang, J. (2018). ESG and corporate financial performance: Empirical evidence from China's listed power generation companies. *Sustainability*, *10* (8), Article 2607. https://doi.org/10.3390/su10082607.

Chapter 5

ESG-Aligned Ownership Types and Corporate Governance: How Institutional, Insider, and Family Investors Drive Sustainable Finance and Ethical Investing

Zahra Mohamed El Shlmani[1,†]
Mushtaq Yousif Alhasnawi[2,†]
and Ibrahim Eriqat[3,‡]
[1]School of Management, Universiti Sains Malaysia, Penang, Malaysia
Libyan Academy for Postgraduate Studies, Benghazi, Libya
[2]Faculty of Administration and Economics, University of Thi-Qar, Nasiriyah, Iraq
[3]Smart University College for Modern Education, Hebron, Palestine

Abstract

This chapter examines the critical link between ownership types—institutional, insider, and family—and corporate governance, with a specific focus on how they mitigate or exacerbate corporate moral hazard and shape ethical investing outcomes, ultimately driving ESG performance. Findings suggest that institutional investors exhibit heterogeneous behaviors despite being theoretically positioned as ideal monitors. Some investors actively engage in governance. However, other investors remain passive or contribute to short-termism due to conflicting incentives. Moreover, insider ownership exhibits contradictory behavior. Although equity alignment can reduce agency costs, it may create

† Corresponding Author's Email: zahrashalmani@student.usm.my, zizishalmani@yahoo.com
† Corresponding Author's Email: alhasnawi78@utq.edu.iq
‡ Corresponding Author's Email: ibrahimeriqat96@gmail.com

In: Environmental, Social, and Governance (ESG) …
Editor: Veena Grover
ISBN: 979-8-90134-138-4

opportunities for expropriation, especially when it is combined with information asymmetries in weak enforcement systems. Meanwhile, family firms emerge as a distinct case. Family firms demonstrate how nonfinancial motives can lead to superior ESG performance. This situation is due to the long-term stewardship that these firms possess. Furthermore, these firms encounter governance challenges in professional oversight and succession planning. These findings challenge traditional shareholder models. Sustainable governance requires moving beyond abstract ownership categories. These models demonstrate how real-world investors exercise their power in practice. This chapter emphasizes the need for independent oversight mechanisms and calls for meaningful enforcement actions tailored to specific ownership types. ESG considerations are constantly redefining corporate goals. Accordingly, this study highlights the importance of developing ownership-sensitive governance frameworks. These frameworks should balance financial and sustainability objectives while protecting minority stakeholders.

Keywords: ESG, ownership types, corporate governance, sustainable finance, ethics, institutional ownership, insider ownership, family ownership

1. Introduction

The increasing emphasis on environmental, social, and governance (ESG) principles has reshaped corporate priorities. ESG factors have transformed investor behavior and reoriented regulatory frameworks worldwide (Jaiswal et al., 2025). Different stakeholders increasingly demand transparency, accountability, and sustainable business practices. Consequently, the role of ownership structures in shaping corporate governance and ESG outcomes has become a critical area of inquiry (Zhu et al., 2025). Ownership concentration and composition, whether institutional, insider, or family-based, significantly influence a firm's strategic decisions, risk management, and long-term sustainability performance. However, the relationship between different types of ownership and governance effectiveness remains complex (Alshbili et al., 2020). Studies show that each ownership provides unique advantages but faces specific governance challenges.

Institutional investors are often viewed as stewards of good governance due to their substantial resources and influence. However, the effectiveness of these institutional investors can significantly vary based on multiple factors. Investment horizons, fiduciary duties, and pressures for short-term profits are well-known drivers. Meanwhile, insider ownership is theoretically intended to align the interests of management and shareholders. However, insider ownership can also lead to the entrenchment of control and enable opportunistic behavior. This situation is particularly observed in environments with weak regulatory oversight. By contrast, family-owned firms have a distinctive combination of long-term orientation and ethical commitment (Chaudhary et al., 2025). Consequently, these firms often outperform their industry peers on critical ESG metrics. Nevertheless, these firms face governance hurdles related to professionalization and succession planning (Villalonga & Amit, 2020).

This chapter investigates how various types of ownership influence the quality of corporate governance and the integration of ESG factors. A systematic literature review methodology is utilized to analyze the relationship between ownership types and ESG-aligned corporate governance. A key concern is how different owners—institutional, insider, and family—affect the ethical behavior of a firm and its exposure to risks like managerial self-interest. The analysis, centered on the U.S. context, examines whether these ownership models promote accountability or enable misconduct. This chapter draws its findings from empirical research and theoretical frameworks, such as agency theory, stewardship theory, and stakeholder theory. The link between ownership structures and ESG performance can be interpreted through agency, stewardship, and stakeholder theories. Agency theory (Jensen & Meckling, 1976) highlights conflicts between owners and managers, suggesting that institutional investors can reduce managerial opportunism when long-term oriented, while excessive insider control may lead to entrenchment. Stewardship theory views owners as trustworthy stewards: family ownership often reflects this logic through long-term and reputational goals but faces risks of nepotism and weak professional oversight. Stakeholder theory broadens both perspectives by recognizing that institutional, insider, and family owners differ in balancing profit motives with social and environmental accountability. Together, these lenses frame ownership not merely as a financial arrangement but as a behavioral system shaping how ESG principles are embedded in corporate governance. Furthermore, this chapter addresses key questions: How do different owners balance financial objectives with sustainability goals? What governance mechanisms can mitigate ownership-related risks? How can regulatory frameworks be adapted to the specific challenges linked to different ownership types? This chapter offers valuable insights for policymakers who aim to enhance corporate accountability by analyzing these dynamics. In addition, this chapter also aids investors in comprehending ESG-driven markets. Lastly, this chapter provides practical guidance for firms that desire to align their ownership models with sustainable growth.

The chapter discussion proceeds as follows: First, this chapter explores the evolving regulatory landscape for ESG criteria and corporate governance. This chapter mainly focuses on the US regulatory system for ESG and corporate governance. This system represents the most advanced framework globally. Accordingly, this chapter highlights persistent enforcement challenges, even within this developed system. Next, this chapter analyzes three types of ownership, including institutional, insider, and family ownership. The analysis thoroughly compares the relation of these ownership types to corporate governance. Finally, this chapter synthesizes policy and research recommendations aimed at optimizing ownership-driven governance in the ESG era. This chapter contributes to ongoing debates about sustainable finance, ethical investing, and the future of corporate accountability.

2. ESG-Related Regulatory Developments

The effectiveness of the board and the management in monitoring company management is influenced by the level of enforcement. In particular, managerial fraud is difficult to prevent in jurisdictions with weak legal systems due to the low probability of detection and the imposition of lenient penalties. In such cases, minority investors are unlikely to pursue legal action against management, as the likelihood of winning is low, and the expected compensation may not cover the expenses and opportunity costs associated with litigation. Scholars, such as Bhattacharya and Daouk (2002, 2005), Berkowitz et al., (2003), and Pistor et al., (2000), argued that law enforcement plays a more crucial role than the written code in promoting financial development. Bhattacharya and Daouk (2005) found that countries that introduce insider trading laws fail to enforce them experience an increase in the cost of capital (Zhang, 2007). Bailey et al., (2022) argued that ESG reporting mandates are ineffective in the absence of enforcement. Soltani (2014) and Coffee (2007) pointed out that the US significantly stands out in terms of enforcement actions and sanctions. The US imposes financial penalties that are unparalleled compared with other jurisdictions, even when considering market adjustments. In addition to public enforcement efforts, the US has a robust and highly active system of private enforcement, including class actions[1]. This unique system of enforcement is unmatched worldwide, with no similar counterpart in other countries. The US pursues criminal prosecution for securities offenses in a systematic manner.

The Fair Pay and Safe Workplaces Executive Order (2014), established under the Obama Administration, mandates that federal contracts may only be awarded to companies that demonstrate a satisfactory track record in performance, integrity, and business ethics (Chatterjee, 2016), para 6. The majority of the companies that are federal contractors have clean records, according to available data. The Department of Labor reported that a significant proportion of firms holding federal contracts have not been involved in any federal workplace violations (corporate lawsuits) over the past 3 years. The decreasing size of companies' records indicates that violators are taking steps to improve their practices.

The Dodd-Frank Act of 2010 and the Sarbanes-Oxley Act of 2002 were issued to restrict and regulate corporate behavior. However, corporate governance failures persisted even after the implementation of these regulations, such as Dynegy (due to executives' fraud in 2022). Accounting failures, risky investments, and inefficient operations have proven to be disastrous for many giant US firms. This notion suggests that addressing corporate governance issues concerning scandals is still worthwhile (Bhagat & Bolton, 2019). The securities market reflects and regulates corporate governance standards. Many jurisdictions use securities markets as a tool to improve corporate governance. The Securities and Exchange Commission (SEC) is responsible for enforcing regulations on companies under its jurisdiction. Meanwhile, the Department of Justice (DOJ) enforces the Act for individuals and domestic entities not regulated by the SEC. However, the actions taken by one agency do not prevent the other from initiating separate enforcement proceedings. In certain cases, the DOJ and SEC have pursued enforcement actions against the same company for violating the Foreign Corrupt Practices Act (FCPA). In 2010, the SEC established a specialized unit dedicated to enforcing the FCPA. The SEC and DOJ jointly released the initial edition of their FCPA guide in 2012, followed by a second edition in 2020. The enforcement of the FCPA is a shared responsibility between the SEC and the DOJ, as it amends the SEC Act and the criminal code. However, the majority of companies face civil penalties, with criminal charges involved in less than half a percent of the cases (0.5%).

---

[1] In a class action suit, a plaintiff sues a defendant(s) on behalf of a class or group of absent parties.

The US Congress passed a new law—the Corporate Transparency Act (CTA)–in 2021. This act requires companies to disclose their ownership structures to the US Treasury as of January 2022. Companies must disclose details about their beneficial owners through a beneficial ownership registry, which is managed by the Financial Crimes Enforcement Network (FinCEN) under the US Treasury Department (Johnson et al., 2022). Under the CTA, a "beneficial owner" is defined as an individual with substantial control over the entity, either directly or indirectly, or one who holds at least 25% of its ownership interests (Federal Register, 2022).

The evidence therefore suggests that, while the U.S. has developed a sophisticated and multi-layered regulatory system for corporate governance and, increasingly, ESG disclosure, its effectiveness is not absolute. Persistent corporate scandals reveal that even within this advanced enforcement environment, regulations alone cannot fully deter misconduct. This underscores a critical theme for the analysis that follows: the formal regulatory framework establishes the rules of the game, but the ownership structure of a firm fundamentally shapes how—and whether—those rules are followed. The subsequent sections will analyse how different ownership types interact with this regulatory landscape to drive ethical and sustainable outcomes.

3. ESG-Aligned Ownership and Corporate Moral Hazard

The ownership structure of a company plays a crucial role in shaping its corporate governance framework. In recent years, noticeable trends have emerged in the ownership structure of US firms, driven by changes in corporate governance practices and an increasing emphasis on the influence of ESG factors on decision-making and stock performance (Keller et al., 2022). This phenomenon results from corporate governance evolution and growing attention to the effect of ESG on corporate decision-making and stock performance. Although governance factors have received the most scholarly attention, ownership structures also exert distinct influences on environmental and social dimensions. Institutional investors frequently shape environmental strategies through sustainability screening, carbon disclosure, and green innovation incentives. Insider ownership, by contrast, has a stronger bearing on social outcomes, such as ethical culture, employee protection, and stakeholder relations, given internal control these owners wield. Family ownership often integrates environmental and social goals into long-term stewardship and community engagement but may lag in governance formalization. Recognizing these differentiated effects helps balance the ESG discussion and situates ownership as a multidimensional driver of corporate sustainability.

Owners, managers, and executives account for a sizeable proportion of those involved in corporate crimes. In US firms, different ownership structures coexist, such as privately/publicly held firms and family firms. The theoretical model of Jensen and Meckling (1976) places managers who own 100% of the firm at one extreme of ownership structure. These firms do not have agency conflicts. On the opposite extreme are firms whose managers are salaried employees with no firm equity. Firms in between are those whose equity is split among managers, families, institutions, and other parties. Ownership structure can be defined based on ownership concentration, where ownership is more or less dispersed. This structure can also be defined based on the nature of the owners. An enhanced ownership structure can align the ultimate controlling of owner's interests with those of the minority owners.

3.1. Institutional Ownership

The literature has introduced corporate governance research based on ownership by institutional investors (Chen et al., 2020; Fernando et al., 2017; Gillan et al., 2021; Nofsinger et al., 2019). Gillan and Starks (2007) reported that the institutional investor ownership in the US increased from 10% in 1953 to 60% in 2005. Lewellen and Lewellen (2022) asserted that institutional ownership in the overall market increased from 32% to 73% between 1980 and 2017. In the US market, a significant number of institutional investors are independent of government affiliations and not easily susceptible to political pressures. However, the absence of state control in US firms has direct implications for the quality of corporate governance. Traditional research in corporate governance highlights the importance of institutional investors in external monitoring and enhancing the standards of corporate governance (Sabbagh, 2016). Chung and Zhang (2011) presented empirical evidence through an examination of US data, demonstrating that the proportion of institutional investor ownership increases with the strength of a company's governance structure.

The literature presents conflicting perspectives on the behavior of institutional owners. One viewpoint portrays these owners as short-sighted investors primarily focused on maximizing short-term profits (Porter, 1992). By contrast, an alternative perspective considers these owners as proactive and vigilant long-term investors (Useem, 1996). Some institutional investors are temporal and shortsighted, with a focus on returns. Consequently, these individuals are opponents of long-term investing. However, some of these individuals own huge long-term holdings, making it complicated and costly to sell off or replace their shares. Accordingly, these individuals have incentives to monitor corporate operations and make strategic decisions. Institutional owners are expected to monitor insiders and families, especially when institutions serve as external directors. These individuals play a role in strengthening the internal control of companies, which in turn controls corporate crime. Thus, institutional owners have a direct influence on the corporate crime rate.

The involvement of institutional investors in a company's corporate governance system is a topic of debate. Certain studies argue that institutional investors should be involved in the corporate governance system, as successful corporate governance relies on their active participation. By contrast, other studies suggest that institutional investors do not necessarily need to be associated with the company's corporate governance system. This disclaimer arises from the company's fiduciary responsibility toward its own investors and beneficiaries. Those critical relationships can lead to conflicts of interest. Specifically, when they assume the role of owners (Khanchel, 2007). Yadav (2020) indicated that the risk behavior of institutional investors is classified into two types: pressure-resistant and pressure-sensitive (Brickley et al., 1988; Ferreira & Matos, 2008). Mutual funds represent the first category of institutional investors that often acquire company shares through market mechanisms. Muniandy et al., (2016), as cited in Yadav (2020), asserted that those investors possess strong incentives to closely monitor corporate activities. These investors actively participate in the processes of firms' strategic decision-making. This classification system highlights the varying degrees of engagement and influence that different institutional investor types may exert on corporate governance. In terms of the institutional ownership effect, Kao et al., (2019) found that when institutional investors increase their ownership of company shares in Taiwan, the company's value increases.

Institutional investors typically play a key role in avoiding future litigation. These investors decrease or eliminate their positions in sued firms before litigation begins (Barabanov et al., 2008). In addition, the trading behavior of institutional investors is influenced by their monitoring ability. For example, independent investment advisors and mutual funds are more proactive than banks, insurance companies, and other institutions (Wu & Wang, 2016). Mispricing in the market is positively related to corporate investment, and this link is amplified in firms with higher institutional investor ownership, particularly insurance firms and trusts (Chen et al., 2008).

Pucheta-Martínez and Chiva-Ortells (2018) indicated that institutional owners have a nonlinear relationship with ESGP. Some institutional owners are temporal and shortsighted, with a focus on returns. Consequently, these institutional owners are opponents of ESG investing. However, some institutional owners own huge long-term holdings, making it complicated and costly to sell off or replace their shares. Accordingly, institutional owners have incentives to monitor corporate operations and make strategic decisions, including ESG activities. Institutional owners are expected to monitor insiders and families, especially when institutions serve as external directors. Moreover, institutional owners play a role in strengthening the internal control of companies, which in turn controls corporate crime. Institutional owners have a direct influence on the corporate crime rate and ESG engagements. The presence of institutional owners is expected to interact with the relationship between corporate moral hazard and ESGP. This study predicts that institutional owners affect the negative influence of corporate moral hazard and ESGP.

Nekhili et al., (2019) suggested that institutional holders exert significant control over managerial activities and enhance the firm's ESGP (Lahouel et al., 2014), which is supported by the findings of Martínez-Ferrero et al., (2021). Borghesi et al., (2014) found a negative relationship between institutional ownership and firms' ESG scores, indicating that institutional ownership is associated with shareholder preferences. Gillan et al., (2010) suggested that institutional ownership actually decreases when firms improve their ESG indices. Nofsinger et al., (2019) concluded that institutional ownership is not positively linked to high environmental and social scores. However, institutional ownership is negatively associated with low environmental and social performance. Chava (2014) observed that companies with irresponsible environmental practices records have low institutional ownership. Fernando et al., (2017) examined the relationship between institutional ownership and environmental performance. They found a connection, but they note that this relationship depends on environmental scores. Specifically, companies with either higher or lower environmental indices have lower institutional ownership compared with companies in the middle range (Gillan et al., 2021). Tang et al., (2021) highlighted a critical concern. They demonstrated that companies linked to rating agencies through institutional ownership, known as "sister firms," receive high scores for ESG indicators. They indicated a cause-and-effect relationship between ownership connections and rating inflation, which results from rating agency acquisitions. The inflation of ESG ratings due to these connections becomes significantly notable when institutional owners hold a large proportion of the rating agency's shares. These findings raise concerns about the credibility of ESG ratings. These ratings are influenced by conflicts of interest within market practices. A possible reason for the rating agency to increase the ESG rating of a sister firm is to enhance its reputation among its key stakeholders. The conflict-of-interest issue faced by ESG agencies aligns with research on other intermediaries, as explored in studies such as Li (2016). He found that Institutional Shareholder Service (ISS), a voting recommendation advisor, provides voting recommendations that are favorable to company management. This preference toward management is influenced by the revenue ISS generates from consultation fees paid by the companies.

3.2. Insider Ownership

In contrast to institutional investors, insiders' ESG influence often stems from internal alignment rather than market pressure, which can produce both ethical coherence and accountability risks. Insiders are frequently involved in illegal corporate behavior, which coincides with a significant amount of loss. In addition, insiders exploit information asymmetry to commit long and ongoing corporate crimes, such as accounting manipulation, illegal pollution, insider trading, and tax evasion, to pursue private gains. They overlook long-term opportunities unless they are optimal for themselves for the same reason.

Insiders, who possess concentrated ownership, are more organized compared with dispersed shareholders and have a higher likelihood of obtaining significant premiums through takeovers (Fauzi & Locke, 2012). The primary concern regarding insider ownership relates to the pursuit of personal gains. Insider ownership exemplifies a governance issue that arises due to the disparity between control rights and cash flow associated with such ownership. In the governance literature, insider ownership is examined from two perspectives. First, insider ownership can be identified as management ownership (manager-owner), where owners grant managers ownership rights as a subsequent incentive mechanism. Second, insider ownership is identified when an insider who also manages (owner-manager) possesses de facto ownership rights. The behavior of insiders in both scenarios, influenced by differences in cash flow and control rights, cannot be compared due to variations in motivations and expectations (BV et al., 2005).

Regarding corporate moral hazard, insiders commit corporate fraud when they take advantage of opportunities to gain private benefits (Cappelli et al., 2012). A survey in 2009 indicated that 76% of economic crimes against US corporations were committed by insiders (Hess & Jr., 2016). ACFE (2010) reported that fraud committed by owners/executives resulted in financial damages that were over three times greater than fraud committed by managers and nine times more costly than employee fraud. Furthermore, fraud carried out at the executive level took significantly longer to be identified. Beck and Bhagat (1999) demonstrated that companies involved in lawsuits under SEC Rule 10b-5 were more prone to experiencing periods of underperformance in their stock prices compared with those who are not subject to such legal action. Rule 10b-5 specifically addresses cases of "insider trading," which occurs when confidential information is exploited to manipulate the stock market for personal gain (Bonini & Boraschi-Diaz, 2013). The influence of insider ownership on corporate governance and performance has been categorized as either positive or negative. The positive perspective asserts that higher levels of insider ownership result in reduced motivation for misappropriation, resulting in improved performance. Meanwhile, the negative perspective argues that lower levels of insider ownership increase monitoring by other stakeholders, particularly blockholders, such as institutional investors, thereby reducing misappropriation by insiders. The agency theory provides that concentrating insider ownership aligns the interests of shareholders with those of managers, thereby enhancing corporate performance. Furthermore, owner/executive perpetrators are responsible for the largest scale of fraud compared with other actors, and their fraudulent schemes often last longer, lasting up to 24 months, according to ACFE (2020). Furthermore, insiders who observed an enforcement action have a reduced likelihood of being convicted in the future compared with their counterparts who have not been exposed to such actions (Davidson & Pirinsky, 2022).

High insider ownership may reduce the external accountability of the firm. When insiders face enforcement actions, they may consider it unnecessary to proactively respond. Insider ownership can lead to conflicts of interest between the interests of insiders and the broader stakeholder community. In addition, enforcement actions may exacerbate these conflicts, hindering positive responses to company concerns (Denis & McConnell, 2009).

Existing literature provides abundant studies on insider ownership's key role in corporate performance (Nekhili et al., 2020). Managerial ownership is an important variable because it implies the possibility of oversight and the compatibility of shareholders' and managers' interests. In particular, managerial ownership reduces agency conflict concerns (Sabbagh, 2016). Kim and Kim (2020) indicated that the increased ownership by insiders is strongly linked to decreased occurrences of insider arrests and charges within the Korean stock market from 2000 to 2015. This finding remains consistent across different measurements of insider ownership, such as cash flow rights, control rights, and managerial ownership. Lee (2019) reported that the opportunistic actions of insider owners are examined. When insiders reduce their shareholding, a notable negative excess return is observed following the disclosure. The study also reveals a significant association between changes in insider shareholdings and the likelihood of delisting. A considerable number of studies have found a positive relationship between insider ownership and corporate performance (Ud Din et al., 2021). Gao et al., (2014) found that insiders avoid profitable insider trading to fulfill their obligation to socially responsible practices. Park (2019) claimed that insider ownership negatively affects US firms' ESG indices at a confidence level of 90%. The percentage of insiders on the board negatively affects the ESG score, as reported by Cooper and Uzun (2022).

3.3. Family Ownership

The most prevalent ownership type in most countries is family ownership (Bammens & Hünermund, 2020). The US Census Bureau indicated that family firms comprise 90% of all business firms in North America. The World Bank reported that public firms in the US have decreased from over 8000 in 1996 to 4400 in 2018 (Villalonga & Amit, 2020). The increase in market concentration resulted from the reduction in the size of initial public offerings and the rise in the number of delisting (Grullon et al., 2019).

Family owners exhibit the potential to engage in opportunistic behavior and exploit company resources to the disadvantage of shareholders with smaller ownership stakes. However, the informal practices, internal ethical cultures, and core values of these individuals contribute to preventing other parties from exploiting company resources. These individuals avoid hurting their image because they are long-term-oriented investors.

Shanker and Astrachan (1996) classified family firms using two different criteria: family management (narrow definition) and ownership proportion (wide definition). In the strict sense, a family-owned company is classified as such when a family member in a prominent managerial position is involved.

In the broad sense, a family-owned firm is one where the owning family exerts substantial control over the strategic decision-making process, determined by the percentage of shares that they possess (Lohwasser et al., 2021). The competitive advantage hypothesis provides that family ownership is prevalent in situations where it maximizes value for family and non-family stakeholders. However, family ownership prevails when it maximizes value specifically for the family, often at the expense of non-family investors who may be subject to expropriation, based on the hypothesis of private control benefits (Villalonga & Amit, 2020). Family firms exhibit key characteristics that distinguish them from other types of companies. These factors encompass the long-term focus of family owners, their aim to preserve wealth within the company, their active participation in management to shape strategies and objectives, and their significant roles on the board and during transitions between generations. The notable influence of family firms across multiple dimensions, including ownership, management, governance, and succession, as well as in shaping the company's goals and strategies, is what truly distinguishes them (Rodriguez-Ariza et al., 2016). Furthermore, family firms have a high proportion of ownership by insiders (Abeysekera & Fernando, 2020).

Bennedsen et al., (2007) reported that family ownership remains remarkably persistent, despite the negative influence of family CEO successors on corporate performance. Moreover, Belenzon et al., (2017) found that firms that include the founder's family name in their branding are associated with superior corporate performance. Faller and Knyphausen-Aufseß (2018), in their analysis of 19 empirical studies, noted that 12 studies indicated a positive link between family ownership and ESG performance, whereas four revealed a negative association, and three found no statistically meaningful connection.

Corporate moral hazard problems result from the allocation of control rights and ownership. Previous research on family ownership indicates that they frequently prioritize non-financial goals and objectives, such as ESG performance (Bammens & Hünermund, 2020). Amalina and Juliarto (2021) found that public ownership does not moderate the relationship between ethical commitment and ROA.

Musallam et al., (2019) analyzed panel data from 139 non-financial listed firms in Indonesia between 2009 and 2013. They reported a significant positive relationship between family ownership and corporate financial performance. Saeed et al., (2022) demonstrated that family-owned firms show great commitment to environmental sustainability, as evidenced by their high propensity to obtain ISO 14001 certification—an internationally recognized environmental management standard. Sun et al., (2023) extended this research stream by examining broad sustainability metrics. They found that family ownership and control structures are positively associated with comprehensive ESG performance scores. These cumulative findings suggest that family firms exhibit distinct strategic advantages in financial and non-financial dimensions of corporate performance.

Sufficient family ownership plays a crucial role in shaping the board's composition, with the CEO and at least one executive position typically occupied by a family member. This arrangement is often driven by the intention to facilitate the transfer of the company to the next generation (Rodriguez-Ariza et al., 2016). Family ownership is widely prevalent in publicly listed companies across various regions worldwide (Musallam et al., 2019). Other papers aimed to elucidate the reasons behind the prevalence of concentrated ownership, particularly with family-controlled owners, across various regions (Villalonga, 2019). Furthermore, numerous studies affirmed the heightened ethical focus of family owners and their inclination to prioritize factors beyond economic or financial considerations to meet the CSR expectations of stakeholders (Martínez-Ferrero et al., 2016). However, family-owned companies influence fraud occurrence among Taiwanese firms (Aghghaleh et al., 2014). Entrenchment theory suggests that auditors perceive great agency conflicts within family enterprises due to the potential for opportunistic behavior by family members. These individuals may seek to extract personal gains and even exploit the company's resources at the expense of other shareholders (Krishnan & Peytcheva, 2019). Given these risks, Avortri and Agbanyo (2020) suggested that the regulator should firmly enforce the shareholding structure specified in the corporate governance to avoid single-person or family ownership, which gives CEOs a high capacity to misappropriate funds. The Global Fraud Report 2022 revealed that family-related fraud accounts for 45% of all cases, which underscores the risks associated with concentrated family control.

Conclusion

This chapter has demonstrated that the influence of institutional, insider, and family ownership on corporate governance is fundamentally shaped by the distinct incentive structures each creates. These structures critically determine a firm's commitment to ethical stewardship versus its vulnerability to self-interest and managerial excess. The analysis reveals several findings that enhance our understanding of the ownership-governance nexus in relation to ESG performance. The evidence shows that the monitoring influence of institutional investors varies based on their investment horizons and fiduciary constraints. The long-term-oriented owners consistently outperform in controlling managerial excesses than transient shareholders. Meanwhile, insider ownership emerges as a double-edged sword. Although equity stakes theoretically align interests, concentrated control rights often enable expropriation strategies that undermine minority shareholders. This situation particularly occurred in environments with weak legal protection. Family-controlled firms present the most nuanced case. These firms exhibit superior ESG performance due to reputational concerns and intergenerational stewardship motives. However, these firms also face governance struggles regarding succession planning and professionalization. These patterns suggest that no single ownership model offers a governance panacea or efficiently works in all contexts. Instead, effective regulatory frameworks must account for these structural differences between ownership types through targeted measures. These frameworks include extensive oversight of related-party transactions, enhanced beneficial ownership disclosures, and incentives for long-term investment. The central challenge, therefore, lies in aligning the inherent incentives of each ownership class with broader goals of accountability and sustainable value creation. This alignment is the primary defense against the ethical breaches and moral hazards that undermine sustainable governance. The persistent governance failures, even in robust regulatory regimes similar to that of the United States, underscore the need for a more sophisticated, ownership-aware approach to corporate oversight. Beyond summarizing the findings, this chapter highlights a deeper insight: ownership structures are not merely governance mechanisms but behavioral systems that shape ethical norms within corporations. Theoretically, this extends agency and stewardship theories by showing that incentive alignment alone cannot ensure sustainable conduct without value-based oversight. From a policy perspective, strengthening ESG-aligned governance requires ownership-sensitive regulatory measures. First, disclosure requirements should be enhanced and tailored to ownership types to improve transparency and accountability among dominant owners. Second, stewardship codes for institutional investors should be encouraged to promote active monitoring, long-term engagement, and ethical alignment with ESG principles. Third, regulators should design family succession governance guidelines that integrate ESG oversight, ensuring continuity of sustainable practices across generations. This means ESG rules must be complemented by mechanisms that internalize ethics—such as stewardship codes and beneficial ownership transparency. For practitioners, particularly corporate boards, embedding ethical accountability into performance metrics is essential to bridge the gap between regulatory compliance and genuine sustainability. Collectively, these policy measures would align ownership incentives with the broader goals of corporate integrity, stakeholder protection, and sustainable value creation. Future research should examine how emerging ownership forms—such as ESG-focused activist investors, sovereign wealth funds, and digital or algorithmic ownership models—reshape the governance–ESG relationship across different institutional settings. Comparative cross-country studies could reveal how variations in legal systems, enforcement intensity, and cultural norms moderate these effects. Additionally, policymakers must address the growing disconnect between formal ownership classifications and actual control structures in an era of dual-class shares and high-frequency digital trading. Such inquiry would deepen understanding of how evolving ownership mechanisms influence sustainable governance and ethical accountability in global markets.

References

Abeysekera, A., & Fernando, C. (April, 2020). Corporate social responsibility versus corporate shareholder responsibility: A family firm perspective. *Journal of Corporate Finance, 61*, 1-22. doi:https://doi.org/10.1016/j.jcorpfin.2018.05.003.

ACFE. (2010). *Report to the Nations on Occupational Fraud and Abuse.* Association of Certified Fraud Examiners, Inc. Retrieved from https://www.acfe.com/-/media/files/acfe/pdfs/rttn-2010.ashx.

ACFE. (2020). *Report to the Nations.* Association of Certified Fraud Examiners. Retrieved from https://legacy.acfe.com/report-to-the-nations/2020/.

Aghghaleh, S., Iskandar, T., & Mohamed, Z. (February, 2014). Fraud risk factors of fraud triangle and the likelihood of fraud occurrence. *Information Management and Business Review, 6* (1), 1-7. Retrieved from https://core.ac.uk/download/pdf/288022279.pdf.

Alshbili, I., Beddewela, E., & Elamer, A. (2020). Ownership types, corporate governance and corporate social responsibility disclosures. *Accounting Research Journal, 33* (1), 48-66. doi:https://doi.org/10.1108/arj-03-2018-0060.

Amalina, Z. G., & Juliarto, A. (February, 2021). The Effect of Companies' Ethical Commitments on Financial Performance: the Moderating Effect of Ownership Structure. *Diponegoro Journal of Accounting, 10* (1), 1-10. Retrieved from https://ejournal3.undip.ac.id/index.php/accounting/article/view/30242/25113.

Avortri, C., & Agbanyo, R. (17 July, 2020). Determinants of management fraud in the banking sector of Ghana: the perspective of the diamond fraud theory. *Journal of Financial Crime, 28* (1), 142-155. doi:https://doi.org/10.1108/JFC-06-2020-0102.

Bailey, M., Glaeser, S., Omartian, J., & Raghunandan, A. (22 August, 2022). Misreporting of Mandatory ESG Disclosures: Evidence from Gender Pay Gap Information. *SSRN*, 1-51. doi:https://dx.doi.org/10.2139/ssrn.4192257.

Bammens, Y., & Hünermund, P. (11 August, 2020). Nonfinancial Considerations in Eco-Innovation Decisions. *Journal of Product Innovation Management, 37* (5), 431–453. doi:https://doi.org/10.1111/jpim.12550.

Barabanov, S., Ozocak, O., Turtle, H., & Walker, T. (2008). Institutional Investors and Shareholder Litigation. *Financial Management, 37* (2), 227-250. doi:https://doi.org/10.1111/j.1755-053X.2008.00011.x.

Beck, J., & Bhagat, S. (28 April, 1999). Shareholder litigation: share price movements, news releases, and settlement amounts. *Managerial and Decision Economics, 18* (7-8), 563-586. doi:https://doi.org/10.1002/ (SICI)1099-1468 (199711/12)18:7/8%3C 563::AID-MDE853%3E3.0.CO;2-A.

Belenzon, S., Chatterji, A., & Daley, B. (2017). Eponymous Entrepreneurs. *American Economic Review, 107* (6), 1638–1655. doi:https://doi.org/10.1257/aer.20141524.

Bennedsen, M., Nielsen, K., Perez-Gonzalez, F., & Wolfenzon, D. (May, 2007). Inside the Family Firm: The Role of Families in Succession Decisions and Performance. *The Quarterly Journal of Economics, 122* (2), 647–691. doi:https://doi.org/10.1162/qjec.122.2.647.

Bhagat, S., & Bolton, B. (October, 2019). Corporate governance and firm performance: The sequel. *Journal of Corporate Finance, 58*, 142-168. doi:https://doi.org/10.1016/j.jcorpfin.2019.04.006.

Bonini, S., & Boraschi-Diaz, D. (2013). The causes and financial consequences of corporate frauds. *Entrepreneurship, Finance, Governance and Ethics, 3*, 295-314. doi:http://dx.doi.org/10.1007/978-94-007-3867-6_13.

Borghesi, R., Houston, J., & Naranjo, A. (June, 2014). Corporate socially responsible investments: CEO altruism, reputation, and shareholder interests. *Journal of Corporate Finance, 26*, 164-181. doi:https://doi.org/10.1016/j.jcorpfin.2014.03.008.

BV, P., Reddy, V., Ramachandran, N., & Bhattacharyya, A. (7 April, 2005). Insider Ownership, Corporate Governance and Corporate Performance. *NSE , Proposal 89.* Retrieved from https://ssrn.com/abstract=696462.

Cappelli, D., Moore, A., & Trzeciak, R. (2012). *The CERT Guide to Insider Threats* (1st ed.). Westford: Addison-Wesley. Retrieved from shorturl.at/hmtKO.

Chatterjee, P. (29 June, 2016). *New Violation Tracker Tool Helps Public Track U.S. Corporate Misconduct.* Retrieved from CorpWatch: https://www.corpwatch.org/article/new-violation-tracker-tool-helps-public-track-us-corporate-misconduct.

Chaudhary, S., Dhir, A., Nguyen, D., Battisti, E., & Kaur, P. (2025). Exploring Family Values, Religion, and Ethical Behavior in Family Businesses: A Multi-Stage Qualitative Investigation. *Journal of Business Ethics*, 1-27. doi:https://doi.org/10.1007/s10551-025-05947-5.

Chava, S. (15 May, 2014). Environmental Externalities and Cost of Capital. *Management Science, 60* (9). doi:https://doi.org/10.1287/mnsc.2013.1863.

Chen, J., Blenman, L., & Chen, D.-H. (2008). Does Institutional Ownership Create Values? the New Zealand Case. *Quarterly Journal of Finance and Accounting, 47*, 109-122. Retrieved from https://api.semanticscholar.org/CorpusID:150825836.

Chen, R., Guedhami, O., Yang, Y., & Zaynutdinovaa, G. (December, 2020). Corporate governance and cash holdings: Evidence from worldwide board reforms. *Journal of Corporate Finance, 65*, 1-25. doi:https://doi.org/10.1016/j.jcorpfin.2020.101771.

Chung, K. H., & Zhang, H. (Feb, 2011). Corporate Governance and Institutional Ownership. *The Journal of Financial and Quantitative Analysis, 46* (1), 247-273. Retrieved from https://www.jstor.org/stable/23018523?seq=1#metadata_info_tab_contents.

Cooper, E., & Uzun, H. (21 Sep, 2022). Busy outside directors and ESG performance. *Journal of Sustainable Finance & Investment*, 1-21. doi:https://doi.org/10.1080/20430795.2022.2122687.

Davidson, R. H., & Pirinsky, C. (2022). The Deterrent Effect of Insider Trading Enforcement Actions. *Accounting Review, 97* (3), 227–247. doi:https://doi.org/10.2308/TAR-2020-0003.

Denis, D., & McConnell, J. (2009). International Corporate Governance. *The Journal of Financial and Quantitative Analysis, 38* (1), 1-36. doi:https://doi.org/10.2307/4126762.

Faller, C., & Knyphausen-Aufseß, D. (2018). Does Equity Ownership Matter for Corporate Social Responsibility? A Literature Review of Theories and Recent Empirical Findings. *Journal of Business Ethics, 150*, 15–40. doi:https://doi.org/10.1007/s10551-016-3122-x.

Fauzi, F., & Locke, S. (January, 2012). Board structure, ownership structure and firm performance. *Asian Academy of Management Journal of Accounting and Finance, 8* (2), 43-67. Retrieved from https://www.researchgate.net/publication/287572483_Board_structure_ownership_structure_and_firm_performance_A_study_of_New_Zealand_listed-firms.

Federal Register. (30 September, 2022). *Beneficial Ownership Information Reporting Requirements.* Retrieved from federalregister.gov: https://www.federalregister.gov/documents/2022/09/30/2022-21020/beneficial-ownership-information-reporting-requirements.

Fernando, C., Sharfman, M., & Uysal, V. (2 October, 2017). Corporate Environmental Policy and Shareholder Value: Following the Smart Money. *Journal of Financial and Quantitative Analysis, 52* (5). doi:https://t.ly/5o6KU.

Gao, F., Lisic, L., & Zhang, I. (May, 2014). Commitment to social good and insider trading. *Journal of Accounting and Economics, 57* (2–3), 149-175. doi:https://doi.org/10.1016/j.jacceco.2014.03.001.

Gillan, S. L., Koch, A., & Starks, L. T. (February, 2021). Firms and social responsibility: A review of ESG and CSR research in corporate finance. *Journal of Corporate Finance, 66*. doi:https://doi.org/10.1016/j.jcorpfin.2021.101889.

Gillan, S., & Starks, L. (12 March, 2007). The Evolution of Shareholder Activism in the United States. *Journal of Applied Corporate Finance, 19* (1), 55-73. doi:https://doi.org/10.1111/j.1745-6622.2007.00125.x.

Gillan, S., Hartzell, J., Koch, A., & Starks, L. (2010). Firms' environmental, social and governance (ESG) choices, performance and managerial motivation. *Unpublished working paper, 10*, 1-44. doi:https://t.ly/gRJo.

Grullon, G., Larkin, Y., & Michaely, R. (July, 2019). Are US Industries Becoming More Concentrated? *Review of Finance, 23* (4), 697–743. doi:https://doi.org/10.1093/rof/rfz007.

Hess, M., & Jr., J. (February, 2016). Fraud risk management: A small business perspective. *Business Horizons, 59* (1), 13-18. doi:https://doi.org/10.1016/j.bushor.2015.09.005.

Jaiswal, R., Gupta, S., & Tiwari, A. K. (2025). Environmental, social and governance-type investing: a multi-stakeholder machine learning analysis. *Management Decision*, 1-40. doi:https://doi.org/10.1108/MD-04-2024-0930.

Jensen, M., & Meckling, W. (1 October, 1976). Theory of the Firm: Managerial Behavior, Agency Costs and Ownership Structure. *Journal of Financial Economics, 3*, 305-60. doi:https://doi.org/10.1007/978-94-009-9257-3_8.

Johnson, F. B., Rybicki, D. C., Snyder, W. H., & Storm, M. M. (8 August, 2022). What Emerging Growth Companies and Investors Need to Know About the Corporate Transparency Act. *The National Law Review, 12* (243), 1-3. Retrieved from https://www.natlawreview.com/article/what-emerging-growth-companies-and-investors-need-to-know-about-corporate.

Kao, M.-F., Hodgkinson, L., & Jaafar, A. (4 February, 2019). Ownership structure, board of directors and firm performance. *CG, 19* (1), 189-216. doi:https://doi.org/10.1108/CG-04-2018-0144.

Keller, A. J., Boland, M. A., & Petty, S. A. (2022). The Growing Use of Alternative Farmland Ownership Methods in the U.S. *Journal of the ASFMRA*, 37-43. Retrieved from https://www.sciencedirect.com/science/article/pii/S0927538X21000408.

Khanchel, I. (18 September, 2007). Corporate governance: measurement and determinant analysis. *Managerial Auditing Journal, 22* (8), 740-760. doi:https://doi.org/10.1108/02686900710819625.

Kim, J., & Kim, J.-S. (23 November, 2020). Arrests and indictments of corporate insiders, ownership structure, and corporate governance: Evidence from Korea. *International Journal of Finance and Economics, 27* (3), 3580-3598. doi:https://doi.org/10.1002/ijfe.2339.

Krishnan, G., & Peytcheva, M. (12 June, 2019). The Risk of Fraud in Family Firms: Assessments of External Auditors. *Journal of Business Ethics, 157* (1), 261–278. doi:https://doi.org/10.1007/s10551-017-3687-z.

Lee, P. (28 Oct, 2019). Information asymmetry and opportunistic behavior of insider : Focusing on fraud event firm. *Journal of the Korea Convergence Society, 10* (11), 345-352. doi:https://doi.org/10.15207/JKCS.2019.10.11.345.

Lewellen, J., & Lewellen, K. (February, 2022). Institutional Investors and Corporate Governance: The Incentive to Be Engaged. *The Journal of Finance, 77* (1), 213-264. doi:https://doi.org/10.1111/jofi.13085.

Li, T. (16 December, 2016). Outsourcing Corporate Governance: Conflicts of Interest Within the Proxy Advisory Industry. *Management Science, 64* (6), 1–21. doi:https://doi.org/10.1287/mnsc.2016.2652.

Lohwasser, T. S., Hoch, F., & Kellermanns, F. W. (23 June, 2021). Strength in Stability: A Meta-Analysis of Family Firm Performance Moderated by Institutional Stability and Regime Type. *Entrepreneurship Theory and Practice, 46* (1), 1–42. doi:https://doi.org/10.1177%2F10422587211026863.

Martínez-Ferrero, J., Lozano, M., & Vivas, M. (November, 2021). The impact of board cultural diversity on a firm's commitment toward the sustainability issues of emerging countries: The mediating effect of a CSR committee. *Corporate Social Responsibility and Environmental Management, 28* (2), 675-685. doi:https://doi.org/10.1002/csr.2080.

Martínez-Ferrero, J., Rodríguez-Ariza, L., & García-Sánchez, I.-M. (1 November, 2016). Corporate social responsibility as an entrenchment strategy, with a focus on the implications of family ownership. *Journal of Cleaner Production, 135*, 760-770. doi:https://doi.org/10.1016/j.jclepro.2016.06.133.

Musallam, S. R., Fauzi, H., & Nagu, N. (20 February, 2019). Family, institutional investors ownerships and corporate performance: the case of Indonesia. *Social Responsibility Journal, 15* (1), 1-10. doi:https://doi.org/10.1108/SRJ-08-2017-0155.

Nekhili, M., Boukadhaba, A., & Nagati, H. (7 September, 2020). The ESG–financial performance relationship: Does the type of employee board representation matter? *Corporate Governance, 29* (2), 134-161. doi:https://doi.org/10.1111/corg.12345.

Nekhili, M., Boukadhabaa, A., Nagatib, H., & Chtiouic, T. (17 June, 2019). ESG performance and market value: the moderating role of employee board representation. *The International Journal of Human Resource Management, 32* (14). doi:https://doi.org/10.1080/09585192.2019.1629989.

Nofsinger, J., Sulaeman, J., & Varma, A. (26 July, 2019). Institutional investors and corporate social responsibility. *Journal of Corporate Finance, 58*, 700–725. doi:https://doi.org/10.1016/j.jcorpfin.2019.07.012.

Park, K. (2019). ESG Rating and Ownership Structure in US Firms. *International Journal of Applied Research*, 372-374. Retrieved from https://core.ac.uk/download/pdf/288280696.pdf.

Porter, M. (1992). Capital Choices: Changing the Way America Invests in Industry. *Journal of Applied Corporate Finance, 5* (2), 4-16. doi:https://doi.org/10.1111/j.1745-6622.1992.tb00485.x.

Pucheta-Martínez, M. C., & Chiva-Ortells, C. (6 June, 2018). The role of directors representing institutional ownership in sustainable development through corporate social responsibility reporting. *Sustainable Development, 26* (6), 835-846. doi:https://doi.org/10.1002/sd.1853.

Rodriguez-Ariza, L., Martínez-Ferrero, J., & Bermejo-Sánchez, M. (7 November, 2016). Consequences of earnings management for corporate reputation: Evidence from family firms. *Accounting Research Journal, 29* (4), 457-474. doi:https://doi.org/10.1108/ARJ-02-2015-0017.

Sabbagh, O. (3 October, 2016). Corporate governance in China. *CG, 16* (5), 866-882. doi:http://dx.doi.org/10.1108/CG-12-2015-0162.

Saeed, A., Riaz, H., Tahiru, L., & Rajwani, T. (May, 2022). Does family matter? Ownership, motives and firms' environmental strategy. *Long Range Planning*, 1-19. doi:https://doi.org/10.1016/j.lrp.2022.102216.

Shanker, M., & Astrachan, J. (1996). Myths and realities: Family businesses' contribution to the US economy. *Family Business Review, 9* (2), 107–123. doi:https://doi.org/10.1111/j.1741-6248.1996.00107.x.

Soltani, B. (March, 2014). The Anatomy of Corporate Fraud: A Comparative Analysis of High Profile American and European Corporate Scandals. *Journal of Business Ethics, 120* (2), 251–274. doi:https://doi.org/10.1007/s10551-013-1660-z.

Sun, J., Pellegrini, M., Dabić, M., Wang, K., & Wang, C. (7 March, 2023). Family ownership and control as drivers for environmental, social, and governance in family firms. *Review of Managerial Science*, 1-32. doi:https://doi.org/10.1007/s11846-023-00631-2.

Tang, D., Yan, J., & Yao, C. (19 November, 2021). *The Determinants of ESG Ratings: Rater Ownership Matters.* doi:http://dx.doi.org/10.2139/ssrn.3889395.

Ud Din, S., Khan, M. A., Khan, M. J., & Khan, M. Y. (8 February, 2021). Ownership structure and corporate financial performance in an emerging market: a dynamic panel data analysis. *International Journal of Emerging Markets, 17* (8). doi:https://doi.org/10.1108/IJOEM-03-2019-0220.

Useem, M. (1996). *Investor capitalism: how money managers are changing the face of corporate America* (1st ed. ed.). NY: Basic Books. doi:http://dx.doi.org/10.1002/9781118785317.weom110175.

Villalonga, B. (October, 2019). On ownership structure and corporate performance. *Journal of Corporate Finance, 58*, 64-67. doi:https://doi.org/10.1016/j.jcorpfin.2019.04.005.

Villalonga, B., & Amit, R. (17 March, 2020). Family ownership. *Oxford Review of Economic Policy, 36* (2), 241–257. doi:https://doi.org/10.1093/oxrep/graa007.

Wu, W., & Wang, L. (2016). Institutional Ownership Mispricing and Corporate Investment. *Open Journal of Business and Management, 4* (2), 282-290. doi:http://dx.doi.org/10.4236/ojbm.2016.42030.

Yadav, S. (26 November, 2020). Institutional Ownership and Corporate Social Performance in Emerging Economies Multinationals. *Indian Journal of CG, 13* (2), 227-252. doi:https://doi.org/10.1177%2F0974686220966812.

Zhang, Y. (22 January, 2007). Law, Corporate Governance, and Corporate Scandal in an Emerging Economy: Insights from China. *SSRN (957549).* doi:https://dx.doi.org/10.2139/ssrn.957549.

Zhu, J., Li, R., Chen, Z., & Zhang, T. (2025). Does Ownership Structure Influence the Financial Performance of Chinese Listed Companies? An Analysis of ESG Practices and Accounting-Based Outcomes. *International Journal of Financial Studies, 13* (2), 48-69. doi:https://www.mdpi.com/2227-7072/13/2/48#.

Chapter 6

Rationalizing the ESG Framework Integration in the Healthcare Sector for Sustainability

Deepa Pillai*
and Prakriti Chahar
Symbiosis School of Banking and Finance, Symbiosis (Deemed) University, Pune, India,

Abstract

Environmental, Social, and Governance (ESG) is gaining importance in the healthcare industry as a significant driver to achieve sustainability. The ESG broadens the scope to achieve economic stability, helps in financial growth, reduces waste, and provides an inclusive healthcare system. Recognizing ESG reporting measures and accountability towards stakeholders is imperative for healthcare companies. The institutional theory highlights how organizations follow specific rules, norms, and behaviours deemed important and have a legitimate bearing on their stakeholders. The importance of ESG can be highlighted by the convergence of institutional and Triple Bottom Line theory (TBL) in healthcare, as institutional theory focuses on the drivers, and TBL defines the scope of sustainable measures. TBL and institutional theory can provide a comprehensive understanding of ESG in healthcare. If the health system follows the ESG reporting, it will align with the SDGs' goals.

Keywords: ESG, sustainable development goals, healthcare

* Corresponding Author's Email: deepa.pillai@ssbf.edu.in

In: Environmental, Social, and Governance (ESG) …
Editor: Veena Grover
ISBN: 979-8-90134-138-4

1. Introduction

Healthcare companies are inherently resource-intensive, which also causes significant environmental impacts. The ongoing global discourse on sustainability has gained momentum, aiding industries across sectors to appraise their practices through Environmental, Social, and Governance principles. Environmental, Social, and Governance (ESG) contemplation becomes imperative for healthcare companies owing to high consumption of resources, provision of communal health facilities, and ensuring transparency and accountability in decisions. ESG integration is significant to the healthcare sector as the sector is crucial for human development; however, paradoxically, it is resource-intensive and environmentally impactful. ESG practices are enablers for customer retention, the realization of sustainable development goals (SDGs), and the accomplishment of societal accountability. ESG considerations in healthcare foster stakeholder reputation, brand value, and adherence to compliance, thereby enhancing the long-term sustainability of the companies. ESG strategies foster a more resilient and ethically grounded healthcare system by addressing environmental impact, social responsibility, and corporate governance.

The carbon footprint of the healthcare sector highlights the pressing need for circular policies, which accentuate reuse, lengthy product life cycles, and resourceful reverse logistics. Furthermore, transitioning to green healthcare solutions, with renewables and the implementation of net-zero plans, is decisive for sustainable progress, drives value creation, and fosters resilience. Healthcare systems encounter challenges to strike an equilibrium of accessibility, quality, and cost-effectiveness in the context of sustainability in their operational and strategic frameworks. Regulators, investors, and collaborators are integrating ESG in their decision-making processes, thus, the evaluation of non-financial performance beyond financial metrics has gained traction, with healthcare companies not being an exception. The transition underscores the recognition of ESG reporting measures and accountability towards stakeholders' imperative for healthcare companies. Beneficiaries of healthcare have become more conscious about the environmental and social impact of goods and services; thus, healthcare companies must align ESG principles in their business practices for competitiveness and consumer confidence. The healthcare sector contributes widely to carbon emissions, medical waste, and energy consumption, exerting substantial pressure on environmental resources. Concurrently, the sector plays a notable social role in safeguarding equitable access to healthcare services, fostering well-being, and the upkeep of public health. Thus, ESG discussions are critical for institutional accountability, transparency, and resilience. Adoption of the ESG framework into healthcare organizations is not just a regulatory choice but also a strategic choice of the organization for long-term sustainability. Healthcare organizations with good ESG scores are considered more responsible towards the community. They can lead investors to support these organizations, leading to increased investment and financial stability, the cornerstone of sustainability. The chapter highlights a holistic view of ESG practices and their adoption in healthcare organizations, which are directed towards sustainability and SDG attainment.

2. Contextual Framework of ESG

2.1. Environmental

The ESG framework is important in collaboration among stakeholders, transparency, and reducing information gaps. The United Nations first introduced ESG as a widely recognized measurement of sustainability. E in ESG refers to the environmental component, which focuses on necessary resources, energy consumption, waste management, and its impact on living beings. S, social component signifies the inclusivity and associations with institutions and communities. G governance components include regulatory compliance and control measures for safeguarding stakeholders' interests (Henisz et al., 2019). ESG scores are used to assess the company's performance based on three critical dimensions: sustainable, ethical, and regulatory practices. A robust ESG strategy allows firms to explore new markets, initiate expansion, and build trust with regulatory authorities, creating significant growth opportunities. A fundamental component of sustainability is the ability to hold diverse communities and the exclusive voices they support. Healthcare organizations' sustainability measures are thoroughly related to justice, diversity, equity, and inclusion in their duties. A comprehensive global analysis by Health Care Without Harm (2019) reports that the healthcare sector was responsible for approximately 2.0 gigatons of carbon dioxide equivalent emissions in 2014, which accounts for 4.4 percent of net global emissions. The proportion of healthcare-related emissions differs across countries, with the United States being the highest contributor to carbon footprint, with 7.6 percent, Switzerland (6.7%), and Japan (6.4%). At the same time, it was lowest in India, 1.5 percent, and Indonesia (1.9%). The data for low- and middle-income countries were limited, but the majority of 43 countries reported carbon emissions close to global.

In healthcare companies, ESG's bottom-up approach allows companies to identify the operational threats and strategic actions to take for improvement (Pratici et al., 2025). The environmental aspect of ESG in the healthcare sector encompasses using sustainable materials, minimizing chemical waste, achieving zero waste targets by reusing and recycling, and improving the management of hazardous waste through better production and disposal practices. It also includes protecting services and ensuring operational and strong infrastructure. The ecological impact of healthcare extends beyond greenhouse gas emissions and the overconsumption of limited resources it also contributes significantly to air, water, and soil pollution (Lenzen et al., 2020; Corvalan et al., 2020). The sector's reliance on energy-intensive technologies and materials leads to considerable waste and ecological harm (Ullah et al., 2023). Globally, the healthcare industry accounts for nearly 4.4% of carbon emissions (Vayalil, 2024). Existing literature underscores the urgent need to embed environmental responsibility within healthcare systems to support climate action and advance Sustainable Development Goals (SDGs) 6 and 12, which focus on clean water and sustainable consumption (Eckelman & Sherman, 2016; Pichler et al., 2019). This focus also extends to SDG 7 (Affordable and Clean Energy) and SDG 13 (Climate Action), highlighting the critical role of healthcare in promoting clean energy use, reducing environmental impact, and building resilience to climate change. While most ESG frameworks in environmental contexts follow international benchmarks, there is a gap in the literature addressing frameworks tailored to Indian demographics, particularly concerning waste management, equitable healthcare access, and affordability.

2.2. Social

Social and governance actions under the ESG framework have positively influenced financial performance, while environmental actions may have a short-term negative influence on financial outcomes (Dossa, 2025). Integration of ESG as a qualitative attribute is essential for endorsing transparency, stakeholder engagement, and fostering social value. Healthcare organizations play a pivotal role in societal well-being through safeguarding patient interests, providing equitable access to healthcare facilities, and advocating diversity, equity, and inclusion among the healthcare workforces.

Social issues impact employees' and communities' safety, well-being, diversity, and inclusion. Fostering a culture that eliminates systemic bias and fosters norms for equitable representation, benefits, and engagement influences the workforce and service quality in the healthcare sector. The increase in technology adoption in the healthcare sector facts the significance of protecting patient data, respect for patient autonomy, and ensuring ethical use of artificial intelligence. Social context prioritizes ethical care delivery, affordability, and community engagement to foster trust and achieve health equity (Schuller et al., 2020; Welch et al., 2023; Kohnke, 2017). Ensuring care is affordable, accessible, and equitable across all socioeconomic groups shall eliminate disparities in healthcare delivery. The social aspect of ESG focuses on upskilling healthcare professionals to achieve quality deliverables. Measures to promote healthcare education, preventive care, and outreach activities echo a strong ESG orientation. health, life, and well-being, and SDGs 10, well-being. Sensitive care is indispensable for improving patient outcomes, which requires a diverse healthcare workforce. Workforce diversity in the healthcare sector can be viewed through the outreach of job advertisements, standardization of recruitment processes, fairness and consistency in human resource practices, and leadership excellence (Shahi et al., 2019; Taylor et al., 2023; Khosa et al., 2024; Young et al., 2022; Kayingo et al., 2024). Fostering cultural capability and modesty among healthcare professionals would enhance the quality of care (Young et al., 2022; Placide et al., 2023). The long-term outcome of social measures would cultivate an inclusive environment and the realization of SDGs 3, health, life.

2.3. Governance

Governance encompasses subjects with a strong organizational structure, including policies and incentives related to conduct, ethics, board diversity, engagement, lapses in ESG issues, compensation, conflicts of interest, reporting, and policy engagement. Governance in healthcare ESG refers to the systems and policies that safeguard accountability, ethical operations, and regulatory compliance. Healthcare companies are expected to uphold transparency in decision-making, manage risks, protect data privacy, prevent corruption, and assume responsible marketing. Strong governance affirms responsiveness to stakeholders and nurtures long-term resilience. Good governance practices in healthcare comprise ethical management, transparency in operations and reporting, and adherence to regulatory standards, which foster trust and demonstrate responsible corporate behaviour (Alhazemi, 2025; Yu et al., 2024). Compliance with regulatory frameworks is essential for maintaining high governance standards and improving overall ESG performance. Governance in healthcare supports key SDGs by ensuring transparency, accountability, and ethical leadership. It aligns with SDG 3 (Good Health) through effective service delivery, SDG 9 (Innovation and Infrastructure) via resilient health systems, SDG 16 (Strong Institutions) through anti-corruption and data protection, and SDG 17 (Partnerships) by enabling cross-sector collaboration. Good governance is essential for achieving sustainable, inclusive, and trustworthy healthcare systems.

3. Antecedents of ESG in Healthcare

The Indian Healthcare Sector significantly contributes to employment generation and revenue, which highlights the need for sustainable business practices. The sector is resource-intensive and caters to communal interests, which mandates alignment of the healthcare sector's mission with ESG principles for the well-being and development of the nation. ESG is a strategic framework that mitigates untenable practices and promotes harmonized economic and environmental development. Integrating ESG principles in healthcare delivers many benefits, from improved patient outcomes to enhanced organizational transparency and stakeholder trust (Leung & You, 2023). As healthcare systems globally face increasing pressure from climate change, resource constraints, and population health disparities, ESG practices provide a structured roadmap to address these challenges while fostering organizational resilience and accountability.

Employing ESG principles in healthcare actions broadens the scope for improved financial stability and growth opportunities. Over time, healthcare providers are integrating smarter technologies in operations and delivery, which have enabled patient safety and accessibility of healthcare services for underserved communities. Tech-enabled solutions also provide telemedicine, which focuses on the affordability of healthcare services, reducing transportation costs and environmental pollution, and demonstrating a forward-looking approach towards energy conservation and minimizing carbon footprints. Reports state that increased usage of reusable materials, zero liquid discharge, and sustainable sourcing have reduced wastages, which reflects adherence to ESG obligations. Organizations are integrating recyclable materials and adopting innovative technologies to ensure safer and more sustainable waste handling.

Adopting digital technologies in hospital administration processes and workflows has led to paperless operations and significantly reduced the industry's negative environmental impact. The expansion of remote healthcare delivery has increased operational efficiency, reduced the demand for physical infrastructure, and allowed prompt healthcare delivery. The evolution towards renewable energy sources and hospital energy administration systems has directly contributed to ESG activities.

4. Theoretical Underpinning of ESG Framework and Sustainability

4.1. Institutional Theory

The relevance of ESG in the healthcare sector can be explained through Institutional theory, as organizations follow certain rules, norms, and behaviours that are deemed important and have a legitimate bearing on their stakeholders. Institutional theory explains how conventional norms, values, and practices, together known as institutions, shape organizations' structure, behaviours, and growth. The ESG framework translates sustainability goals into concrete actions through policies, programs, and regulatory practices. Institutionalizing ESG principles is important for fostering transparency, responsibility, and consistency in healthcare organizations, all of which contribute to stronger and sustainable healthcare systems (Haghighi & Takian, 2024). The country's institutional framework significantly impacts the ESG outcomes; in countries where organizations have higher economic freedom, a good education system, and liberal trade will engage in ESG practices (Pinheiro et al.,2023).

This theory is relevant in the healthcare industry because it explains the strength of traditional techniques and factors that drive the acceptance of innovative and sustainable approaches (Fuenfschilling, 2019). Healthcare organizations adhere to socially recognized standards and how transformation is managed within the institutional frameworks. Due to regulatory mandates and accountability towards stakeholders, healthcare companies are required to include an ESG framework within their organizations. Compliance with regulatory mandates is driven by strong governance practices, which reflect that institutional theory is of great significance for the sustainability of the Healthcare system. Further, the governance framework demands that healthcare organizations align ESG for legitimacy through diversity initiatives and a transparent reporting mechanism. ESG strategies validate institutional theory in practice, where healthcare entities adopt technology for productivity and innovation, reiterating that actions are guided by institutionalized roles rather than moral calculations. The institutional theory explains the trend of ESG integration in healthcare and provides a structured understanding of how external and internal factors influence organizational change.

4.2. Triple Bottom Line Theory and ESG Framework

In the healthcare industry, the ability to maintain sustainability and health services while considering the social, economic, and environmental impact is consistent with the Triple Bottom Line theory. Sustainability in healthcare is defined as an entity's ability to maintain and enhance health services while considering their social, economic, and environmental impacts, consistent with the Triple Bottom Line theory (TBL) (Rezali et al., 2021). The importance of ESG can be highlighted by the convergence of institutional and TBL theory in healthcare, as institutional theory focuses on the drivers, and TBL defines the scope of sustainable measures. TBL and institutional theory can provide a comprehensive understanding of ESG in healthcare. Both theories provide the framework through which motivation and mechanisms of organizational sustainability can be reviewed. Institutional theory theorizes that organizations are not purely driven by economic benefit but also by societal norms, regulatory potentials, and cultural resolutions. These institutions act as guidelines that form and limit the areas in which organizations can operate while improving acceptability and control. Organizations adopt practices that are economically logical and align with what is acceptable to stakeholders. TBL elucidates a broader framework of organizations that go beyond financial outcomes and include environmental and social impacts.

Organizations formulate ESG strategies to comply with institutional expectations and to attain the desired stakeholder outcomes. At the same time, the TBL framework evaluates the effectiveness of ESG initiatives beyond financial metrics to assess the impact across people, the planet, and the environment. Within ESG frameworks, the interaction between these theories becomes evident as ESG criteria emerge in response to institutional pressures. At the same time, TBL sets the direction of balancing economic viability with social equity and environmental responsibility. Institutional Theory clarifies the drivers that validate ESG adoption. TBL provides the metrics that reinforce a responsible, long-term approach; collectively, they constitute a theoretical basis for understanding how and why organizations integrate ESG principles into business operations.

The theoretical framework of ESG in Healthcare aligns with the institutional and triple bottom line theories as elaborated in the Conceptual Framework in Figure 1.

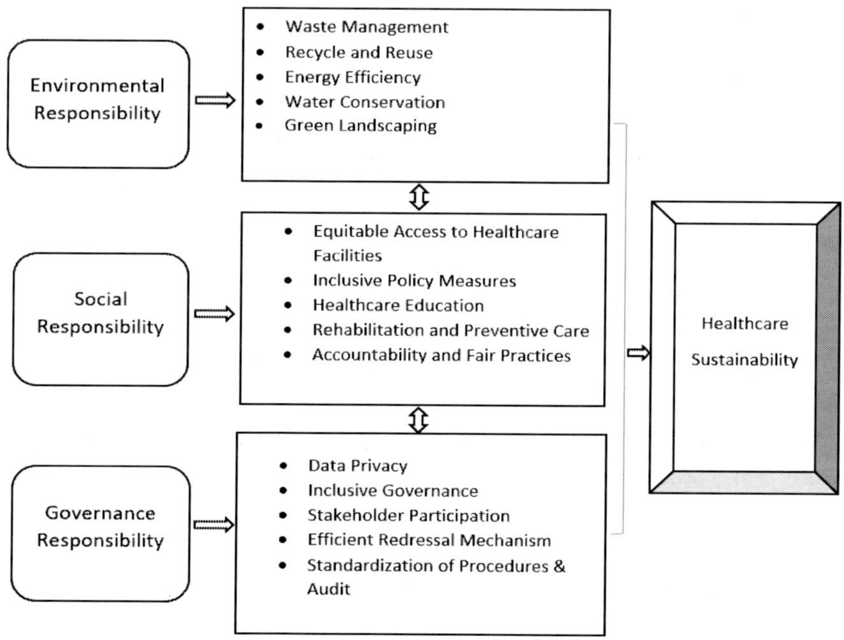

Figure 1. Author's Compilation.

Sustainability is the core of the healthcare industry, guiding its operations and service delivery to guard the long-term health of communities without compromising the environmental ecosystem. Alignment of environmental objectives with operational and financial performance empowers healthcare organizations to implement constructive and responsible practices. Furthermore, embracing inclusive approaches fosters equity and empowers communities, contributing to the widespread well-being of society. The initiatives are grounded in transparent, accountable, and fair governance, they pave the way for a resilient and sustainable healthcare system that reassures the attainment of the Sustainable Development Goals. The ESG framework provides an organized mechanism for measuring and reporting organizational performance. TBL provides a conceptual foundation for how ESG translates these principles into specific, actionable criteria that guide sustainable and ethical operations. The interconnectedness of the theory is examined by case analysis of two companies from the healthcare sector: Novartis Limited and Narayana Health Group.

5. Case Analysis of ESG and TBL Contexts in the Healthcare Industry

5.1. Case 1: Novartis Company

Novartis is a pharmaceutical company and a global leader in innovative medicine. It has an outreach of 296 million patients globally. It has 197 offices in Switzerland, including manufacturing units, R&D facilities, and corporate offices. ESG has been one of the company's foremost underlying agendas, targeting net-zero emissions by 2040. The company is strongly committed to ESG principles, aligning its strategic objectives with global sustainability goals. It has set striving targets to become carbon-neutral transversely in its operations and supply chain by 2030. Also, the company aims to reduce water consumption and waste disposal by 50% in 2025 compared to the Baseline of 2016 through recycling practices and the efficient use of production processes. Novartis worked closely with the manufacturing supplier to manage the water and its impact on the aquatic environment, embarking on the internal water quality standards and eliminating PVC packaging.

The social aspect of a company can be viewed from its ethics code, which promotes a fair and inclusive work environment with no gender, ethnicity, race, or any other bias. The pay disparity has been reduced to -0.3 percent compared to the Bloomberg gender equality index of 17 percent. In Novartis, Women earn nearly the same as men. The company actively engages in mental health support and runs employee awareness campaigns. The company has been at the forefront of promoting the right to health and access to quality medicine.

The company's governance is committed to ethical business practices, transparency, and accountability. Initiatives and policy design to advance healthcare, innovation, and enhance accessibility are the core. Implementation of AI in day-to-day operations focuses on data privacy and transparency. The company introduced an ethical use of information and digital policy through the AI risk and compliance framework.

Novartis' environment focuses on renewable energy, reducing water usage, and minimizing pharmaceutical waste. Socially, the company emphasizes access to healthcare, inclusive healthcare, investment in global healthcare initiatives, and encouraging diversity, equity, and inclusion in the workforce. The company upholds ethical standards through transparent business practices, anti-corruption measures, and a strong commitment to data privacy and patient rights, signifying the role of governance structure. By integrating ESG considerations into its core business strategy, Novartis fosters strong corporate responsibility, resilience, and stakeholder trust. The integration of ESG and TBL is reflected in the company's value-driven strategies for attaining carbon neutrality, reducing pollution, improving access to medicines, and promoting health equity measures. Novartis decodes the abstract principles of TBL into measurable outcomes, empowering accountability and constant development. The alignment supports regulatory compliance and stakeholder expectations and fortifies the long-term value creation, placing the company as a sustainable and responsible healthcare entity.

5.2. Case 2: Narayana Health Group

Narayana Health, a leading private healthcare provider in India, was founded by Dr. Devi Shetty in 2000 and is headquartered in Bangalore. The organization operates a network of hospitals and heart centres across major Indian cities. It is responsible for approximately 15% of the country's heart surgeries, reflecting its significant role in cardiac care. In addition to clinical services, Narayana Health provides affordable health insurance solutions for underprivileged populations, paying premiums in small, flexible instalments, making quality healthcare financially accessible. Narayana Health demonstrated operational resilience by scaling up ICU capacity and enhancing its digital infrastructure through telemedicine and remote monitoring. The organization's commitment to innovation is further exemplified by its collaboration with IIT Kanpur to develop an affordable artificial heart, advancing accessibility and technological progress in medical care. The organization actively incorporates technology into daily operations, enhancing care quality with cost-effective measures.

Narayana Health follows a robust sustainability strategy for resource management through reducing, recycling, and reusing waste, achieving approximately 95% wastewater recycling through water-efficient fixtures, reuse of RO-reject water, and rainwater harvesting. It has also reduced biomedical waste generation by 5 percent through in-house organic composting. Hazardous waste is managed by authorized dealers and through strict protocols, with regular staff training to ensure compliance. The hospital sources 23% of its electricity from renewable energy, and the organization aims to become carbon-neutral by 2040.

Narayana Health is committed to building a future-ready healthcare system supported by strong leadership and statutory guidelines. It uses a five-tier governance structure, which includes the Board of Directors, clinical leadership, quality specialists, auditors, and frontline staff. Seventeen of its hospitals have been accredited by the National Accreditation Board for Hospitals & Healthcare Providers (NABH), and their goal is to achieve 100% accreditation by NABH by 2025. Additionally, the group is improving its cybersecurity infrastructure to support its digital capabilities.

Narayana Health's dedication to environmental responsibility, social fairness, and good governance is due to its ESG policy, which ESG committees at both the corporate and hospital levels support. These bodies ensure the implementation of sustainability initiatives across the organization, ensuring that Narayana Health remains eco-sensitive, socially responsible, and ethically accomplished. This hospital group aims to deliver safe, accessible, and sustainable healthcare for future generations.

The ESG and TBL frameworks reflect the organization's operational practices. The organization exhibits strong and dedicated sustainable practices through recycling wastewater, rainwater harvesting, reducing biomedical waste, and sourcing renewable energy, aligning with the organization's goal to become carbon neutral by 2040. The focus on healthcare accessibility to underprivileged populations proves inclusion through low-cost insurance schemes, telemedicine, and public health innovations. The organization's continuous emphasis on staff training, safety measures, and quality healthcare proves its dedication to social sustainability. Narayana Health has a robust five-layer governance structure that demonstrates adherence to regulatory standards. Through dedicated ESG committees and a structured sustainability agenda, Narayana Health operationalizes the principles of ESG and TBL to build a resilient, inclusive, and environmentally responsible healthcare system.

Conclusion

The healthcare sector is a resource-intensive one. The integration of the ESG framework is the strategic requirement of sustainability. When the healthcare industry follows the ESG framework, we achieve the important global goals called the SDGS goals, which include clean water, better health for all, reducing inequality, responsible consumption and production, and industry innovation and infrastructure. As we can see from both industries, the Implementation enhances their operational and financial performance and supports them in achieving SDG goals. Government policy and society expect them to implement institutional theory, but it also helps financial growth, reduces waste, and provides an inclusive healthcare system.

References

ADEC Innovations. (n.d.). *ESG in healthcare*. ADEC Healthcare. Retrieved April 7, 2025, from https://www.healthcare.adec-innovations.com/our-solutions/esg-in-healthcare/.

Alhazemi, A. (2025). Integrating ESG framework with social sustainability metrics: A dual SEM-PLS formative–reflective model perspective. *Sustainability, 17* (6), 2566.

Corvalan, C., Villalobos Prats, E., Sena, A., Campbell-Lendrum, D., Karliner, J., Risso, A., Wilburn, S., Slotterback, S., Rathi, M., Stringer, R., et al., (2020). Towards climate-resilient and environmentally sustainable health care facilities. *International Journal of Environmental Research and Public Health, 17* (23), 8849. https://doi.org/10.3390/ijerph17238849.

Dossa, J. V. (2025). Can sustainability pay off? Evaluating ESG disclosure and financial outcomes in Chinese health care firms. *Business Strategy & Development, 8* (1), e70061.

Eckelman, M. J., & Sherman, J. (2016). Environmental impacts of the U.S. health care system and effects on public health. *PLOS ONE, 11* (6), e0157014. https://doi.org/10.1371/journal.pone.0157014.

Fuenfschilling, L. (2019). An institutional perspective on sustainability transitions. In *Handbook of sustainable innovation* (pp. 219–236). Edward Elgar Publishing.

Haghighi, H., & Takian, A. (2024) Institutionalization for good governance to reach sustainable health development: A framework analysis. *Globalization and Health, 20* (1), 5.

Health Care Without Harm, & Arup. (2019). *Health care's climate footprint: How the health sector contributes to the global climate crisis and opportunities for action.* https://noharm-global.org/sites/default/files/documents-files/5961/HealthCaresClimateFootprint_092319.pdf.

Henisz, W. J., & McGlinch, J. (2019). ESG, material credit events, and credit risk. *Journal of Applied Corporate Finance, 31* (2), 105–117.

Khosa, M. B. A., Ding, J., & BDS, D. T. (2024). *Equity, diversity, and inclusion in healthcare: From knowledge to practice*. Elsevier Science & Technology.

Kohnke, E. J., Mukherjee, U. K., & Sinha, K. K. (2017). Delivering long-term surgical care in underserved communities: The enabling role of international NPOs as partners. *Production and Operations Management, 26* (6), 1092–1119.

Lenzen, M., Malik, A., Li, M., Fry, J., Weisz, H., Pichler, P.-P., Chaves, L. S. M., Capon, A., & Pencheon, D. (2020). The environmental footprint of health care: A global assessment. *The Lancet Planetary Health, 4* (7), e271–e279. https://doi.org/10.1016/S2542-5196 (20)30121-2.

Leung, T. C. H., & You, C. S. X. (2023). ESG application in sustainable development of the healthcare industry. In *Environmental, social and governance and sustainable development in healthcare* (pp. 47–64). Springer Nature Singapore.

Pichler, P.-P., Jaccard, I. S., Weisz, U., & Weisz, H. (2019). International comparison of health care carbon footprints. *Environmental Research Letters, 14* (6), 064004. https://doi.org/10.1088/1748-9326/ab19e1.

Pinheiro, A. B., dos Santos, J. I. A. S., Cherobim, A. P. M. S., & Segatto, A. P. (2023). What drives environmental, social and governance (ESG) performance? The role of institutional quality. *Management of Environmental Quality: An International Journal, 35* (2), 427–444.

Placide, V., Brown, R. A., Blavos, A., Grover, O., & Chubb, C. S. (2023). The importance of diversity in the healthcare workforce. In *Handbook of Research on Exploring Gender Equity, Diversity, and Inclusion Through an Intersectional Lens* (pp. 374–396). IGI Global.

Pratici, L., Salvatore, F. P., Fanelli, S., Zangrandi, A., & Milone, M. (2025). Using ESG paradigm as a basis for social reporting in nonprofit organizations: Evidence from cases in healthcare. *Management Decision, 63* (2), 586–609.

Rezali, N., Ali, M. H., Idris, F., Yunus, Y. M., & Yunan, Y. S. M. (2021). Exploration of institutional theory in green supply chain initiatives for healthcare industries in Malaysia. *International Journal of Business Continuity and Risk Management, 11* (2–3), 126–141.

Schuller, K. A., Cronin, C. E., Nicks, S. E., Jing, X., Kingori, C., & Morrone, M. (2019). Development and application of a rubric to compare strategies for improving access to health care in rural communities in the United States. *Evaluation and Program Planning, 74*, 61–68.

Shahi, A., Karachiwalla, F., & Grewal, N. (2019). Walking the walk: The case for internal equity, diversity, and inclusion work within the Canadian public health sector. *Health Equity, 3* (1), 183–185.

Taylor, J., Sharma, S., Supersad, A., Miller, E., Lebel, K., Zabihaylo, J., ... & Yong-Hing, C. J. (2023). Recommendations for improvement of equity, diversity, and inclusion in the CaRMs selection process. *Canadian Association of Radiologists Journal, 74* (4), 624–628.

Ullah, Z., Nasir, A. R., Alqahtani, F. K., Ullah, F., Thaheem, M. J., & Maqsoom, A. (2023). Life cycle sustainability assessment of healthcare buildings: A policy framework. *Buildings, 13* (9), 2143.

Vayalil, S. (2024, September 25). The role of ESG in healthcare: Balancing sustainability, care and corporate responsibility. *Saïd Business School, University of Oxford.* Retrieved April 7, 2025, from https://www.sbs.ox.ac.uk/climate-change-challenge/resources/role-esg-healthcare-balancing-sustainability-care-and-corporate-responsibility.

Welch, V., Pottie, K., Gaudet, C., Thuku, M., Mallard, R., Spenceley, S., ... & IMPACT Team. (2023). Realist review of community coalitions and outreach interventions to increase access to primary care for vulnerable populations. *Archives of Public Health, 81* (1), 115.

Young, P., Pinto, D. B., Asher, S., DeSanctis, S., Gardner, K., Geary, S., ... & Pauze, D. (2022). An intensive approach to improving diversity, equity, and inclusion in an academic emergency department. *Western Journal of Emergency Medicine, 23* (4), 557.

Yu, K., Wu, Q., Chen, X., Wang, W., & Mardani, A. (2024). An integrated MCDM framework for evaluating the environmental, social, and governance (ESG) sustainable business performance. *Annals of Operations Research, 342* (1), 987–1018.

Chapter 7

Analyzing the Impact of Socially Responsible Investing in the Indian Stock Market

Karan Rawat[1]
Dipasha Sharma[1,*]
Riidhi Jain[2]
and Shagun Thukral[1]
[1]Symbiosis Centre for Management and Human Resource Development (SCMHRD), Symbiosis International (Deemed) University (SIU), Hinjewadi, Pune, Maharashtra, India
[2]Dr. D. Y. Patil B School Pune, Maharashtra, India

Abstract

This paper aims to analyze the companies' stock compliance with sustainability norms, while comparing them against the stocks of available companies to know whether it is profitable to be sustainable, both for the company and the investor. Moreover, this study also aims to raise awareness about various indices available in the Indian stock market; for instance, people can obtain information about green & non-green stocks. We collected data on the historical stock prices of six indices, including S&P BSE ESG, S&P BSE CARBONEX, S&P BSE GREENEX, CNX NIFTY, S&P BSE SENSEX, & S&P BSE 100, covering a ten-year period (i.e., 2008 to 2019). We compared their monthly returns over these years using risk-adjusted performance evaluation measures to observe whether SRI portfolios outperform conventional stocks. Based on all the performance metrics, the 'S&P BSE GREENEX' index turned out to be the best performing portfolio, as it had high scores on almost every risk-adjusted performance evaluation

* Corresponding Author's Email: dipashasharma20@gmail.com

In: Environmental, Social, and Governance (ESG) …
Editor: Veena Grover
ISBN: 979-8-90134-138-4

measure overall, as well as when it was divided into phases of slowdown and growth. Importantly, other green indices also performed well on the selected criterion, yielding significant returns for a relatively lower risk. This suggests that investing more in a sustainable greenway would positively impact an investor's portfolio and provide added diversification.

Keywords: SRI, socially responsible, environmental, social, and governance (ESG), green indices, emerging market, India

1. Introduction

Socially Responsible Investing (SRI) refers to investing in industries or companies that are concerned about both the positive & negative consequences on the environment & society. Thus, they are more inclined to work within a framework that enables them to make incremental efforts [17]. It is also sometimes referred to as Green or Ethical investing; more recently, it has become known as Sustainable investing or socially conscious investing. In general, Socially Responsible Investors try to promote corporations that they believe are upholding the tenets of environmental stewardship, human rights, and cultural and racial equality by selectively investing in only those specific companies. Such investors envision a world, where everyone would invest only in similar companies, so that other companies that may be detrimental to society cease to exist. Such investors choose their companies based on their ESG (Environmental, Social, and Governance) record.

'SRI' is the exercise of directing investments in such a way that it fulfills the dual purpose of attaining maximum returns for the investor, while ensuring that there's no adverse impact on the surroundings in any environmental, social, or economic way [7]. SRI has become more relevant recently due to the growing personal focus on social issues that affect individuals' investment decisions, such as fair-trade products [10]. According to *the Forum for Sustainable and Responsible Investment (2012), the size of assets in sustainable investment practices has increased by 500%* since 1995. In numbers, it was valued at around USD 639 billion in 1995; by 2011, it had increased to USD 3.7 trillion, representing thereby 11.3% of the USD 33.3 trillion in overall AUM in the US alone. Overall, AUM has further increased to USD 3.74 trillion (11% of USD 33.7 trillion) in the US market and GBP 1.235 trillion (27% of GBP 4.5 trillion) in the UK as of 2014.

The concept of SRI has been in existence for a long time. Still, it was not as widespread as the idea of conventional investing, especially in the context of developing markets like India. In fact, even in developed countries, it gained more traction after the 2007-08 Housing market crash, which resulted in a widespread recession [2]. The belief that investing in companies that follow ethical practices would result in reduced losses, even during a downturn, has effectively strengthened the case for SRI. With each new fraud case coming to light, the belief would likely grow further, and it can only mean good news for such investors. However, it is worth noting that, despite SRI being an established concept, 'large-scale awareness' has still been lacking, possibly due to the scarcity of readily available information on ESG-compliant companies or stocks.

This paper aims to examine and compare the performance of stocks from ESG responsible firms and general or traditional firms listed on the Indian stock markets from 2008 (i.e., post-recession) until Q4 of the calendar year 2019, to capture the immediate effect of the recession. We evaluate two types of portfolios, viz. SRI portfolios & general market portfolios. The SRI portfolio is represented by 'S&P BSE ESG, S&P BSE CARBONEX, and S&P BSE GREENEX indices.' The general company portfolio consists of 'CNX NIFTY, S&P BSE SENSEX, & S&P BSE 100 indices.' The 'S&P BSE CARBONEX' assesses the performance of stocks on the 'S&P BSE 100' index, based on their inclination towards dissipating risks, possibly created due to the issue of climate change. This index, in fact, was initiated to address market demand for a sophisticated approach to portfolio management, incorporating, in the process, environmental risks and opportunities to address them in a sustainable manner. The 'S&P BSE ESG Index' was created to evaluate stocks that meet sustainability investing criteria, while maintaining a risk and performance profile similar to that of the S&P BSE 100. The 'S&P BSE GREENEX' measures the performance of the top 25 'green' organizations in terms of greenhouse gas (GHG) emissions, market cap, and liquidity.

The following sections discuss past studies in this domain and the methodology used to contrast the performance measures of the various portfolios.

2. Literature Review

[15] attempted to determine whether a widespread distinction existed in returns obtained from diverse sustainable and general portfolios. They found that sustainable portfolios generated significantly higher returns than general stocks, implying that sustainable investing becomes more profitable during crises. They also found that the performance of a sustainable portfolio improved considerably, compared to a general portfolio. Thus, sustainable and socially responsible firms could be a more secure bet for risk-averse investors. [16] studied packaged SRI products. They found that, on average, socially responsible mutual funds do not include a larger number of sustainability-compliant firms in their portfolios than general funds. Thus, it is uncertain whether such packaged SRI products serve as the correct measure for finding the connection between the funds' social and financial performance. We assume that ESG would possibly be a better-suited method, as it offers an instantaneous account of Corporate Social Protocols at the organizational level. In fact, various specialized organizations have defined specific criteria for measuring ESG, considering a range of sustainability and societal issues. Organizations operating within those standards receive a particular score that determines their ESG compliance.

Compared to SRI products, ESG rankings yield large datasets that provide unique insights into how sustainability aspects ultimately impact a firm's return. Several organizations have incorporated ESG standards into their existing operational policies and procedures. For others, the façade of aligning ESG with company goals is a way to create good PR, and in reality, does not hold much merit. However, there has been mounting pressure worldwide on corporations to contribute to environmental betterment from diverse "epistemic CSR community," including regulatory agencies, social activists, and NGOs, as observed by [11].

[3] study raised several questions to understand the investors' psyche when it came to 'social investing.' The author found that SRI can be attributed to broad behavioral traits of an individual, such as their value system, economic & social ideas, and religious beliefs. Further, building upon other cognitive studies, [6] aimed to understand the rationale behind making SRI decisions, and divided investors into Financial First Investors (FFIs), who are more inclined towards increasing their financial performance with some consideration for socio-environmental factors; & Impact First Investors (IFIs), who value the ESG impact over financial returns, according to their decision-making and investing psychology. This paper aims to continue exploring this

subject, focusing on data obtained after analyzing the stock returns of both green & non-green portfolios. Notably, the most recent publication on a similar topic was by [14], wherein the authors compared the performance of 'green indices' with that of the general ones. They analyzed the performance of green indices over an 18-year period (1996-2013) using various performance measures. As mentioned earlier, this paper focuses on the immediate aftermath of the 2008 recession on the Indian market, particularly analyzing investors' inclination towards SRI stocks (or lack thereof). In the process, this paper contributes to the extant literature, as there are limited studies on the impact of SRI in various sectors, particularly in the Indian context.

3. Research Methodology

This section outlines the methodology behind data gathering and analysis, defining the data sources and the analysis tools used to generate results.

3.1. Data Gathering

This study begins with gathering data about the historical stock prices of the six indices – 'S&P BSE ESG, S&P BSE CARBONEX, S&P BSE GREENEX, CNX NIFTY, S&P BSE SENSEX, & S&P BSE100' – from 2008 to 2019. Then, it compares their monthly returns over the years through risk-adjusted performance evaluation measures, such as the Sharpe ratio, Treynor ratio, Jensen's alpha, & Information ratio [1]. The six indices are further divided into green & non-green indices, and the results are compared across the classifications to observe whether SRI portfolios outperform conventional stocks. Notably, the three indices—S&P BSE Carbonex, S&P BSE Greenex, and S&P BSE ESG—are classified as green or sustainable indices, while the other three are general/conventional indices. The market portfolio is defined by the S&P BSE ALLCAP, which comprises the S&P BSE SMALLCAP, S&P BSE MIDCAP, and S&P BSE LARGECAP, as well as 877 other company stocks, thereby acting as a comprehensive indicator of the broader Indian stock market. The 91-day T-Bill acts as a proxy for a risk-free instrument, and its primary yield (as given by RBI) would act as a risk-free rate. Analysis was conducted in two phases to illustrate the impact of the post-

2008 crisis on the Indian economy. Observe the graph below (Figure 1) of the Annual GDP growth rate (%) to understand the economic recovery shape of India.

As can be seen from the graph shown in Figure 1, the Indian economy was volatile in 2008, as indicated by the dip in 2010, after which the economy stabilized, and growth remained constant & positive until 2016. We divide our observations into two periods: 2008–2011 (inclusive) and 2012–2016 (inclusive). The conventional indices are compared against S&P BSE GREENEX only for the first period and "S&P BSE GREENEX and S&P BSE CARBONEX" for the second period.

3.2. Research Methods

The generally accepted methodology, as utilized by [8] and [12], involves scrutinizing the stocks/portfolios through the lens of risk-adjusted performance evaluation measures. A brief description of each measure/model used would enlighten the reader about the definition and application of the same. The underlying concept for most of the measures below is that investors require compensation for the additional risk they incur by not holding the risk-free asset and instead investing in risky assets.

3.2.1. The Sharpe Ratio

This ratio represents the excess return for the additional volatility incurred by investing in risky assets. The Sharpe ratio was developed by William Sharpe in 1966 and is one of the most applied formulas for risk and return calculations in finance. The formula for the Sharpe ratio is as follows:

$$Sharpe\ Ratio(r) = \frac{r - R_f}{StdDev\ (r)}$$

In the formula, r stands for the return of a risky asset. R_f gives the risk-free rate. Their difference is divided by the risk associated (or the Standard deviation) with the risky asset, r.

A limitation of the Sharpe Ratio is that it assumes that the distribution of returns is normal, which is not always the case in a volatile stock market. Another notable disadvantage is that it cannot distinguish between upturn & downturn, but focuses on the overall volatility.

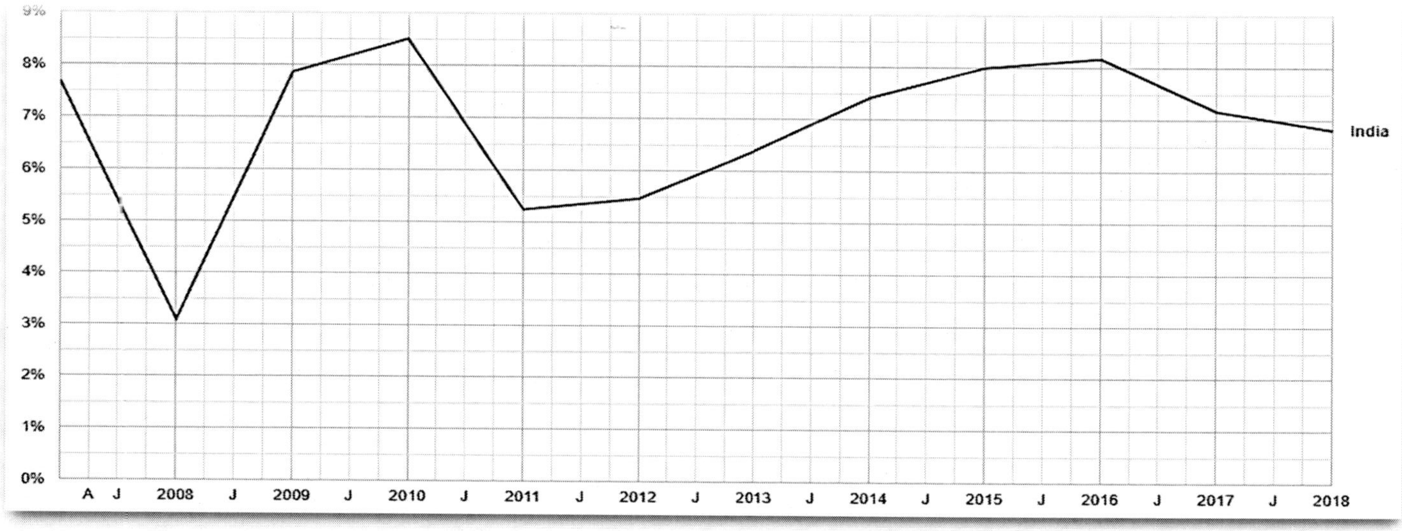

Source: World Bank Group.

Figure 1. Annual GDP growth rate for India (2008-2018).

3.2.2. Sortino Ratio

This ratio better measures an asset's return for a given level of risk (i.e., a downturn). The Sortino ratio is a variation of the Sharpe ratio that addresses a limitation of the Sharpe ratio, which does not distinguish between the upturn & downturn of volatility. Thus, the Sortino ratio differentiates between harmful volatility and overall volatility by focusing on downside deviation (negative portfolio return) rather than total standard deviation or asset value.

3.2.3. Treynor Ratio

The Treynor ratio is a performance evaluation measure that calculates the excess return for an asset/portfolio, while accounting for systematic risk as measured by beta (β). A difference between the Sharpe/Sortino ratio and the Treynor ratio is that the former uses the standard deviation of the asset or portfolio to measure risk. In contrast, the latter uses the asset/portfolio beta. The Treynor ratio is named after Jack Treynor, an American economist who was one of the most acclaimed and influential developers of the Capital Asset Pricing Model (CAPM). The financial formula for the ratio is:

$$Treynor\ Ratio = \frac{Portfolio\ Return - Riskfree\ Return}{Portfolio\ Beta}$$

A limitation of the Treynor ratio is its dependence on appropriate benchmarks for calculating beta. Additionally, the ratio yields non-meaningful results for a negative beta.

3.2.4. Jensen's Alpha

Jensen's alpha, also known as Jensen's performance index, measures the excess return achieved by a portfolio or asset compared to the return predicted by the Capital Asset Pricing Model (CAPM). This is used to verify whether an investor has "beaten the market" or not. The alpha can be positive, negative, or zero, depending on the asset/portfolio. It was first used as a criterion for evaluating portfolio fund managers by Michael Jensen in 1968. The formula for Jensen's Alpha is as follows:

$$\alpha = R_i - \left(R_f + \beta \times \left(R_M - R_f\right)\right)$$

where R_I gives the return of the asset/portfolio, R_f is the risk-free rate, R_M stands for realized market return, and β is the investment beta. A limitation of

Jensen's Alpha is that it does not consider an investment's volatility or drawdown; instead, it focuses on the expected return.

3.2.5. Information Ratio

The information ratio (IR), also referred to as the Appraisal Ratio, estimates portfolio returns above or below those of a benchmark, typically an index, and then compares the volatility/risk associated with those returns. The formula for the Information ratio is:

$$IR = \frac{Portfolio\ Return - Benchmark\ Return}{Tracking\ Error}$$

The tracking error in the above formula is the standard deviation of the difference between portfolio returns & benchmark returns. A limitation of the Information ratio is that it measures risk-adjusted returns, where the level of the required return can have various interpretations depending on the investor.

3.2.6. Fama-French 3-Factor Model

The Fama-French 3-factor model extends the CAPM model to explain the returns attained by a portfolio. The CAPM is a one-factor model, as it considers only the market risk premium. In contrast, the model proposed by Fama & French considers two additional factors in addition to market risk. These factors include the better performance of small-cap companies relative to large-cap companies, as well as the superior performance of high book-to-market value (value) companies compared to low book-to-market value (growth) companies. The idea behind the model is that high-value, small-market-cap companies tend to outperform the overall market historically. The Fama-French three-factor model was developed by University of Chicago professors Eugene Fama and Kenneth French. We use this model to derive the value of alpha adjusted for outperformance tendencies, thereby obtaining a more accurate measure of investment performance. The following formula defines the model:

$$r = R_f + \beta_1(R_M - R_f) + \beta_2(SMB) + \beta_3(HML) + \varepsilon$$

In the above formula, r denotes the expected rate of return, R_f gives the risk-free rate, R_M is the market return, SMB (Small minus Big) signifies the historical excess return of Small market-cap companies over Big market-cap companies; HML (High minus Low) gives the historical excess return of value stocks (high book-to-price ratio) overgrowth stocks (low book-to-price ratio), ε is the risk, and the various β signify the factor coefficients.

4. Analysis and Results

The results obtained using the methodology will be analyzed and elaborated upon here. Overall, the results demonstrate various risk-adjusted evaluation methods and how different portfolios performed in relation to these metrics. We begin with the correlation matrix presented in Table 1 to examine how the multiple indices evolve. We observe that the green indices exhibit a lower correlation compared to the others, while the conventional indices are highly correlated. Thus, according to the Modern Portfolio Theory, we should diversify the portfolio by adding SRI stocks with a lower correlation.

Table 1. Correlations matrix of portfolio

Portfolios	SENSEX	NIFTY 50	BSE 100	GREENEX	CARBONEX	ESG
SENSEX	1.000					
NIFTY 50	0.993	1.000				
BSE 100	0.993	0.992	1.000			
GREENEX	0.832	0.837	0.834	1.000		
CARBONEX	0.615	0.636	0.614	0.682	1.000	
ESG	0.257	0.254	0.240	0.251	0.396	1.000

4.1. Risk-Return Tradcoff

Table 2 presents the results of the average monthly returns and average risks for the various portfolios selected.

We have shown the negative standard deviation to focus on the downturn or the harmful volatility rather than the overall volatility. The upturn in the stock price is considered favorable, so we will only consider the low risk. As is evident from the data, the harmful risk associated with investing in conventional stocks is far greater than that of the sustainable portfolio. The S&P BSE GREENEX portfolio consistently outperforms other indices, even during economic slowdowns. The other two green indices are not too far off from the average return provided by conventional stocks, and they achieve this return at a significantly lower level of volatility. Thus, we can observe that, overall, the returns offered by green stocks may be lower than those of conventional stocks; however, the risk associated with the former is significantly lower than that of the latter.

Table 2. Risk to return measure

Index	Overall		Slowdown (2008-2011)		Growth Period (2012-2016)	
	Annual return (%)	Negative SD (%)	Annual return (%)	Negative SD (%)	Annual return (%)	Negative SD (%)
Market Index	0.76%	3.78%	0.01%	5.63%	1.20%	2.12%
S&P BSE GREENEX	1.18%	2.42%	1.75%	3.12%	1.17%	2.05%
S&P BSE CARBONEX	0.71%	2.33%			1.10%	2.00%
S&P BSE ESG	0.67%	2.16%				
S&P BSE SENSEX	0.78%	3.46%	0.11%	5.13%	0.99%	1.98%
CNX NIFTY	0.79%	3.48%	0.16%	5.18%	1.05%	2.01%
S&P BSE 100	0.76%	3.64%	0.06%	5.46%	1.10%	2.02%

4.2. Risk-Adjusted Performance Evaluation Metrics

Table 3 analyzes various measures we selected earlier for evaluating the performance of the stocks.

Table 3. Sharpe ratio

Index	Overall	Slowdown (2008-2011)	Growth Period (2012-2016)
Sharpe Ratio			
Market Index	0.03196	-0.05034	0.12335
S&P BSE GREENEX	0.10937	0.15058	0.11612
S&P BSE CARBONEX	0.03685		0.10436
S&P BSE ESG	0.03134		
S&P BSE SENSEX	0.03701	-0.04329	0.08663
CNX NIFTY	0.03884	-0.03733	0.09482
S&P BSE 100	0.03325	-0.04631	0.10454

The results for the Sharpe Ratio indicate that the green indices outperform conventional portfolios overall, both during periods of slowdown and growth. We also see that the value is considerably higher, especially for S&P BSE GREENEX over all the observed periods. Additionally, CNX NIFTY seems to have a higher ratio than others among the conventional stocks. The SRI portfolios have a significantly higher Sharpe ratio than the market index, and thus, they outperform the market on this metric. Since the Sharpe ratio is the most basic & primitive way to gauge an investment, we analyze further the stocks through other measures.

Table 4 presents results for the Sortino ratio.

Table 4. Sortino ratio

Index	Overall	Slowdown (2008-2011)	Growth Period (2012-2016)
Sortino Ratio			
Market Index	0.05489	-0.08535	0.26629
S&P BSE GREENEX	0.26343	0.41390	0.26396
S&P BSE CARBONEX	0.07043		0.23327
S&P BSE ESG	0.05588		
S&P BSE SENSEX	0.06446	-0.07514	0.18179
CNX NIFTY	0.06736	-0.06363	0.20556
S&P BSE 100	0.05784	-0.07938	0.23174

We only focus on the bad risk (or negative standard deviation) in the Sortino ratio for our volatility measure. Here, we observe that, despite a downturn, the evaluation measure assigns an even higher rating to the green indices, indicating a greater positive deviation (or upturn) in the case of SRI portfolios. Notably, the Green index has consistently outperformed the market, especially during periods of slowdown. Table 5 exhibits portfolio beta.

Table 5. Portfolio beta

Index	Overall	Slowdown (2008-2011)	Growth Period (2012-2016)
Beta			
Market Index	1	1	1
S&P BSE GREENEX	0.99	1.01	0.96
S&P BSE CARBONEX	0.95		0.95
S&P BSE ESG	0.90		
S&P BSE SENSEX	0.90	0.90	0.87
CNX NIFTY	0.91	0.89	0.92
S&P BSE 100	0.96	0.96	0.96

The SRI portfolios have a similar beta to the market index (represented by S&P BSE ALLCAP). Hence, they move mostly in line with the market, but they still offer higher returns (especially S&P BSE GREENEX) due to their relatively low risk level.

Table 6 exhibits the Treynor ratio for various indices selected for the study.

Table 6. Treynor ratio

Index	Overall	Slowdown (2008-2011)	Growth Period (2012-2016)
Treynor Ratio			
Market Index	0.00208	-0.00481	0.00565
S&P BSE GREENEX	0.00640	0.01286	0.00564
S&P BSE CARBONEX	0.00172		0.00490
S&P BSE ESG	0.00135		
S&P BSE SENSEX	0.00247	-0.00426	0.00414
CNX NIFTY	0.00259	-0.00370	0.00448
S&P BSE 100	0.00218	-0.00453	0.00490

The Treynor ratio is a measure of the reward-to-volatility ratio. It determines the additional return an asset earns over (or below) the risk-free asset for each unit of extra risk. As can be observed from the data, the green index has the highest value for the Treynor ratio, & thus, it would yield the maximum return for every extra unit of risk held by an investor. Importantly, even during the slowdown period, when other conventional stocks underperformed, the SRI portfolio returned over the risk-free asset. Thus, for example, if an investor had invested in this index, they would have outperformed the return on the risk-free asset.

Table 7 presents results for Jensen's alpha for various indices.

Table 7. Jensen's alpha

Index	Overall	Slowdown (2008-2011)	Growth Period (2012-2016)
Jensen's Alpha			
S&P BSE GREENEX	0.00424	0.00181	-0.00001
S&P BSE CARBONEX	-0.00040		-0.00072
S&P BSE ESG	-0.00071		
S&P BSE SENSEX	0.00035	0.00049	-0.00130
CNX NIFTY	0.00046	0.00099	-0.00107
S&P BSE 100	0.00010	0.00027	-0.00072

The alpha in Table 7 signifies the additional return that an asset or portfolio has achieved over the benchmark (in our case, the S&P BSE ALLCAP, which serves as a proxy for the market index). We observe that S&P BSE GREENEX has consistently "beaten the market" compared to conventional stocks. The other green indices cannot outperform the market benchmark, but this is compensated for by their low level of relative risk, as observed earlier. Even during the market's growth period, it consistently outperformed other indices, yielding substantial returns. The alpha is approximately 0, indicating that it yielded returns in line with those of the market, albeit at a lower level of risk (as observed in Table 1).

Table 8. Information ratio

Index	Overall	Slowdown (2008-2011)	Growth Period (2012-2016)
Information Ratio			
S&P BSE GREENEX	0.30476	0.11877	-0.01845
S&P BSE CARBONEX	-0.07617		-0.16998
S&P BSE ESG	-0.09697		
S&P BSE SENSEX	0.01187	0.06773	-0.18729
CNX NIFTY	0.02165	0.08774	-0.18560
S&P BSE 100	0.00514	0.07727	-0.18210

Table 8 presents results for the Information ratio, which is often used to measure the level of skill of a portfolio manager and their ability to generate excess returns relative to a defined benchmark. However, it also aims to identify the consistency of a stock's performance by incorporating a tracking error or standard deviation component into the calculation. In this case, we use it to evaluate the performance of the selected portfolios against each other, as well as the market portfolio, in terms of the risks associated with investing in those portfolios.

Fama – French Three-Factor Model.

Table 9. Fama French 3 Factor Model

Index	Fama - French 3 Factor Model				
	Alpha	Factor Beta			R Square
		Premium	SMB	HML	
S&P BSE GREENEX	0.0052	1.0238	-0.1272	-0.0468	0.9507
S&P BSE CARBONEX	0.0059	0.9926	-0.1148	-0.0547	0.9905
S&P BSE ESG	0.0050	1.0169	-0.2283	-0.0594	0.9719
S&P BSE SENSEX	0.0054	0.9460	-0.1504	-0.0837	0.9760
CNX NIFTY	0.0056	0.9455	-0.1545	-0.0706	0.9763
S&P BSE 100	0.0054	0.9899	-0.1035	-0.0429	0.9955

According to Table 9, results of the 3-factor model proposed by Fama & French, historically, smaller companies have outperformed their larger counterparts (in terms of market cap). High-value companies have beaten high-growth companies. This has mostly been the case in most global markets; hence this model can be applied in such markets. Various studies conducted by Eugene Fama and Ken French led to the conclusion that this model can explain more than 90 percent of a diversified portfolio's return. Similar to the Capital Asset Pricing Model, the 3-factor model assumes that investments carrying extra risk require higher returns. However, in addition to the market risk factor prevalent in the CAPM, this model introduces two further factors. Thus, we attempt to determine whether the portfolio returns are attributable to these inherent factors. We observe the beta coefficients associated with these three factors. If there appears to be a positive beta value on the SMB factor, it indicates that the asset or portfolio performs better when smaller companies outperform. If we observe a negative value on the size factor, specifically the SMB beta, it indicates that the asset/portfolio's performance is better when large companies perform well.

Similarly, for the value factor, if HML beta is positive, it signifies that the performance of the asset/portfolio positively correlates with how high the market (value), whereby stocks seem to be performing. If the beta on the HML factor is negative, it means that our stocks tend to perform well during periods when low book-to-market (growth) stocks seem to perform better. The R-Square factor indicates the proportion of the stock price's volatility that these three factors can explain. Ideally, it should signify that almost all the volatility is due to market factors that cannot be mitigated by further diversification and are not attributable to stock selection for the portfolio.

After our analysis, we note that, on average, the green indices have outperformed conventional stocks. In some cases, where green stocks have lower returns than general indices, this is offset by the lower risk associated with those indices, making them a better investment option when adjusted for risk. The following sections present the research results, recommendations, implications, and limitations.

Conclusion and Recommendations

In this section of the paper, conclusions will be drawn based on the analysis of the earlier sections and the implications for investors and corporations regarding socially responsible investing.

Through this study, we aim to gain a deeper understanding of the scenario of socially responsible investing in the Indian stock market by comparing the performance of stocks listed on various indices, namely conventional & sustainable indices. We collected the monthly adjusted closing returns for six indices, and then used various globally accepted performance evaluation measures, including different performance ratios, metrics, and factors. Furthermore, we analyzed the performance of the six indices. Notably, the indices used provided a good account of investing in established & sustainable companies. Moreover, we aimed to highlight the benefits of incorporating green stocks into a fund portfolio, as demonstrated by the consistently better-performing green indices, specifically the S&P BSE GREENEX index. Additionally, the added diversification can be achieved by incorporating green stocks alongside conventional stocks, as evident from the correlation matrix, which highlights the lower correlation values between the green and general indices. However, we acknowledge that there were certain limitations to the data collection and analysis process, as the sustainable indices were created later than the general indices and therefore incorporate fewer data points.

In some cases, the incorporation was in the middle of the testing period. Comparative assessment was somewhat difficult across all the indices due to the non-uniformity of the data collected between the Green indices. They had a limited set of stock prices. The research also compared the performance evaluation measures and identified the pros and cons of each when used as an evaluator for the index performance. After analyzing the data, we observed a significant difference between the returns obtained from the portfolios of available companies and those of SRI-compliant companies.

The paper also outlines the scope of future research in the area and provides a future outlook for the SRI sector. Based on all performance metrics, the S&P BSE GREENEX index proved to be the best-performing portfolio, achieving high scores across nearly every risk-adjusted performance evaluation measure, both overall and when divided into phases of slowdown and growth. During most periods, the S&P BSE GREENEX outperformed even the S&P BSE ALLCAP (our proxy for the market index). It consistently yielded a positive CAPM alpha (which is the elusive benchmark that every fund manager craves), while keeping the value of R Square factor lower than most, which effectively signifies the performance of the portfolio, other than the easily achievable way of investing in Small value stocks (as the Small Value companies have historically done better, according to the Fama-French model). We also used the Fama-French 3-factor model to consider the return achieved by following the small-value policy, which is then adjusted for in the model to yield an adjusted alpha. The alpha achieved from this model was also positive and relatively high for the S&P BSE GREENEX index. Although we see a significant positive contrast in performance between the types of indices, a substantial portion of India's general population remains unaware of sustainable indices or stocks and has consistently missed out on these gains.

Even as the popularity of investing in certain stocks over others, based on their green or ESG scores, has increased in European and US markets, the same cannot be said for emerging markets, particularly India. This could be because there is limited information that is easily accessible to the general public on such matters. There is also a dearth of general funds or portfolios focused on the socially responsible side of investing.

Nevertheless, in the past few years, especially after the turn of the last decade, many major private financial corporations have introduced funds that focus on ESG-compliant stocks, emphasizing the sustainable side of investing. Although they currently manage smaller stocks, these funds have grown in popularity due to their knack for being less volatile than the market, especially when the market itself is down or bearish, and consistently deliver better risk-adjusted performance even when the market is up or bullish. Based on the findings, we recommend that financial firms allocate more funds to sustainable investing. Mutual funds and other investment funds available today should consider adding stocks with a high ESG quotient to increase diversification and potential returns. Suppose such funds increase their popularity and attract more investors; they would start to positively influence corporations to strive for sustainability, and thereby become eligible to be included in such firms. They could also appeal to such investors, who primarily examine the company's profile and financials before investing.

Future studies can focus on the sectoral effect of sustainable investing. Currently, there is a lack of data to classify green stocks into various sectors, and then study the impact on each sector by comparing green and non-green companies.

As we deal with the novel coronavirus 2019 (COVID-19) pandemic, there is scope for further study to be developed in the SRI sector. As can be seen from the global economies, there is a threat of a prolonged economic slowdown due to the lockdowns enforced by various governments worldwide to curb the transmission of the virus. The effects of an economic downturn due to a non-financial factor can be considered when developing a new study to assess how well or poorly the green portfolios will perform compared to conventional portfolios. The results can be compared to those produced by the stock market following the 2008 subprime mortgage housing crisis. As the slowdown following the last economic crisis proved invaluable in increasing the popularity of SRI products and the inclination of investors towards them, there is a higher chance that this impending crisis could trigger a similar shift in approach, which is undoubtedly good news for proponents of the SRI system.

This study is limited to the period from 2008 to 2019. It focuses solely on the returns of the six indices mentioned earlier, in relation to their performance within the Indian stock market. The study considered the Indian stock market in a bubble. It did not consider global trends in SRI or how international markets might have affected the Indian stock market. Since the Green stocks started later than the timeline of our study, with S&P BSE CARBONEX beginning in November 2012 and S&P BSE ESG starting in November 2017, there are some gaps in the study due to non-uniformity data, as the stock returns of those indices before their incorporation are taken based on the companies listed on those indices which might not give the correct picture but did show approximate results. Importantly, this study does not recommend any investment strategy and instead provides a factual analysis of the performance of the various stocks incorporated in the specified indices through a comparison of monthly returns obtained by those stocks. Thus, the research should not be taken as a recommendation guide, but merely as a suggestion for inculcating ideas. Any investment made based on these results should be at the individual's own risk.

References

Aragon, G. O., & Ferson, W. E. (2007). Portfolio performance evaluation. *Foundations and Trends® in Finance*, 2 (2), 83-190.

Connaker, A., & Madsbjerg, S. (2019). The state of socially responsible investing. *Harvard Business Review*, *17*.

Dunfee, T. W. (2003). Social investing: mainstream or backwater?. *Journal of Business Ethics*, *43* (3), 247-252.

Fama, E. F. (1972). Components of investment performance. *The Journal of finance*, *27* (3), 551-567.

Fama, E. F., & French, K. R. (1993). Common risk factors in the returns on stocks and bonds. *Journal of financial economics*, *33* (1), 3-56.

Glac, K. (2009). Understanding socially responsible investing: The effect of decision frames and trade-off options. *Journal of Business Ethics*, *87* (Suppl 1), 41-55.

Haigh, M., & Hazelton, J. (2004). Financial markets: a tool for social responsibility?. *Journal of Business Ethics*, *52* (1), 59-71.

Hamilton, S., Jo, H., & Statman, M. (1993). Doing well while doing good? The investment performance of socially responsible mutual funds. *Financial analysts journal*, *49* (6), 62-66.

Jensen, M. C. (1968). The performance of mutual funds in the period 1945-1964. *The Journal of finance*, *23* (2), 389-416.

Kitzmueller, M., & Shimshack, J. (2012). Economic perspectives on corporate social responsibility. *Journal of economic literature, 50* (1), 51-84.

Gjølberg, M. (2009). The origin of corporate social responsibility: global forces or national legacies?. *Socio-economic review, 7* (4), 605-637.

Modigliani, F., & Leah, M. (1997). Risk-adjusted performance. *Journal of portfolio management, 23* (2), 45.

Sharpe, W. F. (1994). The sharpe ratio, the journal of portfolio management. *Stanford University, Fall.*

Tripathi, V., & Bhandari, V. (2015). Socially responsible stocks: a boon for investors in India. *Journal of Advances in Management Research, 12* (2), 209-225.

Tripathi, V., & Bhandari, V. (2012). Green is good in Indian stock market. *Colombo Business Journal, 3* (2), 27-45.

Utz, S., & Wimmer, M. (2014). Are they any good at all? A financial and ethical analysis of socially responsible mutual funds. *Journal of Asset Management, 15* (1), 72-82.

Viviers, S., & Eccles, N. S. (2012). 35 years of socially responsible investing (SRI) research-general trends over time. *South African Journal of Business Management, 43* (4), 1-16.

Chapter 8

ESG and Credit Risk

Sarvendu Tiwari*
Management Studies, JIMS Engineering Management Technical Campus, Greater Noida, India

Abstract

ESG considerations transformed during recent years from outside edge issues into fundamental elements that define investment methods alongside credit risk evaluation processes. The analysis studies how ESG metrics influence credit ratings by evaluating sustainability disclosure requirements and investor financial decision-making during current times. Research from over 90 different academic journals, policy publications, and industry reports transforms the sustainable finance industry while explaining its effects on credit evaluations. The proliferation of ESG-related regulations, such as the European Union's Sustainable Finance Disclosure Regulation (SFDR) and the Corporate Sustainability Reporting Directive (CSRD), underscores the regulatory push toward transparency and standardization.

A rising number of investors, alongside corporate issuers and credit rating agencies, have demonstrated their acknowledgment of ESG risks' material influence, with special emphasis on climate-related and transition risks. The market integration of ESG scores continues to expand despite rating discrepancies among agencies because these scores now influence sustainable bond price formation and access to capital and credit rating forecasts. Organizations such as the Climate Bonds Initiative and ICMA have created essential principles that enable green and sustainability-linked bonds to become a fundamental funding method for responsible social and ecological projects. Artificial intelligence, when

* Corresponding Author's Email: sarvendutiwari@gmail.com

In: Environmental, Social, and Governance (ESG) …
Editor: Veena Grover
ISBN: 979-8-90134-138-4

combined with big data technologies, enhances the assessment process for ESG risks at higher levels of complexity.
This study makes an important achievement by studying the differences among ESG scoring techniques along with their effects on market trust and investment choices. Financial institutions use ESG investment assessment methods completely, but investors doubt the validity of quality reporting standards and intentional greenwashing alongside regulatory delays in the financial markets.
Researchers analyze how ESG performance affects firm valuation while studying default probabilities by using three key theoretical references from bankruptcy prediction, cost of capital, and corporate governance analysis. Investors must develop refined knowledge about ESG ratings because they need to understand their constraints. Long-term corporate viability and creditworthiness will depend on ESG as a basic requirement when sustainable finance advances to maturity.

Keywords: ESG, credit risk, EU taxonomy, SFDR, corporate sustainability reporting directive (CSRD)

1. Introduction: Understanding the ESG (Environmental, Social, and Governance)

ESG refers to a collection of non-financial metrics that are traditionally used to gauge an entity's sustainability and ethical impact. Recently, there has been a growing importance of these factors in investment choices and corporate risk considerations (Friede, Busch & Bassen, 2015). ESG is segmented into the following:

- Environmental (E) covers climate change, carbon emissions, pollution, water management, and resource depletion (Schoenmaker & Schramade, 2019).
- Social (S): Considers labor rights, workplace safety, diversity and inclusion, customer relations, and community engagement (Eccles, Ioannou, & Serafeim, 2014)
- Governance (G): Corporate governance (governance) encompasses the mechanisms, processes, and relations by which corporations are controlled and directed. (Bebchuk & Weisbach, 2010).

Based on data until October 2023, ESG is critical in evaluating long-term company sustainability and performance (Clark, Feiner, & Viehs, 2015). Strong ESG practices can help firms reduce risks and enhance their reputation, resulting in improved financial stability (Khan, Serafeim, & Yoon, 2016).

Look at the other node on this page to discover the Definition of Credit Risk and Its Importance in Financial Markets:

Credit risk is the risk of default by a borrower on its financial obligations, resulting in a financial loss for lenders or investors (Jorion, 2007). The topic presents as a primary issue in the financial markets since it can affect asset valuations, interest rates and market stability.

Credit risk is affected by:

- Financial health: Higher leveraged and poor cash-flow companies are more prone to default (Altman, 1968)
- Industry-specific risks: Economic downturn, volatility of the market and regulatory change affect the borrowers' abilities to meet obligations (Merton, 1974)
- Macroeconomic conditions: Default probabilities are impacted by inflation, interest rates, and geopolitical risks (Duffie & Singleton, 2003).

Most credit risk is rated based on credit ratings by agencies such as Moody's, S&P, and Fitch that assess an issuer's credit quality (Becker & Milbourn, 2011). The stability of financial markets is a function of effective credit risk management and the prevention of financial crises (Basel Committee on Banking Supervision, 2006).

1.1. A Direct Relationship Exists between ESG Criteria and Credit Risk Assessment

Many experts recognize the integration process of ESG factors in credit risk evaluations as a necessary step to determine business resilience (Giese et al., 2019). The creditworthiness of firms experiences major changes when they face ESG-related risks, which affect them through these specific aspects:

- Retailers face financial risks from environmental factors, including climate regulations and carbon taxes, along with pollution penalties, because Bolton & Kacperczyk (2021) predicted these factors would increase operational costs and diminish profitability. The transition risks faced by oil and gas companies and other high-emission industries negatively affect their creditworthiness (Caldecott, 2018).

- Social factors such as substandard labor treatment combined with human rights abuses generate damaging effects on corporate reputation, thus creating financial uncertainties for businesses (Henisz, Koller, & Nuttall, 2019). Data security breaches combined with cybersecurity incidents create both legal financial burdens and detrimental damage to customer trust (PwC, 2020).
- The lack of proper corporate governance, combined with fraudulent acts and insufficient transparency, leads to regulatory fines and credit downgrades as well as investor distrust (Black, Jang, & Kim, 2006). The implementation of robust governance principles prevents defaults in firms according to research by Bhojraj & Sengupta (2003).
- Research has proved that organizations delivering high ESG outcomes face reduced credit risks and secure reduced interest rates (Chava, 2014). ESG factors now factor into credit rating methods at various agencies as they work to produce a complete assessment of business risks according to Moody's Investors Service (2020).

2. Overview of Regulatory and Investor Interest in ESG Considerations

Investors alongside regulatory bodies keep rising in their emphasis on ESG disclosure and risk management activities because ESG elements substantially affect business stability and financial outcomes (European Commission, 2021). Key developments include:

- Regulatory Requirements: The European Union's Sustainable Finance Disclosure Regulation (SFDR) mandates ESG disclosures for financial institutions (EU Commission, 2020). The Task Force on Climate-related Financial Disclosures (TCFD) helps organizations publish climate risk reports through established guidelines (TCFD, 2017).
- Investor Demand is rising because institutional investors like pension funds as well as asset managers use ESG criteria for their investment

choices (BlackRock, 2020). Green bonds, along with other ESG-linked debt instruments, experience rising interest because sustainable finance continues its growth trajectory (ICMA, 2021).

- Leading credit rating agencies S&P Global and Moody's have commenced adding ESG elements to their credit rating systems to evaluate sustainability threats (Moody's 2020).
- Standards of ESG performance integrated in credit risk assessment enable companies to strengthen their access to capital while securing diminished financing expenses and superior market position (MSCI, 2021).

Corporate sustainability assessment and financial stability evaluation heavily depend on ESG factors. Lenders together, with investors and regulators introduce ESG considerations into risk analysis due to their immediate influence on credit risk. ESG will continue to define how credit risk assessments unfold while influencing financial market processes because regulatory development and investor preference for sustainable finance increase.

3. Understanding ESG Factors

Environmental Social and Governance (ESG) factors provide a method that assesses business sustainability together with ethical investment effects. Information about ESG factors has been incorporated by investors together with regulators and corporations into financial decision-making because its significance extends to risk control and long-term profitability and societal wellbeing (Friede, Busch, & Bassen, 2015). ESG assessments reveal businesses that will succeed in future challenges and reveal businesses that expose investors to financial and reputational threats (Khan, Serafeim, & Yoon, 2016). This text provides thorough information about the three fundamental elements under ESG evaluation.

3.1. Environmental Factors

Organizations need to assess natural resource effects together with their ability to manage potential risks and exploit necessary opportunities under environmental aspects. Company survival depends heavily on implementing sustainable practices because climate change and resource limitations stand as vital worldwide problems (Schoenmaker & Schramade, 2019). Companies need to monitor their greenhouse gas emissions as part of their climate policy compliance with the Paris Agreement to achieve environment-related performance targets. Organizations face regulatory penalties as well as reputation damages because of their excessive carbon emissions (Bolton & Kacperczyk, 2021).

To create sustainability businesses must make efficient use of their energy inputs and water and raw materials consumption. Optimized resource usage leads firms to reduce their operational costs while minimizing environmental damage (Eccles, Ioannou, & Serafeim, 2014).

Businesses need to manage pollution and waste by establishing proper systems to dispose of waste and control emissions in air, water, and soil. Failure to meet environmental regulations creates legal penalties according to Caldecott (2018).

The protection of biodiversity alongside ecosystems requires industries associated with agriculture, mining, and forestry to adopt policies which stop deforestation along with habitat destruction and biodiversity decline (UNEP 2020).

3.2. Social Factors

The social assessment checks organizational relations with employees, customers, communities, and external stakeholders. A well-developed social strategy results in satisfied employees who contribute to better reputation and operational excellence (Henisz, Koller, & Nuttall, 2019).

Labor policies based on ethics together with fair wage and safe work environments and compliance with laws protect employees from harm while cutting labor turnover rates. Worker rights violations force organizations to face legal consequences alongside reputation damage that might affect their standing within the market (ILO, 2021).

The implementation of diversity and inclusion guarantees equal gender representation and ethnic diversity, together with inclusive hiring, promotes better organizational outcomes. Financial performance numbers demonstrate that organizations with diverse leadership generally exceed their peer organizations according to McKinsey & Company (2020).

Companies need to activate partnerships with local communities through financial backing of social programs and avoidance of project-related displacements. The establishment of positive relationships with the community creates trust while generating brand faithful customers according to Porter & Kramer (2011).

Organizations must guarantee that their products follow legal safety requirements while maintaining ethical supply standards for consumers. Failure to maintain ethical practices leads businesses to face legal disputes while product recalls and damaged customer trust become likely outcomes (PwC, 2020).

3.3. Governance Factors

The assessment under governance factors focuses on the analysis of corporate leadership along with decision-making processes as well as ethical business conduct. Strong governance systems build trust among shareholders and decrease the chances of financial misbehavior (Bebchuk & Weisbach, 2010).

A corporation with diverse independent board membership delivers superior oversight and prevents conflicts while ensuring balanced corporate decisions. The governance failures of organizations with weak board structures indicate the findings of Black, Jang, & Kim (2006).

The practice of clearly disclosing executive pay linked to performance helps executives take appropriate risks and maintain pay alignment with shareholder interests (Jensen & Murphy, 1990).

Organizations that provide transparent financial along with ESG reports maintain high levels of accountability. The Global Reporting Initiative (GRI), together with the Sustainability Accounting Standards Board (SASB), exists to help companies show their sustainability performance (GRI, 2021).

The prevention of fraud alongside unethical conduct becomes possible through the combination of strong anti-bribery policies and whistleblower protection and global anti-corruption law compliance (OECD, 2018).

Recognition of ESG factors serves as a core requirement which businesses together with investors need to understand for sustainable and responsible operations. Organizations that seamlessly incorporate ESG criteria into their planning experience both long-term stability with additional capital inflow while simultaneously enhancing social and ecological wellness. Organizations need to actively manage these elements because ESG regulations develop alongside mounting stakeholder requirements for business success in the contemporary economic market.

4. ESG's Impact on Credit Risk

Companies need Environmental, Social, and Governance factors to determine their credit standing and financial stability. ESG-related risks negatively influence operational performance along with investor loyalty and financial sources, which determine a firm's capacity to fulfill its debt payments (Giese et al., 2019). The increasing market trend toward sustainable finance makes it crucial for lenders and investors to adopt ESG factors during credit risk analysis (Moody's Investors Service, 2020).

4.1. Direct Impact on Creditworthiness

The financial position of companies undergoes change when ESG factors intervene, thus influencing their creditworthiness alongside their interest rates for borrowing. A company's solid ESG performance leads to reduced default risks and narrower credit spreads, as per Chava (2014). Financial distress becomes a reality for businesses that experience ESG-related risks since they have to deal with regulatory penalties plus litigation costs alongside operational inefficiencies (Bolton & Kacperczyk, 2021).

- The financial stability of companies diminishes when they encounter environmental risks from climate change and carbon taxation and resource depletion because this reduction affects cash flow and asset values and intensifies credit risk (Caldecott, 2018).
- The implementation of poor labor practices and community disputes alongside product safety concerns leads to permanent damage of reputation which ends up diminishing trust among customers and enterprise revenue (Henisz, Koller, & Nuttall, 2019).
- The probability of default increases when companies experience weak corporate governance together with fraud and limited transparency as per Bebchuk and Weisbach (2010).

The business faces operational risks in the form of regulatory penalties combined with environmental responsibilities and staffing conflicts.

- Operational risks triggered by ESG issues generate substantial changes to both financial position and credit risk profile of a company.
- Claims from regulatory bodies for noncompliance with environmental regulations together with labor rules put severe financial strain on companies (OECD, 2018).
- The financial viability of companies deteriorates when they need to pay for pollution cleanup expenses and carbon emissions fees and manage their water resources effectively (Schoenmaker & Schramade, 2019).
- Poor workplace environment, alongside pay disagreements and unethical work practices, create employee strikes, which minimize productivity and produce legal challenges against the firm while diminishing their financial stability (ILO, 2021).

4.2. Reputational Risks: Investor Perception and Market Confidence

Market confidence and investor perception both determine how easy it will be for a firm to obtain funding and maintain its financial capabilities. Weak ESG performance results in declining investor trust that causes both increased financing costs and lower credit ratings (Friede, Busch, & Bassen, 2015).

ESG-related controversies that damage environmental systems or trigger corporate scandals result in a decrease of stock prices and lower investor interest, according to Khan Serafeim Yoon (2016).

The actions of credit rating agencies result in downgrades when ESG performance falls short which raises borrowing expenses according to Moody's Investors Service (2020).

The reputation of companies takes harm when media provides unfavorable coverage about ESG missteps which leads to market distrust and enhances business volatility (PwC, 2020).

The ability to obtain capital and the growing interest of investors toward firms with favorable ESG practices constitute liquidity risks.

ESG factors receive elevated importance from the financial market since they shape both business loan options and their ability to access capital. The increased sustainable investment market now draws rising interest from both financial institutions and investors who want to fund businesses demonstrating high ESG performance standards (BlackRock, 2020).

Fluctuating borrowing costs exist for green bonds, sustainability-linked loans, and ESG-related financial products listed with ICMA (2021) for organizations maintaining ESG compliance.

Stable capital follows investors who favor ESG-friendly firms resulting in better market liquidity that enhances financial flexibility (McKinsey & Company, 2020).

Organizations that demonstrate outstanding ESG performance maintain easy access to credit during economic hard times, according to Giese et al., (2019).

The direct influence of ESG factors on elements of credit risk occurs through their impact on financial stability as well as their effect on compliance requirements alongside investor confidence and capital accessibility. Aspects of ESG principles help organizations attract investors who provide advantageous funding terms and operational relief for their businesses. Corporate sustainability principles should become integral to risk management systems to maintain a strong credit rating and market success, while ESG parameters gain significance as financial world drivers.

5. ESG in Credit Ratings and Analysis

Worldwide financial market risk assessment now heavily relies on ESG factors since these elements were integrated into credit ratings systems. S&P Global and Moody's Investors Service, along with Fitch, implement ESG components into their risk-based assessment strategies for business and government creditworthiness (Moody's Investors Service, 2020). The inability of borrowers who face ESG risks results in reduced capacity to fulfill financial obligations which leads credit rating authorities to make new lending decisions (Giese et al., 2019).

5.1. ESG Integration in Credit Rating Agency Methodologies

To analyze ESG risks credit rating organizations created structured systems for their credit evaluation processes. The analysis of ESG factors as they impact corporate financial health and default potential exists within credit rating methods according to Bolton & Kacperczyk (2021).

The ESG Evaluation Score from S&P Global allows organizations to predict their financial sector risks by analyzing ESG factor impacts on their credit profile (S&P Global, 2021).

Moody's Investors Service includes ESG risks into their credit ratings through assessments of governance structures and social elements and climate-related exposure factors which affect credit worthiness (Moody's Investors Service, 2020).

Fitch Ratings uses an ESG Relevance Score to demonstrate how ESG risks generate impact on overall credit assessment by showing ESG drivers (Fitch Ratings, 2021).

5.2. ESG Scoring Models and Frameworks

The assessment of corporate sustainability through financial risk appraisal happens via multiple ESG scoring mechanisms. Investors and lenders can use these models to obtain numerical assessments of ESG risk exposure according to Friede, Busch, and Bassen (2015).

MSCI ESG Ratings provides evaluations through measuring specific ESG risks within industries alongside their risk management capabilities as compared to peer organizations (MSCI, 2020).

The Sustainalytics ESG Risk Rating system examines business exposure to ESG perils and effectiveness in handling risks by rating organizations on a scale from no exposure to severe (Sustainalytics ESG Risk Rating, 2021).

This ESG evaluation system from Bloomberg diagnoses sustainability capabilities through public ESG reports (Bloomberg, 2020).

Companies can receive ESG performance assessments through Refinitiv ESG Scores, which use publicly available information (Refinitiv, 2020).

5.3. Case Studies of Companies Downgraded Due to ESG Risks

ESG factors cause credit rating degradation based on the evidence from multiple scenarios in which companies received downgrades because of their ESG-related issues. Different cases showcase various essential risks that develop from inadequate ESG performance management.

5.3.1. Pacific Gas & Electric (PG&E) – Downgraded due to Environmental Risk

PG&E faced rating downgrades at junk status in 2019 because of wildfires blamed on its equipment which led to major financial liabilities and its eventual bankruptcy process (S&P Global, 2019).

This case demonstrates that environmental hazards, including climate change and severe weather patterns directly, affect credit scores according to Caldecott (2018).

5.3.2. Volkswagen – Governance Failures and Credit Downgrade

A new statement by Moody's and S&P prompted Volkswagen's credit rating reduction after it emerged that the company used problematic emission testing methods during the 2015 emissions scandal (Moody's, 2015).

Weak governance combined with ethical misconduct forced Volkswagen to pay regulatory penalties while facing adverse impact on its reputation and experiencing higher borrowing expenses (PwC, 2020).

5.3.3. Odebrecht – Corruption Scandal and Credit Impact

Odebrecht suffered from multiple credit ratings reductions when Brazilian authorities uncovered massive bribery and corruption schemes involving the company (Fitch Ratings, 2017).

The absence of transparent governance, along with corruption, resulted in the monetary instability of companies and decreased investor trust (OECD, 2018).

5.3.4. British Petroleum (BP) – Environmental Liabilities and Credit Downgrade

It became necessary for Standard & Poor's to lower BP's credit rating because of the 2010 Deepwater Horizon oil spill, which caused significant financial penalties while creating substantial environmental responsibilities (S&P Global, 2011).

Bad environmental risk management practices caused devastating financial outcomes which negatively impacted both market trust and funding availability to capital providers (UNEP, 2020).

Financial market participants now understand sustainability threats because ESG factors have officially entered credit rating methodologies. CEO performance in ESG aspects leads to higher credit costs and enhances the possibility of financial defaults, along with rating downgrades by credit agencies. Organizations involved in rating credit and regulators together with investors have strengthened their focus on ESG elements throughout risk management structures. Organizations need to implement well-developed ESG policies as an essential step to preserve creditworthiness and achieve enduring financial security.

6. Measuring ESG and Credit Risk

These businesses need to measure Environmental Social and Governance risks because sustainability emerged as an essential factor that affects creditworthiness assessments. Recent credit risk analysis techniques incorporate ESG factors because they affect business performance in meeting financial obligations, according to Giese et al., (2019). The process of credit evaluation for sustainability depends heavily on ESG rating providers alongside quantitative ESG assessments and ESG-adjusted credit risk models, according to Bolton & Kacperczyk (2021).

6.1. ESG Rating Providers

Multiple ESG rating entities and data supply sources evaluate sustainability performance of businesses in addition to determining credit risk effects. Different evaluation techniques enable these organizations to assess both ESG risks and their effect on financial stability.

The MSCI ESG Ratings system evaluates specific ESG threats for industries while assessing organizational capability of risk management through a rating scale from CCC (laggard) to AAA (leader) (MSCI, 2020).

The Sustainalytics ESG Risk Rating evaluates corporate vulnerability to ESG factors by determining if risks fall under negligible, low, medium, high, or severe categories (Sustainalytics, 2021).

The evaluation process of Bloomberg ESG Scores utilizes public ESG data to establish corporate sustainability and governance ratings (Bloomberg, 2020).

Refinitiv ESG Scores offers performance assessments of corporations through available public information to reveal ESG-associated credit risks (Refinitiv, 2020).

6.2. Quantitative vs. Qualitative ESG Analysis in Credit Risk Assessment

Financial stability evaluations in credit risk assessment perform quantitative and qualitative ESG examinations.

6.2.1. Quantitative ESG Analysis

Companies use specific quantifiable ESG metrics which include carbon emissions data along with gender diversity measurements and governance score ratings.

Debt-to-equity ratios that adjust for environmental liabilities constitute part of ESG-adjusted financial analyses according to (Giese et al., 2019).

The system applies AI models to predict default possibilities through analysis of ESG movement trends according to Fitch Ratings standards (2021).

6.2.2. Qualitative ESG Analysis

Examines non-numeric factors such as corporate ethics, board effectiveness, and stakeholder engagement.

The evaluation process analyzes both media-related controversies along with credit risk influence from regulatory investigations (OECD, 2018). Expert opinions are used to determine long-term financial risks related to ESG (McKinsey & Company, 2020).

6.3. ESG-Adjusted Credit Risk Models

Financial institutions together, with credit rating agencies, have constructed ESG-adjusted models that aid ESG considerations for credit risk assessment. The incorporation of ESG elements in these credit evaluation systems improves the standard methods for risk assessment.

6.3.1. ESG-Enhanced Probability of Default (PD) Models

Traditional default probability models receive modification through ESG elements, which affect company solvency (Moody's Investors Service, 2020).

Companies affected by substantial ESG risks experience elevated Probability of Default scores (Caldecott, 2018).

6.3.2. ESG-Adjusted Credit Spread Models

The credit spreads of corporations with unsatisfactory ESG scores tend to increase because investors view them as riskier assets (BlackRock, 2020).

ESG leaders receive lower borrowing costs since investors trust their investment-grade sustainability practices (Friede, Busch, & Bassen, 2015).

6.3.3. Sustainability-Linked Loan (SLL) Pricing Models

Sustainability targets of financially stable businesses result in lower interest rates on loans through financing mechanisms (ICMA, 2021).

Current banking institutions together with lenders rely on ESG scores to establish credit conditions and set loan interest rates according to S&P Global (2021).

The evaluation of ESG factors together with credit risk measurement now forms a necessary basis for contemporary financial research. The financial stability of companies becomes clear through the evaluation from ESG rating providers and the combination of quantitative and qualitative ESG assessments with ESG-adjusted credit models. Increasing ESG considerations will necessitate the vital combination of sustainability factors into credit risk evaluations for both investors and lenders as well as regulatory authorities.

7. ESG Regulations and Reporting Standards

The supervision concerning the Environment, Society, Governance (ESG) and their reporting norms have emerged as focal points in enhancing corporate responsibility and business s financial risks. International standards providing frameworks for ESG reporting, such as International Financial Reporting Standards (IFRS), and ISSB (International Sustainability Standards Board) have made efforts to regulate ESG reporting on a global scale. Moreover, local policies like the EU Taxonomy, SFDR, CSRD, SEC Climatic disclosure policies, also impact the organization's disclosure policy from the perspective of their concern relating to default risk.

7.1. IFRS and ISSB (International Sustainability Standards Board):

The IFRS Foundation formed the ISSB with a mandate to create international ESG disclosure requirements that financial markets need. The ISSB functions to make sustainability reports uniform in order to deliver dependable ESG information that investors can compare easily (IFRS, 2021).

Companies should use IFRS Sustainability Disclosure Standards to present ESG-related financial risks together with opportunities for analysis.

Through its role at ISSB the organization ensures sustainability disclosures follow financial reporting standards to improve reporting clarity (ISSB, 2022).

Standardized ESG disclosures enable investors to determine the long-term credit risks that stem from environmental and social factors (BlackRock, 2021).

7.2. EU Taxonomy, SFDR, and Corporate Sustainability Reporting Directive (CSRD)

The EU established various sustainability regulations which work to increase financial market transparency regarding ESG information.

EU Taxonomy functions as a framework that promotes sustainable economic activities while stopping greenwashing processes to direct sustainable investment choices (European Commission, 2022).

The Sustainable Finance Disclosure Regulation (SFDR) makes financial institutions responsible for ESG risk disclosure when selecting investments (ESMA, 2021).

Corporate Sustainability Reporting Directive (CSRD): Expands ESG reporting obligations for companies operating in the EU (European Commission, 2022).

The noncompliance of EU ESG regulations can lead to legal framework violations which causes organizations to face higher borrowing charges and lower credit rating scores (Fitch Ratings, 2022).

7.3. SEC Climate Disclosure Rules

The U.S. Securities and Exchange Commission recently proposed that companies must provide climate-related data to shareholders in order to improve their ESG information disclosure (SEC, 2022).

Publicly traded companies need to submit three key climate-related statements to authorities including GHG emission reporting, financial risk assessments and governance details (SEC, 2022).

The visibility of ESG risks gives investors precise tools to evaluate sustainability impact on their financial investments (Moody's, 2022).

The companies which maintain large carbon emissions combined with weak climate leadership face increased capital costs and credit spread premiums (S&P Global, 2022).

7.4. Impact of Regulatory Changes on Credit Risk Management

The introduction of ESG reporting regulations enhances corporate transparency while raising investor trust so that both factors affect credit risk evaluation directly. The implementation of ESG regulations leads to better creditworthiness for adaptive organizations yet creates financial along with reputational costs for non-compliant firms (McKinsey & Company, 2021).

Standardized ESG disclosures enable rating agencies and investors to conduct better assessment of credit risk because they receive standardized information (Bolton & Kacperczyk, 2021).

The lack of compliance with ESG regulations creates an elevation of credit risk as well as potential litigation costs and regulatory penalties, according to OECD (2021).

Strong ESG policies in companies attract investors who provide better market opportunities along with reduced borrowing expenses (BlackRock, 2021).

ESG regulations together with reporting standards operate as essential management tools for credit risks because they provide clear data visibility, which minimizes corporate governance uncertainties. Financial markets obtain their guidance from essential frameworks, which consist of the IFRS and ISSB, along with EU Taxonomy, SFDR, CSRD, and SEC climate disclosure requirements. Every business needs to follow sustainability reporting standards under current regulations in order to protect credit stability and investor confidence.

8. ESG and Fixed Income Markets

Investors continually turn to Environmental Social Governance (ESG) considerations to influence their fixed income market decisions because they want sustainable and responsible investment choices. The assessment of credit risk and capital allocation process has changed through ESG integration across various bond categories including corporate bonds in addition to green bonds sustainability-linked bonds and social bonds (Bolton & Kacperczyk, 2021). Investor demand for sustainable fixed income products continues to grow therefore financial markets transform to match sustainability targets (BlackRock, 2022).

8.1. ESG Considerations in Corporate Bonds

Corporate bonds function as essential investments because credit risk decisions, alongside investment choices, strongly depend on ESG factors. The strong environmental, social, and governance (ESG) performance of companies leads to lower borrowing expenses combined with better credit ratings because it reduces their regulatory exposure as well as operational risks and reputational risks (Fitch Ratings, 2022).

ESG risks directly influence bond spreads and credit ratings through the evaluation methods of rating agencies, according to Moody's (2022).

Organizations with inadequate ESG practices must deal with higher risk premiums while investors show diminished confidence, according to S&P Global (2022).

The transition risks that affect companies with significant carbon emissions stem from upcoming regulations and market standards as identified by the OECD (2021).

8.2. Green Bonds, Sustainability-Linked Bonds, and Social Bonds

ESG-themed bonds in the fixed income market have expanded rapidly because they bring investments together with sustainable objectives for financing.

- Green Bonds:

Green bonds serve specifically for funding environmentally friendly initiatives, which include projects involving renewable energy, as well as energy efficiency measures and pollution control operations (ICMA, 2022).

Organizations seek third-party verification to validate their adherence to the criteria of green bond principles.

- Sustainability-Linked Bonds (SLBs):

Unlike green bonds, the Sustainability-Linked Bonds provide flexibility in capital fund usage by featuring ESG performance targets as financing criteria (Climate Bonds Initiative, 2021).

The objective performance of sustainable targets by companies enables them to benefit from reduced borrowing rates through financial incentives.

- Social Bonds:

World Bank (2022) states organizations can use bond funding to support projects that build affordable housing, healthcare infrastructure, and educational facilities.

The selection of issuers for investment greatly depends on their demonstrated social impact performance metrics.

Investor Demand for ESG-Integrated Fixed Income Products. Professional investors, together with retail clients, are applying ESG elements to their fixed income investments, which leads to bond issuances and price adjustments throughout markets.

ESG-focused funds represent one of the emerging trends in the investment management space, which asset managers use to satisfy investors who focus on sustainability (Morningstar 2022).

Transparency in ESG bond reporting receives regulatory support, which serves to prevent cases of greenwashing (European Commission, 2022). Investor demand will drive the sustainable bond market beyond $1 trillion, which forecasts annual growth (Bloomberg, 2022).

The fixed income market now operates under a complete transformation because investors have revolutionized their risk management and planning through ESG principles. A company credit rating process incorporates ESG factors that influence bond prices simultaneously with investor judgment and bond score assessments. The sustainable bond market enlarges through three main bond types: green bonds, sustainability-linked bonds, and social bonds, which demonstrate an active financial market focus on sustainability goals. The rising interest in ESG-integrated fixed income product from investors requires market participants to adjust their practices for evolving ESG disclosure requirements and regulatory rules.

9. Case Studies and Empirical Evidence

Examination of practical examples and scientific research demonstrates the effective way ESG elements impact credit risk analysis and investment returns for fixed income investments.

9.1. Companies Benefiting from Strong ESG Practices

Sustainable innovation at Tesla (TSLA) allows the company to maintain strong investor trust, which leads to both advantageous financing terms and reduced credit spreads according to MSCI (2022).

Unilever (ULVR) strengthened its credit ratings through its sustainable practices and ethical business standards, which generated decreased borrowing expenses (Fitch Ratings, 2022).

9.2. Failures Due to Poor ESG Management

When BP Deepwater Horizon suffered the environmental disaster in 2010, it triggered massive financial losses, court-related expenses, and higher credit spreads for their bond holdings (Moody's, 2011).

Volkswagen Emissions Scandal (2015) caused ethical and governance misconduct that led S&P Global to quantify through credit downgrades and higher borrowing expenses (S&P Global, 2016).

9.3. Empirical Studies Linking ESG Scores with Credit Risk Metrics

Companies that demonstrate high ESG ratings exhibit stronger creditworthiness together with lower default probabilities based on Friede, Busch, & Bassen (2015). The research conducted by Giese et al., (2019) showed ESG leaders receive better credit market conditions through narrower spreads, which support better bond performance as time passes.

Based on documented evidence, businesses demonstrating strong ESG practices achieve lower credit risks; however, financial instability occurs when they perform poorly in ESG management. The growing need among investors for ESG-integrated fixed income tools requires all market stakeholders to change their practices so they follow updated ESG disclosure rules and legal standards.

10. Challenges and Criticisms of ESG in Credit Risk

Several issues continue to confront ESG factor implementation in credit risk evaluations despite their growing incorporation in credit risk evaluations.

10.1. ESG Data Inconsistency and Subjectivity

Different provider companies, including MSCI, Sustainalytics, and Bloomberg, use separate rating systems, which complicates assessment consistency (Berg, Kölbel, & Rigobon, 2022). Subjective ESG assessments occur because organizations lack standard methodologies to measure their ESG performance (OECD, 2021).

10.2. Greenwashing and Misleading ESG Disclosures

The practice of creating false or deceptive ESG presentations persists among certain organizations for obtaining sustainable investment capital (Morningstar, 2022). The SEC together with the European Commission, has started to strengthen their disclosure requirements for ESG information to reduce the risks of greenwashing (European Commission, 2022).

10.3. Difficulty in Quantifying Social and Governance Risks

The measurement of environmental risks, including carbon footprint, represents a more straightforward process compared to social and governance risks, including labor rights and ethical leadership (Gibson, Krueger, & Schmidt, 2021). Investors face difficulties computing the financial consequences of governance malfunction before such issues result in scandals or widespread crises (Moody's, 2022).

11. Case Studies and Empirical Evidence

The transition risks that affect companies with significant carbon emissions stem from upcoming regulations and market standards as identified by the OECD (2021).

11.1. Companies Benefiting from Strong ESG Practices

Two instances showcase Tesla (TSLA) as a prime example of positive ESG impact through clean energy development, which earned the company lower financing expense costs according to MSCI (2022) ratings. Unilever achieved higher credit ratings and cut down borrowing expenses because of its sustainable and ethical sourcing (Fitch Ratings, 2022).

11.2. Failures Due to Poor ESG Management

BP Deepwater Horizon Oil Spill caused BP's bonds to face higher credit spreads and legal liabilities and enormous financial losses during 2010 (Moody's 2011). The Volkswagen Emissions Scandal (2015) caused credit rating agencies at S&P Global to downgrade Volkswagen while increasing borrowing expenses due to governance and ethical failures (S&P Global, 2016).

11.3. Empirical Studies Linking ESG Scores with Credit Risk Metrics

Friede, Busch, & Bassen (2015) performed research that discovered that businesses scoring well on ESG assessments show reduced default risks, together with superior creditworthiness. Giese et al., (2019) established through their study that ESG leadership produces credit spread reductions and positive bond returns both short- and long-term.

Multiple obstacles present in ESG implementation for credit risk assessment include unreliable data and deception tactics, along with difficulties in measuring social and governance aspects. Market participants must shift their ESG-integrated fixed income product methods to respond to increasing investor demand for integrated ESG standards and developing ESG disclosure requirements.

12. Future Trends in ESG and Credit Risk Management

ESG considerations now serve as the cornerstones of financial markets since they determine how credit risk is assessed along with investment strategy decisions. Credit risk management develops superior ESG integration capabilities through combining regulatory changes with better data analytics technologies.

The paper analyzes artificial intelligence and big data applications within ESG credit risk assessments in addition to regulatory transitions and future directions of sustainable finance practices.

13. The Role of AI and Big Data in ESG Credit Risk Analysis

ESG credit risk assessment undergoes transformation with technological breakthroughs, including artificial intelligence (AI) and big data, that supply immediate insights, together with improved predictive power, as well as bias reduction in the decision-making process.

1. AI-Driven ESG Analysis: Enhanced ESG risk analyses now result from processing vast amounts of structured and unstructured data using AI algorithms, according to Deloitte (2023).

Machine learning systems can forecast how ESG-linked dangers affect organizational financial health, together with creditworthiness (PwC, 2022).

2. The monitoring of ESG risks benefits from Big Data analysis because it gathers and evaluates extensive quantities of structured and unstructured information. Time-sensitive ESG indicator analyses, including carbon footprint assessments, labor practice reviews, and regulatory standards monitoring, become possible through big data with modernized tracking systems, according to BlackRock (2022).

The combination of artificial intelligence tools that implement sentiment analysis and NLP technology uses public social media evaluations, news sources, and official regulatory documents for performing reputational risk assessments (Bloomberg, 2023).

3. AI systems now perform ESG assessment tasks and credit rating activities through automated methods. The credit rating organizations Moody's and S&P now use AI-powered ESG assessment tools to transform ESG risk factors into numerical attributes for bond rating purposes (Moody's, 2023).

The automated ESG scoring process through artificial intelligence continues to update assessment ratings as new events related to ESG arise, thus enhancing the transparency levels for investors according to S&P Global (2023).

14. Evolution of the Regulatory Landscape

Governments and regulatory organizations enhance ESG credit risk disclosure standards because these considerations have become more vital in credit risk assessment.

14.1. Global ESG Reporting Standards

ESG disclosure standards are developed through a combined framework created by IFRS and ISSB that provides global reporting norms for explanations (IFRS, 2023).

Companies must report their climate-related risks and opportunities because of the regulatory policies inspired by the Task Force on Climate-Related Financial Disclosures (TCFD) (TCFD, 2023).

14.2. Regional Regulatory Developments

The Corporate Sustainability Reporting Directive (CSRD) of the European Union (EU) requires large companies to make detailed ESG disclosures, which significantly affects the process of evaluating credit risks (European Commission, 2023).

The United States Securities and Exchange Commission (SEC) has created climate disclosure regulations to provide investors with standardized ESG data through new regulations (SEC, 2023).

Japan and China, together with other Asia-Pacific countries, strengthen their ESG disclosure rules to achieve higher market transparency as well as investor confidence, according to the Asian Development Bank (2023).

14.3. Impact on Credit Risk Management

The strengthening of regulations requires companies to demonstrate good ESG compliance; otherwise, they will experience negative effects such as decreased credit rating, elevated borrowing expenses, and limited capital availability (Fitch Ratings, 2023). Financial institutions incorporate regulatory ESG assessments for performing stress tests that help determine long-term credit risk exposure (World Bank, 2023).

15. The Future of Sustainable Finance and Its Impact on Credit Markets

Sustainable finance will define credit markets because ESG-integrated financial instruments are becoming more important to investors, while regulatory requirements strengthen sustainability accountability.

15.1. Growth of ESG-Themed Bonds

Sustainable financing through green bonds will reach more than $2 trillion by 2030 because public entities and corporate organizations enhance their sustainable investment programs (Climate Bonds Initiative, 2023).

The integration of sustainability-linked bonds (SLBs) into financial markets is expected to grow significantly because they provide adaptable financing options that reference ESG performance metrics (IMF, 2023).

15.2. ESG in Credit Portfolio Management

Through the implementation of ESG risk factors in credit risk models, financial institutions adjust their loan prices as well as distribute their capital (Morningstar, 2023).

Financial institutions utilize expanded ESG stress testing as a method to determine credit risk through evaluation of multiple climate change scenarios (Bank for International Settlements, 2023).

15.3. Investor Demand for ESG Transparency

Institutional investors such as pension funds, together with sovereign wealth funds, have demanded standardized ESG disclosure reports to solve issues with information mismatch (OECD, 2023). Many shareholders now actively push companies to strengthen their ESG initiatives while determining bond market prices and evaluating credit risks (S&P Global, 2023).

The implementation of ESG-based practices in credit risk management advances because of technological innovations and regulatory changes, along with sustainable financial patterns. Big data technology working with AI allows ESG credit risk analysis to develop into real-time persistent monitoring that generates predictive modeling systems. Organizations need to establish universal ESG reporting systems since regulatory bodies insist on better industrial transparency.

ESG-linked financial products are experiencing rapid momentum while sustainable finance stands as the main theme in credit markets. ESG elements plan to transform credit risk management approaches and both investment patterns and business decision processes in a lasting way.

Conclusion

Financial institutions are now defining modern finance through their adoption of ESG factors for credit risk evaluation. This paper reveals the fast-developing relationship between sustainability and credit ratings through ESG factors that serve as the main determinants of financial health and creditworthiness benchmarks. Capital markets experience increased complexity because ESG factors gain power from regulatory requirements and market need.

The main discovery shows how ESG risks notably affect the ratings, along with environmental and climate-related risks. The ESG relevance scores, along with risk indicators, have become an essential part of Moody's as well as S&P Global and Fitch evaluation frameworks. New evidence confirms ESG achievements positively affect financial strength, together with regulatory needs, create these advances. Strong ESG scores in corporate entities lead to improved operational readiness against regulatory obligations and market risks, together with efficiency problems.

This strategic market placement helps businesses obtain better financial backing and reduced debt costs while earning increased investor confidence.

Although a seamless transition towards complete ESG adoption exists, there are various obstacles which stand in the way. The main difficulty in using ESG ratings centers on the wide differences that persist between rating organizations. The varied ratings between ESG score agencies weaken investor confidence and produce conditions for deceptive ESG marketing practices, also known as greenwashing. Standardization problems occur as a result of limited ESG disclosure process standardization.

The market-wide harmonization efforts for reporting continue as a work in progress, even though initiatives like IFRS Sustainability Disclosure Standards, ISSB frameworks, and the European Commission's CSRD attempt to standardize reporting.

Industry adoption of sustainable debt instruments is evident through three main debt instruments, including green bonds, social loans, and sustainability-linked bonds. The financial tools provided improved corporate access to funding that matches ESG criteria, and they reward organizations that reach sustainability goals. Sustainable debt instruments perform according to the reliability of ESG data alongside the reporting systems they use. The credibility of sustainable finance instruments might decline when there is no proper verification system combined with effective enforcement measures.

The research puts significant weight on technological progress in ESG analytics. The contemporary ESG risk evaluation system heavily depends on artificial intelligence machinery utilizing machine learning and analyzing large datasets. Financial organizations can process massive data sets so that newly detected ESG indicators might bypass typical business analysis methods. Corporate governance, too, plays a pivotal role in ESG implementation. Corporate executives with board members must fuse ESG principles throughout organizational strategic plans and risk analysis systems, as well as performance assessment methods. Business entities with effective governance systems that include diverse leadership get better results on ESG assessments, which strengthens the relationship between governance structures and sustained financial success.

Policy-wise, global momentum is undeniable. The regulatory organizations, including the SEC, ESMA and European Commission, are harmonizing their policies to make climate disclosure requirements, along with ESG fundamental standards, mandatory for organizations. The new regulations are forcing corporate organizations to make behavioral changes, and investors and credit rating agencies must now evaluate risk with ESG perspectives. Financial regulations exhibit an evident ESG integration trend due to the fact that sustainable targets are now essential for banking stability as well as resilience. ESG integration into credit ratings has had a profound impact on financial market operations. The complete potential of sustainable finance will become accessible through the standardization of ESG measures, innovative technology, and strong disclosure framework development. ESG success requires investors, policymakers, and corporates to unite their efforts both to boost credit ratings and create genuine alterations in the actual economic conditions.

References

Altman, E. I. (1968). Financial ratios, discriminant analysis and the prediction of corporate bankruptcy. *Journal of Finance*.

Asian Development Bank. (2023). ESG reporting trends in Asia-Pacific.

Bank for International Settlements. (2023). ESG stress testing in credit risk management.

Bebchuk, L. A., & Weisbach, M. S. (2010). The state of corporate governance research. *The Review of Financial Studies*.

Berg, F., Kölbel, J., & Rigobon, R. (2022). Aggregate confusion: The divergence of ESG ratings. *The Review of Finance*.

Black, B. S., Jang, H., & Kim, W. (2006). Predicting firms' corporate governance choices: Evidence from Korea. *Journal of Corporate Finance*.

BlackRock. (2020). Sustainable investing: Reshaping capital markets.

BlackRock. (2021). Sustainable investing and ESG disclosure standards.

BlackRock. (2022). AI and ESG risk analytics.

Bloomberg. (2020). Bloomberg ESG disclosure scores.

Bloomberg. (2022). Growth of the sustainable bond market.

Bloomberg. (2023). The role of big data in ESG risk monitoring.

Bolton, P., & Kacperczyk, M. (2021). Do investors care about carbon risk? *Journal of Financial Economics*.

Bolton, P., & Kacperczyk, M. (2021). ESG and credit risk in fixed income markets. *Journal of Financial Economics*.
Caldecott, B. (2018). *Stranded assets and the environment*. Routledge.
Chava, S. (2014). Environmental externalities and cost of capital. *Management Science*.
Climate Bonds Initiative. (2021). Sustainability-linked bonds: A growing market.
Climate Bonds Initiative. (2023). Growth projections for green bonds.
Deloitte. (2023). AI and ESG risk management.
Eccles, R. G., Ioannou, I., & Serafeim, G. (2014). The impact of corporate sustainability on organizational processes and performance. *Management Science*.
European Commission. (2021). EU sustainable finance strategy.
European Commission. (2022). ESG regulations and financial market transparency.
European Commission. (2023). Corporate sustainability reporting directive.
ESMA. (2021). SFDR: Sustainable finance disclosure regulation.
Fitch Ratings. (2017). The impact of corruption on credit ratings.
Fitch Ratings. (2021). ESG relevance scores.
Fitch Ratings. (2022). ESG and credit ratings.
Fitch Ratings. (2023). ESG factors in credit ratings.
Friede, G., Busch, T., & Bassen, A. (2015). ESG and financial performance: Aggregated evidence from more than 2000 empirical studies. *Journal of Sustainable Finance & Investment*.
Gibson, R., Krueger, P., & Schmidt, P. (2021). ESG and credit risk: Challenges in measurement. *Financial Analysts Journal*.
Giese, G., Lee, L., Melas, D., Nagy, Z., & Nishikawa, L. (2019). Foundations of ESG investing. *MSCI Research*.
Henisz, W., Koller, T., & Nuttall, R. (2019). Five ways ESG creates value. *McKinsey Quarterly*.
IFRS. (2021). IFRS sustainability disclosure standards.
IFRS. (2023). Global sustainability reporting standards.
IMF. (2023). Sustainable finance trends in emerging markets.
ICMA. (2022). Green bond principles and guidelines.
ISSB. (2022). Global ESG reporting framework.
Khan, M., Serafeim, G., & Yoon, A. (2016). Corporate sustainability: First evidence on materiality. *The Accounting Review*.
McKinsey & Company. (2020). Diversity wins: How inclusion matters.
McKinsey & Company. (2021). ESG regulations and financial performance.
Moody's Investors Service. (2015). Volkswagen credit downgrade.
Moody's Investors Service. (2020). ESG factors in credit ratings.
Moody's Investors Service. (2022). Climate risk and credit ratings.
Moody's Investors Service. (2023). AI and ESG credit ratings.
Morningstar. (2023). ESG risk integration in credit portfolios.
MSCI. (2022). ESG ratings and impact on corporate credit.
OECD. (2021). Transition risks and ESG investing.
OECD. (2023). Investor demand for ESG transparency.
PwC. (2022). The role of big data in ESG analytics.
S&P Global. (2011). BP credit rating downgrade following Deepwater Horizon spill.

S&P Global. (2021). ESG evaluation score.

S&P Global. (2023). ESG scoring and credit risk assessment.

Schoenmaker, D., & Schramade, W. (2019). *Principles of sustainable finance.* Oxford University Press.

SEC. (2022). Climate disclosure rules and financial transparency.

SEC. (2023). Climate disclosure rules.

Sustainalytics. (2021). ESG risk ratings.TCFD. (2023). Climate-related financial disclosures.

UNEP. (2020). Global biodiversity outlook 5.

World Bank. (2022). Social bonds and their impact on global development.

World Bank. (2023). ESG regulatory developments and credit risk implications.

Chapter 9

Private Equity and ESG Investing - Pathways to Long-Term Value Creation

Deepa Gupta[1,*]
Mukul Gupta[1]
and Parth Mukul Gupta[2]
[1]GL Bajaj Institute of Management, Greater Noida, India
[2]Birla Institute of Technology and Sciences, Pilani, Rajasthan, India

Abstract

Private equity (PE) has been a core source of funding for private companies beyond public markets for decades, serving as a driving force for growth, innovation, and reorganization. The last decade saw environmental, social, and governance (ESG) considerations integrated into investment strategies across sectors, private equity included. This article investigates the nexus of private equity and ESG investing and how PE firms are aligning ESG values with their investment processes and the value implications and long-term societal payoffs. The article explains how ESG standards—environmental considerations, social responsibility, and governance practices—inform investment decisions and help reduce risks. The study also discusses how the integration of ESG has influenced the financial success of private equity investments and includes case studies showing the correlation between good ESG performance and excellent financial return. Additionally, it describes approaches to ESG-friendly investing like screening, active ownership, and impact investing and challenges of standardization, greenwashing, and short-termism. The paper winds up with a focus on the increasing

* Corresponding Author's Email: dr.deepaguptadg@gmail.com

In: Environmental, Social, and Governance (ESG) …
Editor: Veena Grover
ISBN: 979-8-90134-138-4

relevance of ESG in private equity as a catalyst for sustainable finance, with PE companies coming more and more into alignment with the rising call for responsible investment, while coping with global environmental and social issues. The future of private equity is, in turn, linked to how ESG investing evolves, where technology becomes even more critical for improving due diligence, reporting, and real-time tracking of the ESG parameters (Clark, 2021; Garcia, 2022).

Keywords: ESG investing, sustainable finance, ESG, responsible investment, ESG integration, impact investing, active ownership, greenwashing, ESG reporting, due diligence

1. Introduction

Private equity (PE) is one of the defining features of contemporary finance, being an important source of funds for firms that might not be publicly listed on stock exchanges. The last ten years have seen tremendous momentum for environmental, social, and governance (ESG) investing across a range of investment categories, including private equity. The increasing awareness of sustainability risks and opportunities has compelled private equity companies to integrate ESG factors into their investment policies. This chapter examines the crossroads of private equity and ESG investing, examining how private equity companies are embracing ESG principles, value creation implications, and long-term advantages for investors and society alike (Harrison & Molitor, 2020; Rutter, 2021).

1.1. Understanding Private Equity

Private Equity is the investments that are undertaken in businesses which are not publicly listed on an exchange. The investments are generally undertaken by institutional investors, private equity houses, and individual high-net-worth investors. Private equity encompasses a broad set of strategies, ranging from investments in infant companies (venture capital) to acquisitions and restructuring of mature businesses (buyouts) (Peterson, 2019).

1.2. Key Characteristics of Private Equity

1. Private Ownership: Investments by PE firms are in private companies, or listed companies which are delisted and become private.
2. Active Participation: PE investors tend to be actively involved in running the firms they invest in, enhancing operational efficiencies, and promoting growth.
3. Exit Strategy: PE companies seek to exit their investment within a specific time horizon (usually 4-7 years) through diverse mechanisms, for example, by selling to some other investor, an IPO, or a merger/acquisition (Turner & Simons, 2020).

Table 1. Comparison between private equity and public equity

Feature	Private Equity (PE)	Public Equity
Ownership	Private companies or public companies taken private	Publicly traded companies
Investment Horizon	4-7 years (short-term to medium-term)	Long-term ownership
Investment Size	Large capital investments	Smaller, individual investments
Risk Level	High (due to illiquidity and complexity)	Moderate to low (due to market liquidity)
Control	High control over the company	Low control (shareholder influence only)

1.3. Structure of Private Equity Investments

Private equity investments are made in a variety of ways, based on the approach being taken and the particular requirements of the target firm. Following are the most prevalent types of PE investments:

1. Venture Capital (VC): In this, one invests in potential high-growth companies in their early stages. VCs tend to invest in start-ups or small companies that have not yet established strong revenues but have a bright future ahead.
2. Growth Equity: This investment strategy targets existing companies with revenues that are in need of capital to drive growth. Taking a minority position in a firm is often involved in this type of investment.

3. Buyouts: It is the most prevalent type of private equity in which investors take a controlling stake in a mature, established business. The businesses are frequently underperforming or require restructuring in operations.
4. Distressed Assets: Investing in distressed or bankrupt companies. PE firms can purchase these companies at a discount and try to turn them around.

Table 2. Types of private equity investments

Type of Investment	Description	Target Companies
Venture Capital (VC)	Investment in early-stage, high-growth companies	Start-ups and emerging companies
Growth Equity	Investment in mature companies looking to expand	Established, growing businesses
Buyouts	Acquisition of controlling interest in a company	Underperforming, mature companies
Distressed Assets	Purchase of financially troubled companies at a discount	Companies in bankruptcy or distress

1.4. The Role of Private Equity in the Financial Market

Private equity has an important function in the financial market through the provision of capital to firms that would otherwise find it difficult to raise capital from public markets or conventional banking. Such companies facilitate the linkage between start-ups and large businesses, usually creating innovation and growth. Some of the most important functions of private equity in the financial market are outlined below:

1. Capital for Expansion: PE infuses firms with the capital required to increase operations, venture into new territories, or fund research and development.
2. Turnarounds and Restructuring: Taking over underperforming firms, PE companies can restructure and bring in efficiencies to enhance profitability.
3. Employment Generation: By turning around ailing firms or providing fast growth to start-ups, private equity can generate employment and stimulate economic productivity.

4. Market Liquidity: Private equity also improves market liquidity through facilitating buyouts, mergers, and acquisitions that aid in the redistribution of capital to more productive or efficient purposes.
5. Exit Strategies: Through IPOs or disposal to other investors, PE gives rise to a liquidity event for investors to gain returns on their investments.

2. Understanding ESG Investing

ESG investment is concerned with the three vital factors:

a) Environmental: This factor looks at the way a business handles its effect on the environment, such as carbon footprint, waste management, water consumption, and renewable energy use. It also looks at the way businesses handle climate change, depletion of resources, and how they are sustainable (Jones & Roberts, 2021).
b) Social: This aspect measures how a firm treats its workers, consumers, suppliers, and communities. It addresses areas such as labour practices, human rights, diversity and inclusion, product safety, and community involvement (Adams & Green, 2020).
c) Governance: Governance evaluates the internal practices and organization of a firm. It encompasses executive pay, board composition, shareholder rights, transparency, and compliance with ethical business practices (Barker, 2021).

ESG investing seeks to generate financial returns alongside fostering sustainability and ethical business practices (Thompson & Williams, 2022).

2.1. The Importance of ESG Criteria in Modern Investment

In today's investment environment, ESG considerations have become increasingly important because of their ability to influence long-term financial performance (Allen & Smith, 2021). A number of factors explain why ESG considerations are critical in investment decisions:

1. Risk Management: ESG considerations assist investors in recognizing and avoiding potential risks that can influence long-term profitability, including environmental catastrophes, regulatory penalties, or unsafe labour practices that can harm the reputation of a company (Bennet, 2022).
2. Regulatory Changes: Governments and regulatory agencies are paying more attention to ESG standards, and non-compliant companies can expect legal battles or fines. The inclusion of ESG criteria allows investors to anticipate regulatory changes.
3. Consumer Demand: With consumers becoming increasingly aware of environmental and social concerns, companies with good ESG performance tend to be more appealing to customers, which results in higher demand for their products or services.
4. Access to Capital: Strong ESG-rated companies might enjoy improved access to capital based on reduced risk, enhanced reputation, and investor trust, and hence be more attractive to ESG investors.
5. Sustainable Long-Term Growth: ESG investment prioritizes sustainable long-term growth rather than short-term returns. By encouraging ethical conduct, it ensures the building of companies on a foundation favourable to long-term economic, environmental, and social stability.

2.2. Overview of ESG Ratings and Standards

ESG standards and ESG ratings are tools used to gauge and benchmark the ESG performance of companies. ESG ratings are provided by various organizations and are meant to help investors make decisions based on ESG considerations. Some of the key ESG ratings and standards are described below:

a) ESG Ratings Providers

There are numerous organizations providing ESG ratings, each having its methodology. Some of the key ESG rating agencies are:

- MSCI ESG Ratings: MSCI rates companies according to their ESG performance in comparison to their industry peers, from AAA (best) to CCC (worst).
- Sustainalytics: This firm provides ESG risk ratings, concentrating on how a firm handles its ESG-related risks.
- ISS ESG: ISS rates companies on their environmental, social, and governance policies, providing both ratings and information on firms' ESG performance.
- FTSE Russell: FTSE offers ESG ratings and benchmarks to assist investors in incorporating sustainability factors into their investment choices.

b) Common ESG Standards and Frameworks

Table 3. ESG ratings comparison chart

Provider	Rating Scale	Focus Areas	Key Features
MSCI ESG	AAA to CCC	Environmental, Social, Governance	Industry-relative ratings, comprehensive ESG coverage
Sustainalytics	Low to High Risk	Environmental, Social, Governance	ESG risk ratings, identifying risk exposure
ISS ESG	High to Low	Governance, Social, Environmental	Corporate governance focus, broad ESG analysis
FTSE Russell	0 to 5	Environmental, Social, Governance	ESG ratings with benchmarks, focuses on corporate transparency

Several frameworks assist in standardizing the measurement and reporting of ESG factors:

- Global Reporting Initiative (GRI): GRI framework is most widely used in the context of sustainability reporting. It provides advice on how firms can report their ESG performance in a comparable and transparent way.
- Sustainable Accounting Standards Board (SASB): SASB emphasizes financially material ESG data and gives industry standards to direct businesses within their sustainability reports.
- Task Force on Climate-related Financial Disclosures (TCFD): This framework focuses on the financial impacts of climate-related issues and provides guidance on how and what climate-

related issues and opportunities need to be disclosed by companies.

- Principles for Responsible Investment (PRI): PRI is an international initiative that promotes institutional investors to factor in ESG considerations in their investment decisions.

3. The Rise of ESG Investing

ESG investing refers to the inclusion of environmental, social, and governance factors in investment choices. Environmental factors examine how a company impacts the planet, social factors examine how it interacts with stakeholders, and governance factors examine the quality of management and governance at a company.

ESG investing has turned mainstream from being a niche approach as increasing evidence indicates that companies with sound ESG performance are superior long-term investments. In addition, increasing regulatory pressures, changing consumer preferences, and increased awareness of global concerns, such as climate change and social injustice, have driven the broad application of ESG standards.

4. The Integration of ESG in Private Equity

Private equity companies are also increasingly incorporating ESG considerations into their investment activity. There are a number of ways that ESG principles are being implemented across the private equity industry:

a) Screening and Due Diligence:
   - ESG factors are incorporated at an early stage in the investment process, with thorough due diligence on prospective investments. This involves examination of the environmental impact, labour practices, governance arrangements, and wider societal effects of a business (Rodgers & Moore, 2021).
   - Investors are increasingly relying on ESG scores and ratings to evaluate risk factors and spot firms with good sustainable practices.

b) Active Ownership and Engagement:
   - Compared to public market investors, private equity firms often have a more direct involvement in the management of the companies they invest in. This allows them to directly impact ESG practices, leading to improvements in governance and sustainability in their portfolio companies.
   - Many PE firms nowadays have ESG policies at the portfolio company level, working with management to transform in waste minimization, energy conservation, diversity and inclusion, and ethical hiring practices.

c) Impact Investing:
   - Impact investing is a type of ESG investing, whose purpose is to generate direct, positive environmental or social impact alongside financial return. Impact investing, in particular, is done by private equity participants where investments are made to tackle issues related to society such as climate change, poverty alleviation, or healthcare access.
   - Private equity impact investing is generally structured to focus on the most critical sectors, such as clean energy, sustainable agriculture, and affordable housing, and with the twin objectives of creating financial returns and societal impact.

d) ESG Performance Metrics and Reporting:
   - With increasing demand for transparency, private equity players are now embracing greater ESG performance criteria and reporting standards. The Global Reporting Initiative (GRI) and Sustainability Accounting Standards Board (SASB) standards enable firms to monitor and report on ESG-related results.
   - Some private equity players have pledged to release ESG reports from time to time in order to prove their commitment to sustainable investment objectives, thereby being more responsible towards investors.

4.1. Benefits of ESG Integration in Private Equity

a) Risk Mitigation:
   - ESG factors are increasingly being considered as material risks to financial performance. For example, environmental

regulations and regulations may influence the profitability of companies, while governance failure results in financial loss or embezzlement.
- With the inclusion of ESG standards, these risks can be minimized by private equity companies by investing in those companies that have strong ESG processes or by helping their portfolio companies improve their sustainability performance.

b) Enhanced Long-Term Value Creation:
- Firms that are actively managing ESG matters have superior operational performance and economic resilience. Private equity investors who invest in companies with strong ESG systems are positioning these companies to thrive in a shifting market environment.
- ESG improvements stimulate cost reduction, improved brand loyalty, entry into emerging markets, and the power to attract best-in-class talent, all creating value over the long term.

c) Access to Capital:
- With ESG investing being mainstreamed, investors are driving their funds into responsible use. Through the institution of ESG standards, private equity firms are able to source capital from the very investors that would want to merge their investment and values, such as family offices, institutional investors, and pension funds.
- Strong ESG performance from companies can also be rewarded with preferential financing terms or government incentives, particularly in the renewable energy industry.

d) Positive Societal Impact:
- Private equity can drive constructive change in climate action, gender empowerment, and community development through a focus on social governance and sustainability. This is particularly important since customers and society now increasingly demand more accountability from business and investors.
- Further, the ability of the private equity industry to grow and influence business practices has the potential to significantly drive industry-wide ESG shifts towards broader sustainability goals.

5. Impact of ESG on Private Equity Performance

ESG factors have emerged as an essential priority for investors, particularly private equity (PE). With increasing awareness of sustainable business principles, private equity firms are increasingly incorporating ESG factors into their investment choices. This article discusses the different effects of ESG on private equity performance, including financial results, case studies, risk management, and strategic strategies (Miller, 2020).

5.1. The Financial Performance of ESG-Integrated Private Equity Investments

One of the primary concerns of private equity investors is whether or not the inclusion of ESG considerations affects financial performance. Years of evidence have indicated that ESG-focused investments not only create positive societal effects but also generate sound financial outcomes. Increasing amounts of research identify that well-performing companies in terms of ESG perform better in profitability, valuation, and risk-adjusted returns compared to their peers.

Table 4. Financial performance comparison - ESG vs. non-ESG investments

Metric	ESG-Integrated PE	Non-ESG PE	Difference (%)
Average Annual Return (%)	15.2	12.8	+2.4%
Total Return (5 years)	78.5	62.3	+16.2%
Risk-Adjusted Return	9.4	7.1	+2.3%

Source: ESG Impact Study by Private Equity International (PEI).

As seen from the Table above, ESG-integrated private equity investments outperform non-ESG investments on both annual and overall risk-adjusted returns.

5.2. Case Studies: Successful ESG-Driven Private Equity Investments

- Case Study 1: Brookfield Asset Management

Brookfield Asset Management, a top-tier private equity firm, incorporated ESG into its investment strategy through the pursuit of renewable energy and sustainable infrastructure opportunities. The ESG-based investments by the firm have resulted in huge financial returns alongside helping curb climate change.

- Case Study 2: Blackstone Group's ESG Commitment

Blackstone, which is one of the world's largest private equity firms, has been concentrating on minimizing environmental footprints in its portfolio companies, which has meant lower costs of operation and greater revenue growth. Their emphasis on responsible governance and social responsibility has yielded positive financial returns.

Table 5. Comparison of investment returns – ESG vs. traditional investments (case study analysis)

Investment Firm	ESG Portfolio Return (%)	Traditional Portfolio Return (%)
Brookfield Asset Mgt.	14.3	9.5
Blackstone Group	11.8	8.0

Source: Company Reports & ESG Performance Reviews.

5.4. The Relationship Between ESG and Risk Management in PE

ESG factors possess the potential to add significantly to improving risk management techniques of private equity houses. By taking ESG considerations, companies are able to identify potential risks early, e.g., environmental exposures, governance policy, and social tensions, which would negatively affect a portfolio business.

Table 6. ESG risk mitigation in private equity

ESG Factor	Risk Mitigation Impact	Examples
Environmental	Reduced exposure to fines and regulatory risks	Carbon emissions policies, renewable energy investments
Social	Improved reputation, fewer employee-related disputes	Diversity programs, labour rights compliance
Governance	Decreased risk of management scandals and legal issues	Transparent reporting, ethical business practices

Source: ESG Risk Management Analysis.

6. Strategies for ESG-Aligned Private Equity Investing

To effectively implement ESG-based strategies, private equity companies employ different strategies:

1. Screening and Selection: Select investments with alignment through intensive screening of ESG factors.
2. Engagement: Proactively work with the portfolio companies to enhance their ESG standards.
3. Impact Investing: Prioritize investments that produce social and environmental returns in addition to financial gains.

6.1. Screening and Selection: Selecting ESG-Compliant Investments

Table 7. ESG screening criteria

ESG Factor	Screening Methodology	Key Performance Indicator
Environmental	Carbon footprint assessment	Greenhouse gas emissions
Social	Labour rights audit, community impact	Employee satisfaction, diversity metrics
Governance	Board structure review, compliance checks	Corporate governance rating

Source: ESG Screening Best Practices Report.

Private equity firms are experts in scrutinizing and selecting companies with high ESG scores. This involves extensive due diligence, for example, examining environmental trends, governance structures, and social responsibilities.

6.2. Active Ownership: The Role of Private Equity Firms in Driving ESG Change

Active ownership is the most effective strategy for the private equity firm for inducing ESG change. Private equity firms have the capability, through active involvement with portfolio businesses, to direct business practice, company culture, and governance structure towards improved aggregate ESG performance.

6.3. ESG-Impact Funds: Investing for Social and Environmental Outcomes

ESG-impact funds have the objective of contributing a positive environmental and social impact as well as competitive performance. ESG-impact funds have the objective of investing in sectors like sustainable agriculture, renewable resources, and healthcare.

Table 8. ESG-impact funds performance

Fund Type	Social Impact Focus	Average Annual Return (%)
Renewable Energy Fund	Clean energy generation	16.5
Healthcare Fund	Affordable healthcare access	12.7
Agriculture Fund	Sustainable farming practices	14.2

Source: ESG Impact Funds Performance Study.

7. Challenges and Risks of ESG Investing in Private Equity

While the benefits are obvious, there are challenges to integrating ESG principles into private equity investment:

1. Lack of Standardization:
   - The absence of consistent frameworks and standards for ESG reporting makes it difficult for private equity companies to compare and measure ESG performance across firms. While there has been increasing agreement on some of the ESG metrics, no single, universal standard has yet been established that can be used across industries and geographies.

2. Greenwashing:
   - Greenwashing, where businesses or corporations misrepresent themselves as more sustainable or socially responsible than they actually are, is still a worry. Private equity companies need to be careful when doing ESG evaluations so that they do not end up investing in corporations that are not genuinely interested in sustainable practices.
3. Short-Term Pressure:
   - Numerous private equity investments are aimed at generating returns in a given term, usually 3-7 years. Maintaining the desired short-term return against long-term ESG aspirations can prove trying, particularly where sustainable change does not yield all financial benefits initially.

8. Private Equity's Role in Advancing Sustainable Finance

Private Equity (PE) is now a strong force in facilitating the global movement towards sustainable finance. Through bringing in Environmental, Social, and Governance (ESG) aspects to investment, private equity firms are not merely earning money, but they are also addressing many of the biggest issues in the world. In the following, we examine PE's role to drive sustainable finance, its overlap with ESG, and its attempt in tackling green and social issues.

8.1. Contribution to Sustainable Development Goals (SDGs)

Private Equity (PE) firms play a critical role in supporting the United Nations Sustainable Development Goals (SDGs). PE can drive growth while promoting environmental stewardship, social justice, and economic participation through strategic investment. The SDGs are 17 global goals to a more sustainable and equitable world by 2030. PE assistance to the goals is in the following primary areas:

Table 9. Primary areas where PE assist the goals

SDG	PE's Role
SDG 7: Affordable and Clean Energy	PE firms are investing in clean energy companies and renewable energy infrastructure to help address climate change.
SDG 9: Industry, Innovation, and Infrastructure	Investment in sustainable technologies, eco-friendly manufacturing processes, and infrastructure development.
SDG 12: Responsible Consumption and Production	Funding companies that promote circular economy models, reduce waste, and focus on sustainable production practices.
SDG 13: Climate Action	PE supports businesses in climate adaptation and mitigation, investing in solutions to reduce carbon footprints.
SDG 16: Peace, Justice, and Strong Institutions	PE can enhance corporate governance, focusing on accountability, transparency, and ethical practices.

8.2. Creating Long-Term Value through ESG Integration

ESG integration for Private Equity is not a trend but a transformation towards generating long-term sustainable value for the investors and society. By taking environment, social, and governance into account while making investments, PE companies are best placed to reduce risk, enhance return, and facilitate change in harmony with long-term global sustainability agendas.

Table 10. ESG factors and its impact on long-term value

ESG Factor	Impact on Long-Term Value
Environmental	Investing in eco-friendly technologies and energy-efficient systems helps businesses reduce operational costs and minimize risk associated with environmental regulations.
Social	Emphasizing employee welfare, diversity, and community engagement enhances brand reputation and fosters customer loyalty.
Governance	Strong governance structures ensure accountability, transparency, and long-term risk management, reducing the likelihood of scandals or legal issues.

8.3. The Role of Private Equity in Addressing Global Environmental and Social Challenges

Private Equity's concern in addressing global environment and society problems is high. PE companies can invest money in firms and projects with a direct interest in addressing issues such as poverty, inequality, and climate change.

- Environmental Impact: The PE firms are now more and more investing in companies that work on green technology, renewable energy, and waste management. Such investment reduces the negative environmental impact of industries and increases sustainability.
- Social Impact: Most of the PE-backed companies are giving back to society, ranging from better health, education, and working conditions. PE firms are also forcing an equal society by investing in business divisions specializing in diversity and inclusiveness.

Table 11. Private equity's role in addressing the global challenges

Global Challenge	Private Equity's Role
Climate Change	Investment in renewable energy, energy storage, and carbon capture technologies.
Access to Clean Water	Supporting water management and filtration solutions in developing regions.
Affordable Healthcare	Funding healthcare start-ups that make quality healthcare affordable in underserved areas.
Education and Skills Development	Backing Ed-tech start-ups that expand access to education in low-income communities.

9. The Future of Private Equity and ESG Investing

The future of Private Equity also depends heavily on the growing interest in ESG investing. The trend is reshaping investment strategy, and new innovations are arising that are making it possible to create a more sustainable investment landscape.

9.1. ESG Investing Trends and Innovations in Private Equity

Private Equity firms are more and more emphasizing ESG as an integral part of their investment approach. Some of the most important trends are:

- Impact Investing: Investment that delivers financial return as well as beneficial social or environmental outcomes has become increasingly popular. Most PE firms now specialize in impact funds targeting particular SDGs.

- Sustainable and Green Bonds: PE companies are investing in green bonds and sustainable financial instruments to invest in green initiatives.
- Data-Driven Investment Decisions: Usage of big data and analytics is gaining traction in ESG investing. PE firms are using AI and machine learning platforms to scan for ESG drivers and spot high-potential investments.

9.2. The Role of Technology in ESG Due Diligence and Reporting

Technology is more and more becoming the catalyst to enhance the process of due diligence for ESG investment. Technology enables PE firms to be able to measure and monitor ESG opportunities and risks in their portfolios accurately.

- ESG Data Platforms: AI, blockchain, and data analytics technologies are enabling the gathering and analysis of ESG data for PE firms to gain deeper insights into the businesses and sustainability efforts of companies.
- Real-Time Monitoring: IoT sensors and smart technology are enabling real-time monitoring of environmental impact, such as energy consumption, waste production, and water usage.

Table 12. Impact of technology on ESG due diligence

Technology	Impact on ESG Due Diligence
AI and Machine Learning	Helps process vast amounts of ESG data to uncover hidden risks and opportunities.
Blockchain	Provides transparency and accountability in tracking ESG metrics and commitments.
IoT Sensors	Tracks environmental impact in real-time, providing accurate data for assessment.

9.3. The Increasing Demand for ESG-Aligned Investment Vehicles

There is increasing demand for investment funds based on ESG values. Investors want ways to deploy their capital in a way that aligns with their values, and PE firms are responding by offering more ESG-focused funds.

- ESG-Friendly Funds: The majority of PE firms are launching ESG-compatible funds that invest in businesses meeting some ESG criteria. These funds are catering to the rising need of retail and institutional investors for a responsible investment.
- Transparency and Reporting: Investors are now needing greater transparency from ESG reporting. PE firms are adopting standard reporting frameworks such as Global Reporting Initiative (GRI) and Sustainability Accounting Standards Board (SASB) to address ESG expectations.

Conclusion

Private equity and ESG investing walk in sync with one another, and private equity firms recognize the necessity to address ESG factors in order to generate long-term value, mitigate risks, and be accountable to society. With investors and regulators increasingly focusing on sustainable approaches, private equity organizations will have to embrace integrated ESG strategies in order to remain competitive and meet the increasing demand for responsible investment. By successfully integrating ESG values, private equity can be a key driver of sustainable finance with the added benefit of generating strong financial returns.

References

Adams, S., & Green, P. (2020). *Social responsibility in business: Measuring impact.* Oxford Press.

Allen, J., & Smith, K. (2021). Investment strategies for the future: ESG integration in financial markets. *Journal of Sustainable Finance,* 13 (2), 120-136.

Barker, J. (2021). Corporate governance and its role in modern finance. *Financial Management Review*, 45 (6), 32-48.

Bennet, R. (2022). The role of ESG in financial risk management. *Journal of Risk Assessment*, 22 (3), 112-128.

Clark, M. (2021). Sustainable finance: The rise of ESG in private equity. *Green Business Journal,* 9 (4), 68-85.

Garcia, L. (2022). Private equity and sustainability: The growing importance of ESG. *Financial Perspectives*, 19 (1), 45-59.

Harrison, T., & Molitor, D. (2020). Understanding the dynamics of private equity investments. *Harvard Business Review*, 58 (1), 22-40.

Jones, P., & Roberts, M. (2021). Environmental impact and the ESG revolution. *Environmental Business Studies*, 12 (3), 145-160.

Miller, A. (2020). ESG factors in private equity: The link to performance. *Private Equity Research Journal,* 35 (2), 77-90.

Peterson, L. (2019). Introduction to private equity investments. *Finance Insights*, 28 (2), 5-19.

Rodgers, C., & Moore, D. (2021). Due diligence in the age of ESG: What private equity needs to know. *Journal of Financial Law and Practice*, 34 (1), 50-65.

Rutter, B. (2021). The shift towards responsible private equity investing. *Journal of Corporate Finance*, 29 (4), 85-99.

Thompson, J., & Williams, M. (2022). Governance in the 21st century: Corporate responsibility and its financial implications. *Global Governance Review*, 17 (2), 112-124.

Turner, P., & Simons, G. (2020). Private equity and venture capital: Understanding the key differences. *Business Finance Review*, 44 (3), 28-42.

Chapter 10

Exploring Critical Success Factors (CSF) for Environmental Social and Governance (ESG) Implementation in Banking and Financial Institutions: A TISM Approach

Pooja Tyagi[1,*]
Sachi Rana[2,†]
Veena Grover[3,‡]
Rajasve Kaushik[4,||]
Meetu Kumar[5,¶]
Preeti Bhardwaj[6,#]
and Komal Tyagi[7,**]

[1]Noida Institute of Engineering and Technology, Greater Noida, India
[2]Dewan Institute of Management, Studies, CCS University, Meerut, Uttar Pradesh, India
[3]Lloyd Business School, Greater Noida, India
[4]Manipal University, Manipal, Karnataka, India
[5]KIET Group of Institutions, Uttar Pradesh, India
[6]Swami Vivekanand Subharti University, Delhi, India
[7]Royal Melbourne Institute of Technology, Melbourne, Australia

[*] Corresponding Author's Email: poojatyagi2008@niet.co.in
[†] Corresponding Author's Email: drsachirana@gmail.com
[‡] Corresponding Author's Email: Veena.grovere@gmail.com
[||] Corresponding Author's Email: 2020ht4583@alumni.bits-pilani.ac.in
[¶] Corresponding Author's Email: meetu.kumar@kiet.edu
[#] Corresponding Author's Email: preeti22121985@gmail.com
[**] Corresponding Author's Email: mail2komal@gmail.com

In: Environmental, Social, and Governance (ESG) …
Editor: Veena Grover
ISBN: 979-8-90134-138-4

Abstract

Business leaders, consumers, investors, and all the stakeholders belonging to the corporate world and regulators alike are clamoring and committing themselves to climate action, lower carbon footprint, ethical business practices, justifiable labor, and manufacturing gig. Consequentially, an increasing number of organizations and business sojourns are eyeing and aligning their financial interests and practices with socially sound concerns. This has made them vie for aligning the Environmental Social and Governance (ESG) factors, to commensurate with a set of standards for organizations, representing organizations' corporate financial interests related to their sustainability and ethics. Moreover, it guarantees their goodwill for business in the larger dynamic world of cutthroat competition for profits. Keeping ESG as the focal point, banks like other businesses, to have several incentives to align their operations with ESG metrics. However, there are not fully developed and unanimously agreed upon criteria for uniformity of Critical Success Factors (CSFs). There is a dearth of responsible research in identifying the critical success factors for ESG implementation in banking and financial institutions. To this end, the present research endeavors to explore the critical success factors for ESG implementation in banking and financial institutions by adopting of modified TISM (Total Interpretative Structural Modeling) approach, which provides a hierarchical method of identifying and arranging factors in order of their strategic importance.

Keywords: environmental, social, governance (ESG), stakeholders, ethical, organizations, financial, total interpretative structural modeling (TISM)

1. Introduction

ESG has lately emerged and is recognized as one of the most sensitive issues (Shutong & Koblianska, 2024; Xu, 2024), which has attracted the attention of corporate and regulatory bodies alike (Chernykh et al., 2024; Raval, 2024; Rizki & Putra, 2024). Despite regulations having been in place, ESG has not been recognized and implemented in the way and manner it should have been. Moreover, notwithstanding the stated and demonstrated maxim that ESG contributes towards firms' cumulative abnormal returns (De Souza, 2024; Horobet et al., 2024; Misnikova et al., 2024; Li et al., 2022) and liquidity of stocks (Astuti et al., 2024; Kruger et al., 2021), companies still fall short in promotion of sustainability ideals due to challenges they stuck upon and perform unsatisfactorily (Moessa, 2024; Abramova, 2024). However, there is a running consensus about achieving the required level of ESG for cumulative profitability (Kholjigitov, 2024; Gonzalez-Ruiz et al., 2024) and growth in the long run due to pressure from regulators and stakeholders (investors, customers, employees, regulators, and regulators) (Abramova, 2024; Borodako, 2023; Misnikova et al., 2024). They are exerting pressure to ensure a greater degree of transparency and accountability on the part of corporations so that all the stakeholders can come closer to the achievement of sustainability and profitability for all (Gonzalez-Ruiz et al., 2024; Adi et al., 2023; Tashtamirov, 2023; Ostonaqulova, 2023; Ziolo et al., 2023; Pavlova et al., 2022; Zahid et al., 2023). Consequential to this, there has been increased interest in the achievement of ESG practices and policies in recent years (Khamisu & Paluri, 2024; Dragomir et al., 2022; Yuen et al., 2022; Bruno & Lagasio, 2021; Bătae et al., 2020), which is expected to bring in visible changes about ESG practices in coming decades. Hence, it is pertinent to identify the critical success factors for the ESG implementation for the common good and welfare of all.

2. Literature Review

The growing prominence and weight of ESG principles reflects the global recognition of sustainability as a crucial determiner and harbinger of economic-social progressive trend (Abramova, 2024; Gonzalez-Ruiz et al., 2024; Raval, 2024; Xu, 2024; Shutong & Koblianska, 2024; Chernykh et al., 2024; Rizki & Putra, 2024; Horobet et al., 2024; De Souza, 2024; Astuti et al., 2024; Moessa, 2024; Kholjigitov, 2024; Abramova, 2024). Scholars and practitioners have increasingly explored the adoption of ESG frameworks within banking and financial institutions (Misnikova et al., 2024; Gonzalez-Ruiz et al., 2024; Adi et al., 2023; Tashtamirov, 2023; Ostonaqulova, 2023; Ziolo et al., 2023; Pavlova et al., 2022; Dragomir et al., 2022; Yuen et al., 2022; Bruno & Lagasio, 2021; Bătae et al., 2020) due to their pivotal role in channeling resources towards sustainable development (Misnikova et al., 2024). Research highlights that ESG implementation enhances organizational performance by mitigating risks, improving regulatory compliance, and fostering stakeholder trust (Kholjigitov, 2024). Studies by Freeman (1984) and Carroll (1991) laid the foundation for understanding corporate social responsibility (CSR) as a precursor to ESG, emphasizing the importance of balancing economic, social, and environmental responsibilities.

In recent years, banking institutions (Astuti et al., 2024; Moessa, 2024; Kholjigitov, 2024; Abramova, 2024; Borodako, 2023) have been identified as key actors in promoting sustainable finance (Abramova, 2024) through green lending, impact investing, and corporate governance reforms (Chernykh et al., 2024; Rizki & Putra, 2024; Horobet et al., 2024; De Souza, 2024; Astuti et al., 2024; Moessa, 2024; Kholjigitov, 2024; Abramova, 2024; Borodako, 2023). Empirical studies have demonstrated that banks integrating ESG principles often outperform their peers in terms of long-term financial stability and market competitiveness. The work of Khan, Serafeim, and Yoon (2016) underscores the materiality of ESG factors, asserting that firms focusing on financially relevant ESG issues achieve superior financial outcomes. However, the successful implementation of ESG in financial institutions depends on understanding and addressing various critical success factors (CSFs).

Methodological contributions in this domain have also been significant. Researchers have employed frameworks such as ISM, and TISM to analyze and prioritize the interdependencies among CSFs for ESG implementation (Ziolo et al., 2023; Pavlova et al., 2022; Dragomir et al., 2022; Yuen et al., 2022; Bruno & Lagasio, 2021; Bătae et al., 2020). Studies utilizing these techniques, such as those by Singh and Kant (2008) and Govindan et al., (2014), highlight their robustness in handling complex decision-making processes. While extensive research exists on ESG's financial and operational benefits, there remains a gap in understanding the structural relationships among CSFs specific to the banking and financial sectors (Moessa, 2024; Kholjigitov, 2024; Abramova, 2024; Borodako, 2023; Misnikova et al., 2024; Gonzalez-Ruiz et al., 2024; Adi et al., 2023; Tashtamirov, 2023; Ostonaqulova, 2023).

The study proposes to fill in the gap extant in previous studies by employing the TISM approach to explore and model the CSFs for ESG implementation. Doing so not only advances the theoretical understanding of ESG integration but also provides actionable insights for practitioners in banking and financial institutions seeking to enhance their sustainability initiatives. This literature review establishes the need for a holistic, methodologically robust investigation into ESG implementation, positioning the study within the broader discourse on sustainable finance and governance.

3. Methodology

This paper utilized TISM Modelling, which is based on ISM and has been used to map the relationship between multiple elements in a complex situation where the interlinkages between the factors can be manifold (Rizvi et al., 2019). Also, given the qualitative nature of the research, to develop an evaluation framework from multiple viewpoints having multiple inter-linkages, a modified version of ISM, i.e., TISM (total interpretive structural modeling) is used, which is a framework and methodology that is used to delineate the hierarchical relationship among the identified factors. TISM is developed and built on the ISM technique introduced by Warfield (1973, 1974) and later on developed by other scholars (Parameswar et al., 2023; Jayalakshmi & Pramod, 2015; Srivastava & Sushil, 2013, 2014; Sushil, 2012; Harary et al., 1965). In addition to the perks of ISM, TISM involves the exploration of independent utility and the interrelationship of variables. In the TISM model, the interlinkages are more transparent as the experts and the respondents build on the underlying interpretive logic in the model itself when responding to the questionnaire. TISM helps in the incorporation of subjective judgments of the respondents in a systemic manner, the option of revisiting the judgment, eliciting managerial insights, and helps in the identification of order and direction among the factor relationships. Further, the respondent need not have prior knowledge about the process of research.

TISM follows the steps shown below:

1. Firstly, the key variables are identified through a thorough literature review of extant literature.
2. Thereafter, a contextual relationship between the identified factors is tried to be established.
3. Once the above steps are completed, the interpretation of influence is carried on.
4. After this pair-wise comparisons are done.
5. This is followed by the construction of a reachability matrix which is based on paired comparison by undertaking variables.
6. On completion of this step, factors are designated separate hierarchical levels.
7. This leads to the construction of a diagram called diagraph which also shows transitive links with the help of interpretative insights.
8. At last, the comprehensive mapping of inherent complex relationships assists in eliciting managerial insights.

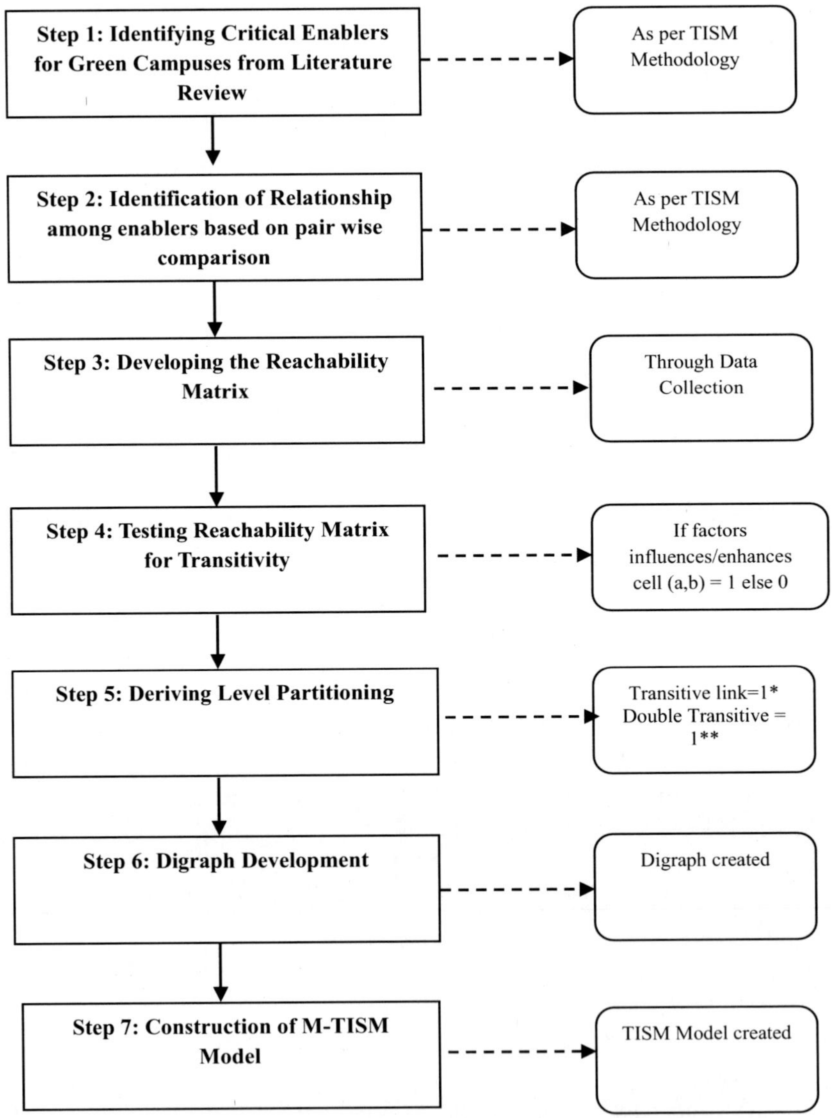

Figure 1. Steps in M-TISM Model for this study.

4. TISM for the Present Study

CSF for ESG implementation in Banking and Financial Institutions identified in the present study:

Table 1. Critical success factors

Sl. No.	Critical Success Factors
1.	Stakeholders
2.	Industry
3.	Strategic ambition
4.	Customers and segments
5.	Products and services
6.	Risk and regulation
7.	Competitor activity
8.	Data and management information
9.	Brand and communications and reporting

4.1. Stakeholders

The role of stakeholders is critical in shaping the direction and success of ESG, and its implementation in the banking industry (Khamisu et al., 2024). They include customers, investors, employees, regulators, and the community in operation at large (Abramova, 2024). Each of these have unique thoughts and expectations about sustainability and ethical norms attached to them. For example, investors are interested in ESG to evaluate the long-term sustainability and utility of their investments and hence they push banks to adopt and disclose the practices that are responsible for performance (Gonzalez-Ruiz et al., 2024). Customers on the other hand are concerned about ethical standards of banking services and expect transparency in the usage of funds, which aligns with values and sustainable goals (Rizki & Putra, 2024). Regulators take cognizance of compliance with evolving ESG practices and related legislation that shows banks' accountability for social and environmental impact. Employees are drawn to ESG prioritization for the sustenance of their livelihood and job retention (Misnikova et al., 2024). This accounts for the interest of diverse stakeholders in ESG regulations and their implementation.

4.2. Industry

The banking industry is primarily responsible for driving ESG transformation as it has an insurmountable influence on the allocation of capital and factors responsible for economic development (Gonzalez-Ruiz et al., 2024). Banks and financial institutions in this regard act as intermediaries and direct funds towards sustainable projects (Xu, 2024). For that, they seek businesses which are favorable for environmental conservation and social equity (Shutong & Koblianska, 2024). Moreover, they emphasize undertaking ventures, which promote green financing, renewable energy, and infrastructure development. Banking also adapts to industry-wide challenges, which range from climate challenges to technological advancements and societal shifts etc. This sort of industry-wide commitment to ESG leads to a ripple effect that inspires the setting of higher standards for contemporary players and promises global progress (Astuti et al., 2024).

4.2. Strategic Ambition

Banks and financial institutions are driven by strategic ambitions, which set the tone for prioritizing ESG principles and the optimum operation of banks (Hanganu, 2023). ESG strategy and ambition attached to them help integrate the corporate strategy and provide direction for meaningful outcomes (Raisa, 2024). With the help of strategic ambition, banks can decide on long-term goals, such as enhancing workforce diversity, achieving net-zero emissions, and increasing the financial inclusion of the general populace (Huang, 2024). For the realization of these goals, they need to be supported by leadership commitment, resource allocation, and performance tracking at different stages of operations. Banks and financial institutions with the help of strategic ambitions, create value beyond profitability and address societal challenges such as poverty, inequality, climate change, etc. Furthermore, strategic ambitions help banks to align their functions with global frameworks provided by the United Nations Sustainable Development Goals, which showcase a proactive and forward-thinking approach.

4.3. Customers and Segments

ESG priorities bear high on customer and market segments as they act as focal points of ESG shaping. Banks and financial institutions in modern times have to tailor products to the liking of customers and follow ethical banking practices to lure customers and maintain faith to earn their loyalty (Napolitano, 2024). Moreover, banks and financial institutions need to cater to the diverse clientele ranging from corporate to normal retail customers (D'Este, 2024). To maintain this base, they have to design products, which offer sustainable financing options and green investment products (Chow & Ho, 2024). This understanding of customer preferences and product alignment with ESG helps banks strengthen their relationships and drives large-scale innovation of financial products (Kulińska-Sadłocha, 2024). For instance, they provide financing options for small and medium enterprises, which help them maintain sustainable practices and show commitment to customer-centric ESG initiatives. Banks and financial institutions adopt different means to meet customer demand, promote affordability, inclusivity, and accessibility, and ensure ESG principles in the realm of core banking services.

4.4. Products and Services

ESG implementation largely depends on the design and delivery of products and services in baking and financial institutions (Horobet et al., 2024). For that, banks and financial institutions design products such as green bonds, carbon-neutral credit cards, and social impact funds and offer opportunities to align with sustainable goals and ESG principles (Edunjobi, 2024). Through such innovative solutions, banks and financial institutions lead to the enhancement of their reputation, grab better market opportunities, and address pressing global issues while pursuing them (Saviano et al., 2024). Responsible lending practices followed by banks and financial institutions in alignment with ESG credentials ensure credibility in the long run. In addition, they help in curbing the finances for environmentally harmful and socially unethical activities. This helps in attracting socially conscious customers and investors and helps competitive differentiation of banking products and services. Banks and financial institutions, which invest in sustainable product portfolios, have better prospects and are better positioned to lead their functions in the ESG-focused market landscape in the long and short run.

4.5. Risk and Regulation

ESG has an integral relationship with banking and financial institutions' compliance with regulations and implementation (Joosen, 2024). The risks covered under ESG include reputational damage, climate risk, governance failures, industrial failures, and economic challenges in the industry (Adeniran et al., 2024). For example, the climate-related risks of the failure of the economy to mitigate it can cause or result in financial losses due to increased defaults on loans in sectors, which are heavily vulnerable to climate changes in nations. In this regard, regulators have resorted to enforcement of stricter ESG disclosure requirements and disclosures (Gonzalez-Ruiz et al., 2024). This leads to compelling bans for the adoption of unaccountable practices for investment and lending by banks and financial institutions. Moreover, banks and financial institutions are held responsible for adopting responsible and transparent services. In case of non-compliance of these ESG norms banks can face legal penalties and confront loss of investor confidence and reputational harm, which can result in decreased trust and consumer loyalty and economic losses. Hence, banks are required to adopt robust risk management frameworks and function in alignment with the regulatory requirements laid down by ESG norms. In this regard, they are required to follow the norms of Task Force on Climate-Related Financial Disclosures (TCFD) guidelines. Through proper enforcement of ESG norms and addressing the risks by adhering to regulatory expectations banks and financial institutions enhance their respective resilience, which helps them safeguard their long-term viability.

4.6. Competitor Activity

ESG commitments are core to the competitor activity and help banks and financial institutions to remain abreast of competition in the dynamic field, such as that of banking and financial institutions (Xing, 2024). Moreover, the competitor activity among banking contemporaries helps to dive into innovative activities and encourages banks and financial institutions to elevate and undertake ESG commitments at a higher level. Industry leaders in banking and financial institutions often adopt and follow ESG strategies, which create unique competitive pressure on banking contemporaries in the banking industry and financial institutions (Maside-Sanfiz et al., 2024). For example, a peer bank launching successful green finance initiatives can act as an inspiration to competitors and develop a sense of innovation among other banks, and they may follow suit by adopting ESG practices. In addition, competitor benchmarking leads banks to identify gaps in their ESG adoption and practices which helps them learn from their failures and adopt better ESG practices (Korzeb et al., 2024). This competitive dynamic of ESG implementation forces the banking industry and encourages them to adopt ESG practices for sustainable performance. Banking firms and financial institutions adopt ESG to remain competitive in the market and reinforce the overall market of the banking industry (Tarkhanova et al., 2024). Lastly, it helps in establishing banking as a forward-thinking and responsible institution.

4.7. Data and Management Information

ESG implementation relies heavily on comprehensive and accurate data. With the help of data-driven insights, banks can measure their respective ESG performance and identify areas where in improvement is possible (Gherghina, 2024). In addition, it helps them to communicate and relate that progress to stakeholders (Nikolić et al., 2024). For instance, monitoring carbon emissions across operations and investments helps banks set goals and targets on realistic grounds and maintain their investments and operations in alignment with ESG norms and practices (Edunjobi, 2024). Moreover, the advanced data analytics and information management systems aided by the industry 4.0 revolution help and support risk assessment and its mitigation. Reliable data enhances transparency and enables banks and financial institutions to lend responsibly and fulfill their commitments. In addition, the regulatory bodies also work with the help of ESG disclosures to make robust data management compliances and follow ESG norms with robust compliance. In this regard, the banks, which invest diligently in state-of-the-art data management systems, can stay ahead in the ESG journey and ensure better accountability and continuous improvement.

4.8. Brand, Communications, and Reporting

Banks and financial institutions in today's era with the help and compliance of ESG norms act as trailblazers of improvement in the financial sector (Neumann & Forthmann, 2024). When banks and financial institutions follow measures and regulations by aligning their functions and operations with ESG norms they enhance their reputation and elevate their ethical standards, which leads to greater attraction of investors and building of customer loyalty (Mohammad, 2024). With the help of transparent communication about ESG goals, challenges, and achievements, stakeholders' interest in banks and financial institutions is elevated, and it reinforces the credibility of banks (Nickerson & Georgiadou, 2024). In addition, the fast and flawless reporting frameworks enable banks and financial institutions to showcase their competitiveness and commitment to ESG principles (Ferri, 2024). This sort of clear and consistent reporting with honest and trustworthy intent helps build the positions of banks and financial institutions and helps them become leaders in sustainable finance.

Hence, the integration of critical success factors in alignment with ESG implementation enables banks and financial institutions to undertake cognizance of sustainable economic development. In this manner, they can meet the economic expectations of stakeholders and fulfill regulatory requirements. This holistic approach helps banks to properly align their strategy, communications, and operations with ESG principles. Moreover, it helps the banking industry act as a catalyst for positive environmental, economic, and social transformation.

5. Diagraph for Model

Table 2. Reachability matrix

	T1	T2	T3	T4	T5	T6	T7	T8	T9
T1	1	1	1[a]	1[a]	1[a]	1[a]	1[a]	1[a]	1
T2	1	1	1[a]	1[a]	1	1[a]	1[a]	1[a]	1[a]
T3	0	0	1	0	0	1[a]	1[a]	1	1
T4	0	0	1	1	1	1[a]	1[a]	1[a]	1[a]
T5	0	0	1	1	1	1[a]	1[a]	1[a]	1[a]
T6	0	0	0	0	0	1	0	0	0
T7	0	0	0	0	0	1	1	0	0
T8	0	0	0	0	0	1	0	1	0
T9	0	0	0	0	0	1	1	0	1

Table 3. Levels of critical success factors

Sl. No.	CSF for ESG implementation in Banking and Financial Institutions	Level
1.	Risk and regulation (6)	Level I
2.	Competitor activity (7)	Level II
3.	Data and management information (8)	Level II
4.	Brand and communications and reporting (9)	Level III
5.	Strategic ambition (3)	Level IV
6.	Products and services (5)	Level V
7.	Customers and segments (4)	Level V
8.	Stakeholders (1)	Level VI
9.	Industry (2)	Level VI

It can be witnessed from Figure 2 given below that the CSF for ESG implementation in Banking and Financial Institutions interact among themselves and give rise to a hierarchical relationship.

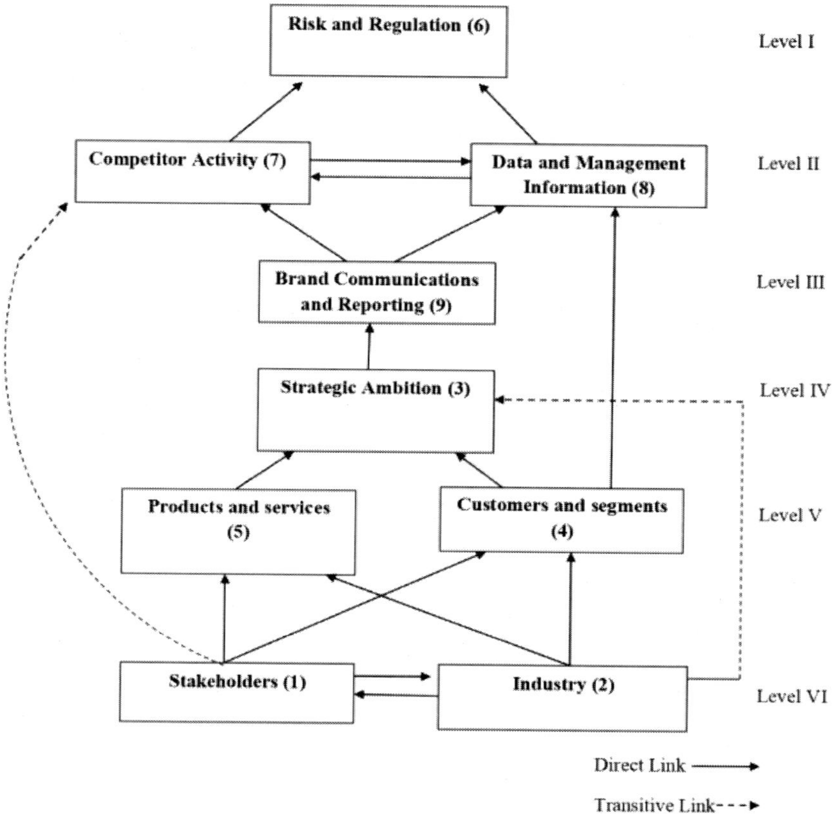

Figure 2. Diagraph of CSF for ESG implementation in Banking and Financial Institutions.

6. Discussion of the Model and Diagraph

- Level VI

Figure 2 Level VI comprises Stakeholders (1) and Industry (2), which shows that Stakeholders (1) Level VI impacts Industry (2) Level VI and Industry (2) Level VI affects Stakeholders (1) Level VI. It can also be seen that Stakeholders (1) Level VI impacts Products and Services (5) Level V and Customers and Segments (4) Level V for ESG implementation in Banking and Financial Institutions. Similarly, Industry (2) Level VI also impacts Products and Services (5) Level V and Customers and Segments (4) Level V for ESG implementation in Banking and Financial Institutions.

- Level V

Level V comprises Products and Services (5) Level V and Customers and Segments (4) Level V for ESG implementation. Products and Services (5) Level V impacts the Influence of Strategic Ambition (3) Level IV for ESG implementation, and Customers and Segments (4) Level V for ESG implementation and also impacts Strategic Ambition (3) Level IV for ESG implementation given at level IV.

- Level IV

Level IV comprises the Influence of Strategic Ambition (3) Level IV and its impacts Brand Communications and Reporting (9) Level III for ESG implementation in Banking and Financial Institutions.

- Level III

Level III consists of Brand Communications and Reporting (9)., Brand Communications and Reporting (9) Level III for ESG implementation impacts the Competitor Activity (7) Level II and it also impacts Data and Management Information (8) Level II for ESG implementation in Banking and Financial Institutions.

- Level II

Level II has two main critical success factors and that is Data and Management Information (8) Level II for Competitor Activity (7) Level II for ESG implementation in Banking and Financial Institutions.

- Level I

Level I have Risk and Regulation (6) as its main component, which is very important forESG implementation in Banking and Financial Institutions.

Business leaders, consumers, investors, and all the stakeholders belonging to the corporate world and regulators alike are clamoring and committing themselves to climate action, lower carbon footprint, ethical business practices, justifiable labor, and manufacturing gig. Consequentially, an increasing number of organizations and business sojourns are eyeing and aligning their financial interests and practices with socially sound concerns. This has made them vie for aligning the Environmental Social and Governance (ESG) factors, to commensurate with a set of standards for organizations, representing organizations' corporate financial interests related to their sustainability and ethics. Moreover, it guarantees their goodwill for business in the larger dynamic world of cutthroat competition for profits. Keeping ESG as the focal point, banks like other businesses, to have several incentives to align their operations with ESG metrics. However, there are not fully developed and unanimously agreed upon criteria for uniformity of Critical Success Factors (CSFs). There is a dearth of responsible research in identifying the critical success factors for ESG implementation in banking and financial institutions. To this end, the present research endeavors to explore the critical success factors for ESG implementation in banking and financial institutions by adopting of modified TISM (Total Interpretative Structural Modeling) approach, which provides a hierarchical method of identifying and arranging factors in order of their strategic importance.

Conclusion

The study underscores the role of ESG in fostering social and economic benefits to the society to attain sustainability in operations and forward economic growth of the nation as a whole. It proposes for lowering the carbon footprint of all the tasks undertaken by business leaders, investors, consumers, and all the stakeholder. Furthermore, it calls for alignment of operations in financial fields so the socially, and financially sound steps result in sustenance and sustainability of operations. This paper strongly proposes for alignment of environmental, social and governance factors, for setting standards for organizations' corporate financial interests that are related with sustainability and ethics.

Implications

Social Implications of the Study

If scrutinized on the social front, the ESG implementation guarantees to foster unprecedented social benefits. Financial institutions and banks, which endeavor to invest and operate on ESG principles, stand to gain in social terms in terms of the image they create in society and among customers (Pavlova et al., 2022). If they invest and provide funds for community development projects that enhance housing, clean energy, and education, they stand to gain a lotin terms of finances they generate by being a party to such ventures (Misnikova et al., 2024). In this process, they create and promote workforce engagement by creating inclusive and equitable workplaces, which help improve and attain greater employee engagement and satisfaction, which in turn leads to greater retention of employees. In addition, institutions with greater adherence to robust ESG principles help build greater trust, loyalty, and credibility among stakeholders (Moessa, 2024). This, in turn, providesthem them with an invisible social license to operate in financial matters. By laying greater emphasis on works that help underserved communities ESG ESG-driven financial practices can lead to a reduction in social and economicinequality and attain equitable access to financial services (Moessa, 2024). This helps financial institutions to work towards greater environmental responsibility and ethical governance and helps in the establishment of banks and financial institutions as harbingers of sustainable societal progress.

Economic Implications of the Study

The present study has far-reaching economic implications for the banking sector in enhancing its image and performance on an overall basis. Firstly, the implementation of ESG frameworks in banking and financial institutions is particularly profound about the balance that is being promised with the help of the alignment of banking functions with the ESG (Abramova, 2024).

Secondly, it promises good economic yield through robust financial performance by attracting environmentally conscious investors. These investors tend to reduce operational costs by following sustainable resource management (Ziolo et al., 2023). Moreover, the integration of ESG would actively assist in the mitigation of capital risks that are involved in banking operations. In addition, by following ESG principles banking sector would gain credibility and praise from the general community and bring loyalty and trust to the whole banking sector, which again would add to the robust economic performance of banks and financial institutions (Ostonaqulova, 2023). Furthermore, it would lessen and avoid the reputational damage of banks and financial institutions, and mitigate financial instability, fostering long-term resilience of banks (Kholjigitov, 2024). These practices would majorly impact the turnover of banks, to bring in access to more capital for long-term investments and help gain investments. It would also help in prioritizing sustainability and channeling funds toward green bonds and ESG-focused ventures (Rizki & Putra, 2024). This would help in gaining sustainability and enhance economic growth by supporting green industries and infrastructural projects. Lastly, operational efficiencies would lead to cost optimization, and greater degree of competitive marketing, and elevated financial performance of banks and financial institutions.

Research Implications of the Study

On the research front, the study contributes significantly to the growing body of knowledge and literature about sustainable finance and governance practices. A TISM approach too has its usability and charm in bringing about the interrelationship of CSF for ESG implementation in Banking and Financial Institutions. Through the identification and modeling of critical success factors for ESG implementation, the research provides a theoretical framework that helps enrich the understanding of how financial institutions can effectively and efficiently integrate ESG principles. Moreover, this study assists in bridging the gap between theoretical discourse and practical application of ESG principles. Furthermore, it offers insights into hierarchical relationships and interdependencies among the critical success factors that have been identified in the study. Additionally, the adoption of the TISM approach helps in the introduction of a novel methodological lens for ESG research in the realm of banking and financial institutions. By emphasizing the structural complexity and layered interaction of factors it offers a novel understanding of factors, which are crucial for the operation and economic growth of banking and financial institutions. This contributes robustly to the methodological realm for future studies, which can refine the TISM framework for analyzing complex and multidimensional phenomena in finance and governance. In addition, the research is particularly relevant for practitioners and scholars who are interested in exploring the interaction of sustainability of organizational performance in banking and finance areas of research. This study in particular highlights the actionable pathways for embedding ESG principles and considerations into the strategic analysis and decision-making of banks. It also opens venues for studies in the realm of different industries, across different regions, structures, and disciplines, which promise to deepen the understanding of ESG principles, norms, and nuances. Lastly, focusing on banking and financial sectors, the research underscores the pivotal role played by ESG in shaping the operation of banking and financial intuitions. In addition, it helps in understanding the balance that is created through following the ESG rules and how they assist in attaining and fostering environmental stewardship, robust governance, and social equity. These contributions position this study as a cornerstone for further exploration in the field of sustainable finance.

References

Abramova, A. (2024). Environmental, Social, and Governance (ESG) *Principles in the Banking Sector. Development, Integration, and Risk Management Strategies: a case study of a Finnish banks' approach to ESG Framework.*

Adeniran, I. A., Abhulimen, A. O., Obiki-Osafiele, A. N., Osundare, O. S., Agu, E. E., & Efunniyi, C. P. (2024). Strategic risk management in financial institutions: Ensuring robust regulatory compliance. *Finance & Accounting Research Journal*, *6* (8), 1582-1596.

Adi, H. K., Haryadi, A., Wiadi, I., Mayasari, I., Mudrika, S., & Mila, S. (2023, October). Organizational Learning Perspective Analysis in Accelerating Environmental, Social & Governance (ESG) Orientation: Studies in the Banking Industry. In *e-Proceedings* (p. 35).

Astuti, W. T., Ani, D. A., Subranta, A., Solissa, F., & Wiriatmaja, N. U. (2024). Sustainable Financial Strategies: Analysing the Role of ESG in Corporate Financial Performance and Risk Management. *The Journal of Academic Science*, *1* (6), 813-820.

Bătae, O. M., Dragomir, V. D., & Feleagă, L. (2020). Environmental, social, governance (ESG), and financial performance of European banks. *Accounting and Management Information Systems*, *19* (3), 480-501.

Borodako, A. (2023). *ESG integration in banking: A qualitative study on the impact of regulation on banks' operations* (master's thesis, NTNU).

Bruno, M., & Lagasio, V. (2021). An overview of the European policies on ESG in the banking sector. *Sustainability, 13* (22), 12641.

Carroll, A. B. (1991). The pyramid of corporate social responsibility: Toward the moral management of organizational stakeholders. *Business Horizons, 34* (4), 39–48. https://doi.org/10.1016/0007-6813 (91)90005-G *(JED), 6* (3), 656-667.

Chernykh, D., Ezangina, I., Khryseva, A., Kozhukhova, M., & Vorotilova, O. (2024). ESG financing instruments in the context of sustainable development of regional infrastructure. In *E3S Web of Conferences* (Vol. 548, p. 03017). EDP Sciences.

Chow, M. Y. C., & Ho, S. P. S. (2024). Investigating the effect of ESG on retail banks' customer equity. *Journal of Financial Services Marketing*, 1-15.

de Souza, L. M. (2024). Benchmarking of National ESG Banking. *Sustainable Finances and the Law: Between Public and Private Solutions, 16*, 27.

D'Este, L. (2024). The effects of sustainable practices on customer loyalty: an analysis of the banking sector through PLS-SEM.

Dragomir, V. D., Bătae, O. M., Ionescu, B. Ș., & Ionescu-Feleagă, L. (2022). The Influence of ESG Factors on Financial Performance in the Banking Sector During The Covid-19 Pandemic. *Economic Computation & Economic Cybernetics Studies & Research, 56* (4).

Edunjobi, T. E. (2024). Sustainable supply chain financing models: Integrating banking for enhanced sustainability. *International Journal for Multidisciplinary Research Updates 2024, 7* (02), 001-011.

Ferri, I. G. M. P. A. (2024). Linking strategic communication and sustainability reporting. Exploring corporate websites of Georgian Banks.

Freeman, R. E. (1984). *Strategic management: A stakeholder approach*. Boston: Pitman.

Gherghina, Ș. C. (2024). Corporate finance and environmental, social, and governance (ESG) practices. *Journal of Risk and Financial Management, 17* (7), 308.

Gonzalez-Ruiz, J. D., Ospina Patiño, C., & Marín-Rodríguez, N. J. (2024). The Influence of Environmental, Social, and Governance Issues in the Banking Industry. *Administrative Sciences, 14* (7), 156.

Govindan, K., Khodaverdi, R., & Jafarian, A. (2014). A fuzzy multi-criteria approach for measuring the sustainability performance of a supplier based on a triple bottom line approach. *Journal of Cleaner Production, 47 (3)*, 345–354. https://doi.org/10.1016/j.jclepro.2012.04.014.

Hanganu, A. C. (2023). *Key Regulatory Initiatives in EU Sustainable Banking*. BRILL.

Harary, F., Norman, R., & Cartwright, D. (1965). Structural models: An introduction to the theory of directed graphs. New York: Wiley.

Horobet, A., Rahat, B., Floarea, A. M., & Belascu, L. (2024). Green banks, golden returns? Unravelling the ESG–Financial performance nexus in European banking. *Review of Accounting and Finance*.

Huang, L. (2024). A Comparative Analysis of Five Frameworks Guiding Banks Towards Sustainable Finance Practices–SDGs, CSR, UN Global Compact, ESG and ECG.

Jayalakshmi, B., & Pramod, V. R. (2015). Total interpretive structural modelling (TISM) of the enablers of a flexible control system for industry. *Global Journal of Flexible Systems Management, 16* (1), 63–85.

Joosen, B. P. (2024). Prudential Requirements for ESG Risks of Banks. In *Sustainable Finance in Europe: Corporate Governance, Financial Stability and Financial Markets* (pp. 291-374). Cham: Springer International Publishing.

Khamisu, M. S., Paluri, R. A., & Sonwaney, V. (2024). Environmental social and governance (ESG) disclosure motives for environmentally sensitive industry: an emerging economy perspective. *Cogent Business & Management, 11* (1). https://doi.org/10.1080/23311975.2024.2322027.

Khan, M., Serafeim, G., & Yoon, A. (2016). Corporate sustainability: First evidence on materiality. *The Accounting Review, 91* (6), 1697–1724. https://doi.org/10.2308/accr-51383

Kholjigitov, G. (2023). Note on preparation and implementation of ESG strategy for banks and financial institutions. *Available at SSRN 4672230.*

Korzeb, Z., Niedziółka, P., Szpilko, D., & De la Torre, A. (2024). A bibliometric analysis of ESG performance in the cooperative banks: from the current status to future directions. *Economics and Environment.*

Krueger, P., Sautner, Z., Tang, D. Y., & Zhong, R. (2021). The effects of mandatory ESG disclosure around the world, vol. 754. *European Corporate Governance Institute–Finance Working Paper*, 21–44.

Kulińska-Sadłocha, E. (2024). The banking sector and the Sustainable Development Goals (SDGs). In *The Role of Financial Markets in Achieving the Sustainable Development Goals* (pp. 61-92). Edward Elgar Publishing.

Li, Z., Feng, L., Pan, Z., & Sohail, H. M. (2022). ESG performance and stock prices: evidence from the COVID-19 outbreak in China. *Humanities and Social Sciences Communications, 9* (1), 242. https://doi.org/10.1057/s41599-022-01259-5.

Maside-Sanfiz, J. M., Iglesias-Casal, A., Mazahreh, Q. A. S., & López-Penabad, M. C. (2024). The impact of competition on environmental and social performance in the MENA banking sector. *Corporate Social Responsibility and Environmental Management.*

Misnikova, L., Aleksandrov, I., Parshukov, A., Maksina, S., Ilina, V., Terentyev, A., & Ol, E. (2024). State regulation of the use of ESG methodology. In *E3S Web of Conferences* (Vol. 549, p. 09010). EDP Sciences.

Moessa de Souza, L. (2024). Benchmarking of National ESG Banking Regulations: State of Art and Remaining Challenges. *Sustainable Finances and the Law: Between Public and Private Solutions*, 27-61.

Mohammad, N. (2024). Environmental, Social, and Governance (ESG) Integration: Evidence from an Emerging Economy. In *Cases on Uncovering Corporate Governance Challenges in Asian Markets* (pp. 133-152). IGI Global.

Napolitano, G. (2024). The Integration of Sustainability in the Banking Sector. In *Place Based Approaches to Sustainability Volume II: Business, Economic, and Social Models* (pp. 79-107). Cham: Springer Nature Switzerland.

Neumann, M., & Forthmann, J. (2024). ESG Reporting in Corporate Communication. *Springer Books.*

Nickerson, C., & Georgiadou, E. (2024). Shifting sands: the use of marketing communication strategies in corporate social responsibility disclosure in the United Arab Emirates. *Journal of Islamic Marketing*.

Nikolić, J. L., Mirković, V., & Dudić, B. (2024). CHALLENGES AND OPPORTUNITIES FOR NON-FINANCIAL AND ESG REPORTING THROUGH THE LENS OF DIGITAL TECHNOLOGIES. *PUBLISHERS: • FACULTY OF ECONOMICS AND ENGINEERING MANAGEMENT–FIMEK, NOVI SAD, SERBIA; • EDUCATIONAL AND BUSINESS CENTER FOR DEVELOPMENT OF HUMAN RESOURCES*, 100.

Ostonaqulova, G. (2023). Integrating ESG-Criteria in Project Selection: A Strategic Approach for Enhancing Investment Efficiency in Commercial Banking.

Parameswar, N., Hasan, Z., Shri, C., & Saini, N. (2023). Exploring the barriers to ESG adoption using a modified TISM approach. *Kybernetes*.

Pavlova, S. A., Pavlov, I. E., & Milyukhina, N. V. (2022). Development of ESG concept in the Russian banking sector. *Международный научно-исследовательский журнал*, (7-3 (121)), 198-202.

Raisa, K. K. (2024). Navigating Sustainable Finance in Bangladesh: The Role of Banks and Financial Institutions.

Raval, M. (2024). ESG Integration in Banking: Navigating Principles, Risks, and Regulations. *Risks, and Regulations (February 28, 2024)*.

Rizvi, N. U., Kashiramka, S., Singh, S., & Sushil. (2019). A hierarchical model of the determinants of non-performing assets in banks: an ISM and MICMAC approach. *Applied Economics, 51* (35), 3834-3854.

Saviano, M., Russo, G., Farina Briamonte, M., & Di Nallo, L. (2024). The challenges in integrating ESG factors into banks' credit department: a knowledge management enhanced framework. *Journal of Knowledge Management*.

Shutong, D., & Koblianska, I. I. (2024). *ESG policy in banking and finances sector: cases of European companies* (Doctoral dissertation, Sumy State University).

Singh, M. D., & Kant, R. (2008). Knowledge management barriers: An interpretive structural modeling approach. *International Journal of Management Science and Engineering Management, 3* (2), 141–150. https://doi.org/10.1080/17509653.2008.10671034.

Srivastava, A. K., & Sushil. (2013). Modeling strategic performance factors for effective strategy execution. *International Journal of Productivity and Performance Management, 62* (6), 554–582.

Srivastava, A. K., & Sushil. (2014). Modeling drivers of adapt for effective strategy execution. *The Learning Organization, 21* (6), 369–391.

Ştefan, C. G. (2024). Corporate Finance and Environmental, Social, and Governance (ESG) Practices. *Journal of Risk and Financial Management*, *17* (7), 308.

Sürücü, B., & Caylan, S. (2024). Banking Sector on Sustainability: Evolution, Trends, and Regional Disparities in CSR Practices (2000-2024). *International Journal of Social and Humanities Sciences Research (JSHSR)*, *11* (107), 1019-1034.

Sushil. (2012). Interpreting the interpretive structural model. *Global Journal of Flexible Systems Management, 13* (2), 87–106.

Tarkhanova, E. A., Tarkhanova, A. V., Fricler, A. V., Pelkova, S. V., & Koltsova, T. A. (2024). Comparative Analysis of ESG Transformation of Banking Sector in Asian Countries and Russia. *Pacific Business Review International*, *16* (8).

Tashtamirov, M. (2023). The place of sustainable development in ESG risks formation in banking sector. In *E3S Web of Conferences* (Vol. 371, p. 03051). EDP Sciences.

Warfield, J. N. (1973). On arranging elements of a hierarchy in graphic form. *IEEE Transactions: System, Man and Cybernetics, 3* (2), 121–132.

Warfield, J. N. (1974). Towards interpretation of complex structural models. *IEEE Transactions: System, Man and Cybernetics, 3* (2), 121–132.

Xing, T., Li, X., & Feng, N. (2024). Is bank competition conducive to corporate ESG performance? *International Review of Financial Analysis*, *95*, 103509.

Xu, J. (2024). AI in ESG for Financial Institutions: An Industrial Survey. *arXiv preprint arXiv:2403.05541.*

Yuen, M. K., Ngo, T., Le, T. D., & Ho, T. H. (2022). The environment, social and governance (ESG) activities and profitability under COVID-19: evidence from the global banking sector. *Journal of Economics and Development*, *24* (4), 345-364.

Zahid, R. M. A., Taran, A., Khan, M. K., & Chersan, I.-C. (2023). ESG, dividend payout policy and the moderating role of audit quality: empirical evidence from Western Europe. *Borsa Istanbul Review, 23* (2), 350–367. https://doi.org/10.1016/j.bir.2022.10.012.

Zioło, M., Bąk, I., Cheba, K., Filipiak, B. Z., & Spoz, A. (2023). Environmental, social, governance risk versus cooperation models between financial institutions and businesses. Sectoral approach and ESG risk analysis. *Frontiers in Environmental Science*, *10*, 1077947.

Chapter 11

Sustainable Finance in Emerging Markets: ESG Integration, Regulatory Innovation, and Pathways to Inclusive Climate Resilience

Madhusudan Narayan[1,*]
Pooja Shukla[2]
Bhavna Taneja[2]
and Sumeer Ranjan[2]
[1]Amity Business School, Amity University Jharkhand, Ranchi, India
[2]Amity College of Commerce and Finance, Amity University Jharkhand, Ranchi, India

Abstract

Sustainable finance is increasingly recognized as a catalyst for inclusive economic growth, climate resilience, and social equity in emerging markets. This study examines how financial tools such as green bonds, impact investing, and microfinance are shaping development outcomes in China, India, and Latin America. Through qualitative analysis of literature and case studies, it finds that investments in renewable energy, sustainable infrastructure, and social finance initiatives contribute significantly to job creation, emissions reduction, and financial inclusion. Regulatory innovation such as China's green bond standards and Brazil's BNDES-led financing for environmentally beneficial projects demonstrates how clear, supportive policies can successfully mobilize capital toward sustainability goals. However, inconsistent enforcement, fragmented ESG data, and institutional capacity gaps remain major barriers. To scale sustainable finance effectively, the study recommends

* Corresponding Author's Email: msnarayan07@gmail.com

In: Environmental, Social, and Governance (ESG) …
Editor: Veena Grover
ISBN: 979-8-90134-138-4

tailored regulatory reforms, standardized ESG reporting frameworks, and stronger multi-stakeholder collaboration. Clear rules and local adaptation are critical to aligning financial systems with long-term sustainability objectives and unlocking inclusive development across emerging economies.

Keywords: sustainable finance, emerging markets, green bonds, ESG regulation, climate resilience, inclusive growth, public-private partnerships

1. Introduction

Sustainable finance has emerged as a pivotal strategy for reconciling economic growth with environmental stewardship and social equity in emerging markets. By integrating Environmental, Social, and Governance (ESG) criteria into financial decision-making, this approach transcends traditional profit-centric models, addressing systemic challenges such as climate change, resource depletion, and inequality (Bril et al., 2020; Joshipura et al., 2025). Emerging economies, characterized by rapid industrialization and infrastructural deficits, are uniquely positioned to leverage sustainable finance to bridge developmental gaps while aligning with global frameworks like the Paris Agreement (UNFCCC, 2015) and the Sustainable Development Goals (SDGs) (Goel et al., 2022; Agyemang et al., 2025). However, the transformative potential of this paradigm remains constrained by fragmented regulatory frameworks, inconsistent ESG data, and socio-political complexities a paradox that underscores the urgency of context-sensitive solutions (Boiral et al., 2024; Khan & Yaghoubi, 2020).

The global shift toward ESG-aligned investments reflects a growing recognition of financial systems' role in mitigating systemic risks (Hong et al., 2023; Ali et al., 2025). Instruments such as green bonds and impact investments have mobilized capital for renewable energy, sustainable agriculture, and green infrastructure, sectors critical for reducing carbon footprints and fostering job creation (World Bank, 2008; Zhou et al., 2020). For instance, the global green bond market surged to $470 billion in 2020, signalling investor confidence in climate-aligned projects (World Bank, 2008). Yet, emerging markets often lag in harnessing these opportunities due to structural barriers, including underdeveloped regulatory ecosystems and limited institutional capacity (Van Lerven & Ryan-Collins, 2017; Gangwani & Kashiramka, 2024).

Emerging economies face a dual imperative: meeting immediate developmental needs while ensuring long-term sustainability. Rapid urbanization and industrialization frequently exacerbate environmental degradation and social disparities, perpetuating cycles of vulnerability (Malakar et al., 2023; Siddiqi et al., 2024). Sustainable finance offers a pathway to disrupt these cycles by directing investments toward projects with co-benefits. Renewable energy initiatives, such as India's solar power expansion, reduce fossil fuel dependence while generating employment (Taghizadeh-Hesary & Yoshino, 2019; Taneja et al., 2025). However, the absence of standardized ESG reporting and region-specific policies stifles progress. Brazil's Green Protocol and India's fragmented ESG guidelines exemplify challenges in enforcement and transparency, deterring investor confidence (Zhou et al., 2020; Boiral et al., 2024).

International agreements like the Paris Agreement have catalysed efforts to align financial flows with sustainability, yet implementation in emerging markets remains uneven. Climate finance mechanisms, such as the Green Climate Fund (GCF), aim to address funding gaps, but bureaucratic inefficiencies and governance challenges delay progress (Ameli et al., 2021; Gucciardi, 2024). Socio-political dynamics including political instability and cultural norms further compound these issues. For example, Latin American microfinance institutions, despite advancing financial inclusion, face operational hurdles due to regulatory ambiguities (Zhou et al., 2020; Kyrdoda et al., 2024). Addressing these barriers demands multi-stakeholder collaboration and capacity-building initiatives tailored to local contexts (Kurniawan & Kurniawan, 2022; Edu et al., 2025).

Despite growing scholarly interest, critical gaps persist in understanding the interplay between sustainable finance and emerging market dynamics. Existing studies often prioritize macro-level regulatory challenges while overlooking micro-level socio-political drivers, such as community engagement and cultural norms (Jamali & Karam, 2018; Rataj et al., 2024). Additionally, standardized frameworks like the Global Reporting Initiative (GRI) remain understudied in emerging contexts, limiting their applicability (Boffo & Patalano, 2020; Biju et al., 2025). This study addresses these gaps by investigating how tailored regulatory innovation, enhanced ESG data transparency, and stakeholder collaboration can optimize sustainable finance adoption. Through qualitative analysis of case studies from China, India, and Latin America, the research evaluates sustainable finance's economic, environmental, and social impacts, identifies systemic barriers, and proposes actionable strategies for scalability.

This study contributes to the discourse in three key ways. First, it establishes a holistic framework for assessing ESG implementation challenges in heterogeneous markets, integrating macro-level policies with micro-level socio-political factors. Second, it underscores the role of multi-stakeholder partnerships in bridging governance gaps, drawing on examples such as Brazil's BNDES green bonds and India's Tata Power initiatives (Zhou et al., 2020; Martinez & Williams, 2021). Third, it offers policy recommendations emphasizing the interdependence of regulatory coherence, data integrity, and community engagement, positioning sustainable finance as a strategic tool for inclusive growth and climate resilience (Luo et al., 2025; Vandana et al., 2024). By grounding its analysis in empirical evidence and regional case studies, this research advances a nuanced understanding of sustainable finance's potential to transform emerging economies while addressing the unique challenges they face.

2. Literature Review

Sustainable finance has evolved from a niche concept rooted in ethical investing to a mainstream strategy integral to global economic resilience. Its theoretical and practical foundations are anchored in the recognition that financial systems must address environmental degradation, social inequities, and governance risks to ensure long-term viability (Bril et al., 2020). This review synthesizes existing scholarship on sustainable finance, focusing on its historical trajectory, regulatory frameworks, data challenges, and socio-political dynamics in emerging markets, while identifying critical gaps in current research.

- Historical Evolution and Theoretical Foundations

The origins of sustainable finance trace back to the Brundtland Report (1987), which redefined development as a process that meets present needs without compromising future generations. This paradigm shift laid the groundwork for integrating sustainability into financial systems, culminating in frameworks like the United Nations Principles for Responsible Investment (UNPRI, 2006) and the Paris Agreement (UNFCCC, 2015). Early ethical investing focused on excluding harmful industries, but modern sustainable finance emphasizes proactive ESG integration, driven by stakeholder theory's assertion that firms must balance the interests of all societal actors (Freeman, 1984). Institutional theory further explains how external pressures such as regulatory mandates and investor expectations shape corporate adoption of ESG practices (DiMaggio & Powell, 1983). Meanwhile, the resource-based view (Barney, 1991) posits that sustainability-oriented resources and capabilities can confer competitive advantages, particularly in resource-constrained emerging markets (Goel et al., 2022).

- Regulatory Frameworks: Progress and Pitfalls

Robust regulatory frameworks are critical for scaling sustainable finance, yet emerging markets often grapple with fragmented policies. International initiatives like the EU Sustainable Finance Disclosure Regulation (SFDR) and the Task Force on Climate-related Financial Disclosures (TCFD) have standardized ESG reporting in developed economies, enhancing transparency and investor confidence (Weber, 2016). However, emerging markets such as India and Brazil face enforcement inconsistencies and regulatory gaps. For example, India's ESG guidelines lack alignment with global standards, while Brazil's Green Protocol suffers from regional disparities in implementation (Zhou et al., 2020; Van Lerven & Ryan-Collins, 2017). Scholars argue that regulations must be tailored to local socio-economic contexts to avoid "carbon copy" policies that ignore institutional weaknesses (Kahn & Yaghoubi, 2020; Choudhury & Das, 2021). The Paris Agreement's emphasis on climate finance underscores the need for adaptive frameworks that channel funds toward climate-resilient infrastructure in developing regions (Ameli et al., 2021).

- ESG Data Challenges and Capacity Building

The effectiveness of sustainable finance hinges on reliable ESG data, yet emerging markets struggle with inconsistent metrics and disclosure practices. Non-standardized reporting frameworks and varying definitions of ESG criteria create comparability issues, complicating risk assessments (Chatterji et al., 2016; Eccles & Serafeim, 2013). For instance, while developed markets benefit from platforms like Bloomberg ESG indices, emerging economies often lack localized data infrastructure (Boffo & Patalano, 2020). Capacity-building initiatives led by institutions like the International Finance Corporation (IFC) aim to address these gaps by training stakeholders in ESG risk management and green bond issuance (IFC, 2019). However, persistent technical and financial constraints limit their reach. Hossain et al., (2021) advocate for AI-driven data analytics to improve ESG transparency, while Turner and Lang (2019) stress the need for localized training programs to enhance financial literacy among policymakers and investors.

- Socio-Political Dynamics and Implementation Barriers

The adoption of sustainable finance is deeply intertwined with socio-political contexts. Political instability, weak governance, and corruption in emerging markets deter long-term investments and exacerbate greenwashing risks (Jamali & Karam, 2018). For example, in Latin America, microfinance institutions like Banco Compartamos face operational hurdles due to regulatory ambiguities, despite their potential to advance financial inclusion (Zhou et al., 2020). Similarly, renewable energy projects in Sub-Saharan Africa often stall due to bureaucratic delays and land rights disputes (Martinez & Williams, 2021). Boubaker et al., (2020) emphasize that stakeholder engagement and participatory governance are vital for aligning ESG initiatives with community needs. Cultural norms also play a role: in Southeast Asia, communal land ownership models require tailored financing approaches to avoid displacing indigenous populations (Kurniawan & Kurniawan, 2022).

- Opportunities and Transformative Potential

Despite challenges, sustainable finance offers transformative opportunities for emerging markets. Green bonds, pioneered by the World Bank (2008), have mobilized billions for renewable energy and sustainable infrastructure, demonstrating their scalability (Sullivan & Gouldson, 2017). Case studies from China and India highlight how solar and wind projects generate jobs while reducing carbon footprints (Taghizadeh-Hesary & Yoshino, 2019). Impact investing further bridges funding gaps in sectors like affordable housing and healthcare, directly contributing to SDG targets (Zhou et al., 2020). Moreover, ESG integration enhances corporate resilience by mitigating risks such as regulatory penalties and reputational damage (Mian et al., 2024). Campiglio (2016) and Ameli et al., (2021) argue that sustainable finance can decouple economic growth from resource depletion, fostering low-carbon transitions in energy-intensive economies.

2.1. Research Gaps

Existing studies on sustainable finance in emerging markets prioritize macro-level regulatory and technical barriers, neglecting micro-level socio-political drivers such as cultural norms and community engagement (Jamali & Karam, 2018; Malakar et al., 2023). While frameworks like the Global Reporting Initiative (GRI) are well-established in developed economies, their applicability in emerging contexts remains underexplored (Boffo & Patalano, 2020). Additionally, systemic reforms addressing governance gaps and political economy constraints lack empirical validation in local settings, particularly for blended finance and public-private partnerships proposed by global institutions (World Bank, 2018; UNEP, 2020). Future research must bridge these gaps to develop context-sensitive strategies that align global standards with local realities.

3. Problem Statement

Emerging markets face systemic barriers in leveraging sustainable finance to achieve inclusive growth and climate resilience. Despite the proliferation of ESG frameworks, inconsistent data reporting standards and evolving regulatory environments create uncertainty for investors and policymakers (Zhou et al., 2020; Van Lerven & Ryan-Collins, 2017). Capacity constraints, such as limited technical expertise and inadequate infrastructure, further impede effective implementation (IFC, 2019). Compounding these challenges are socio-political dynamics, including governance gaps and cultural norms, which influence stakeholder trust and investment prioritization (Martinez & Williams, 2021; Kurniawan & Kurniawan, 2022). There is an urgent need to standardize ESG metrics, strengthen institutional capacity, and foster multi-stakeholder collaboration to align financial flows with sustainability goals. Addressing these issues is critical for ensuring emerging markets contribute equitably to global climate targets while achieving socio-economic development.

4. Research Questions

1. How does sustainable finance influence economic growth, job creation, and sectoral development in emerging markets?
2. What are the primary regulatory, technical, and socio-political challenges hindering sustainable finance adoption, and how can they be mitigated?
3. How have historical trends in sustainable finance shaped its current application and effectiveness in emerging economies?
4. What role do regulatory frameworks, ESG data availability, and socio-political factors play in the implementation of sustainable finance across diverse markets?

5. Research Objectives

1. To evaluate the economic impacts of sustainable finance by analysing its contributions to GDP growth, employment, and sectoral innovation in emerging markets.
2. To identify systemic barriers to sustainable finance adoption and propose context-specific solutions for regulatory coherence, data standardization, and capacity-building.
3. To trace the historical evolution of sustainable finance and assess its alignment with contemporary practices in emerging economies.
4. To analyze the influence of regulatory frameworks, ESG data quality, and socio-political dynamics on the effectiveness of sustainable finance initiatives.

6. Research Methodology

This study employs a qualitative methodology to investigate the role of sustainable finance in addressing developmental challenges in emerging markets. A systematic literature review was conducted using peer-reviewed articles, policy reports, and case studies from databases including ScienceDirect, JSTOR, and SpringerLink, focusing on publications from 2013–2023 to ensure relevance. Theoretical frameworks from institutional theory (DiMaggio & Powell, 1983) and stakeholder theory (Freeman, 1984) guided the analysis of regulatory and socio-political dynamics. Data were synthesized through thematic coding to identify patterns in three core areas: (1) regulatory challenges, (2) ESG data inconsistencies, and (3) socio-political barriers. Case studies from China, India, and Latin America selected for their diverse regulatory landscapes and ESG adoption trajectories were analysed to contextualize findings (Taghizadeh-Hesary & Yoshino, 2019; Zhou et al., 2020). Thematic analysis emphasized intersections between policy frameworks, data transparency, and community engagement, aligning with the research objectives. The study acknowledges potential biases from reliance on secondary data and the rapid evolution of ESG regulations, which may affect the timeliness of recommendations. Future empirical research is needed to validate findings in real-time settings.

7. Results and Discussion

7.1. Sustainable Finance and Its Revolutionary Power in Emerging Markets

Sustainable finance has emerged as a transformative force in emerging markets, integrating environmental, social, and governance (ESG) considerations into investment strategies to address systemic challenges such as climate change and inequality. By aligning financial flows with long-term sustainability goals, this approach fosters inclusive growth while mitigating environmental degradation (Bril et al., 2020). For instance, renewable energy projects in countries like India and Brazil have reduced reliance on fossil fuels, creating jobs in green technology sectors and enhancing economic resilience (Van Lerven & Ryan-Collins, 2017). These investments not only diversify economies but also position emerging markets as key players in the global transition to low-carbon systems.

However, the revolutionary potential of sustainable finance is tempered by structural barriers. Regulatory frameworks in emerging markets often lack clarity and enforcement, leading to inconsistent implementation. Brazil's Green Protocol, for example, suffers from regional disparities in compliance, while India's fragmented ESG guidelines hinder standardization (Taghizadeh-Hesary & Yoshino, 2019). Additionally, limited access to reliable ESG data complicates risk assessments, undermining investor confidence (Zhou et al., 2020). Political instability and governance challenges further exacerbate uncertainties, deterring long-term investments in sustainability projects (Weber, 2016). Addressing these issues demands collaborative efforts to strengthen regulatory coherence, improve data transparency, and engage stakeholders a theme explored further in subsequent case studies.

7.2. Benefits and Challenges of Sustainable Finance

Sustainable finance delivers multifaceted benefits across economic, environmental, and social dimensions. Economically, it channels capital into sectors like renewable energy and green infrastructure, driving job creation and technological innovation. India's Tata Power, for example, has leveraged green bonds to expand its solar and wind portfolios, contributing to national renewable energy targets while generating employment (Zhou et al., 2020). Environmentally, initiatives such as green bonds fund projects that enhance energy efficiency and reduce emissions, aligning with global climate goals (Taghizadeh-Hesary & Yoshino, 2019). Socially, impact investing promotes financial inclusion and equitable development, as seen in Latin American microfinance programs that support sustainable agriculture and community welfare (Zhou et al., 2020).

Despite these advantages, significant challenges persist. High upfront costs for sustainable projects, such as transitioning to renewable energy, strain the limited financial resources of emerging markets (Van Lerven & Ryan-Collins, 2017). Regulatory inconsistencies and weak enforcement mechanisms further impede progress, as observed in Brazil's uneven adoption of the Green Protocol (Weber, 2016). Socio-political dynamics, including governance gaps and cultural norms, also influence stakeholder engagement. For example, land acquisition disputes in India delay renewable energy projects, highlighting the need for community-centric approaches (Martinez & Williams, 2021). Overcoming these barriers requires enhanced international cooperation, standardized ESG reporting, and capacity-building initiatives themes elaborated in later sections.

7.3. Historical Development of Sustainable Finance and Its Application to Emerging Markets

The evolution of sustainable finance traces back to 20th-century ethical investing, which excluded industries like tobacco and firearms. Over time, this exclusionary approach evolved into proactive ESG integration, driven by frameworks such as the UN Principles for Responsible Investment (UNPRI) and the Paris Agreement (Weber, 2016). The introduction of green bonds by the World Bank in 2008 marked a pivotal shift, enabling capital mobilization for climate-aligned projects (Zhou et al., 2020). Today, standardized reporting tools like the Global Reporting Initiative (GRI) enhance accountability, though their application in emerging markets remains uneven.

Emerging economies face unique challenges in adopting these historical advancements. Regulatory environments in countries like India and Brazil remain underdeveloped, with enforcement gaps undermining policy effectiveness (Van Lerven & Ryan-Collins, 2017). Limited access to financing and inconsistent ESG data further hinder progress. International organizations like the IFC have supported capacity-building efforts, yet technical and financial constraints persist (Taghizadeh-Hesary & Yoshino, 2019). Despite these hurdles, emerging markets are increasingly innovating, as seen in China's green bond market and Latin America's microfinance initiatives examples explored in subsequent case studies.

7.4. Legislative Frameworks, ESG Data Availability, Capacity-Building Programs, and Sociopolitical Factors

The efficacy of sustainable finance hinges on robust legislative frameworks. Developed markets like the EU benefit from regulations such as the Sustainable Finance Disclosure Regulation (SFDR), which standardizes ESG reporting and reduces greenwashing risks (Weber, 2016). In contrast, emerging markets struggle with fragmented policies. Brazil's Green Protocol and India's ESG guidelines, while progressive, face enforcement challenges, creating investor uncertainty (Taghizadeh-Hesary & Yoshino, 2019). International collaboration, exemplified by the UNDP's technical assistance programs, is critical to strengthening local regulatory ecosystems (Zhou et al., 2020).

ESG data availability remains a cornerstone of sustainable finance. Developed markets utilize platforms like Bloomberg ESG indices, while emerging economies grapple with inconsistent disclosure practices and language barriers (Van Lerven & Ryan-Collins, 2017). Initiatives such as the Sustainable Stock Exchanges (SSE) aim to bridge this gap, yet progress is slow. Capacity-building programs, including the CFA Institute's ESG certifications, are vital for enhancing expertise. In emerging markets, organizations like the IFC provide training on green bond issuance, though scalability remains a challenge (Zhou et al., 2020).

Sociopolitical factors further shape implementation. Political stability in developed markets attracts responsible investment, whereas regulatory instability in regions like Latin America deters long-term commitments (Martinez & Williams, 2021). Addressing these issues requires culturally sensitive strategies, such as respecting indigenous land rights in renewable energy projects, to ensure inclusive development (Kurniawan & Kurniawan, 2022).

7.5. Case Studies of Sustainable Finance from China, India, and Latin America

7.5.1. Green Bonds in China

China's Agricultural Bank of China (ABC) exemplifies leadership in sustainable finance through its 2019 green bond issuance, raising capital for renewable energy and green infrastructure. Adhering to international standards, these bonds funded solar farms and energy-efficient buildings, reducing emissions while stimulating economic growth (Zhou et al., 2020). Despite success, challenges like regulatory ambiguities and opaque impact assessments persist, underscoring the need for standardized reporting (Tang et al., 2023).

7.5.2. Renewable Energy Investments in India

Tata Power's renewable energy projects highlight India's commitment to sustainability. Leveraging green bonds and partnerships, the company has expanded its solar and wind capacity, contributing to India's 175 GW target (Taghizadeh-Hesary & Yoshino, 2019). However, land acquisition disputes and grid integration hurdles reveal the socio-political complexities of scaling clean energy (Martinez & Williams, 2021).

7.5.3. Green Bonds in Latin America

Brazil's BNDES has driven green bond adoption, financing renewable energy and biodiversity projects. These initiatives align with the Paris Agreement, fostering regional resilience and job creation (Zhou et al., 2020). Challenges include inconsistent impact reporting and underdeveloped legal frameworks, necessitating capacity-building support from global institutions (Kurniawan & Kurniawan, 2022).

7.5.4. Microfinance Institutions in Latin America

Microfinance institutions like Mexico's Banco Compartamos integrate ESG criteria to promote sustainable agriculture and financial inclusion. These programs empower marginalized communities but face hurdles such as regulatory bottlenecks and funding shortages (Zhou et al., 2020). Strengthening stakeholder collaboration and financial literacy is key to scaling impact.

8. Findings of the Study

This study reveals the transformative potential of sustainable finance in emerging markets, emphasizing its role in driving economic growth, environmental sustainability, and social equity. The findings underscore both opportunities and systemic barriers shaping its implementation.

Sustainable finance significantly stimulates economic growth by channelling investments into renewable energy, green infrastructure, and sustainable agriculture. These sectors foster innovation, create jobs, and enhance resilience. For instance, India's renewable energy projects have reduced fossil fuel dependency while generating employment in solar and wind sectors (Taghizadeh-Hesary & Yoshino, 2019). Similarly, green infrastructure investments in Brazil improved local productivity and economic diversification (Zhou et al., 2020).

Sustainable finance is pivotal in mitigating climate change. Green bonds and renewable energy investments have lowered carbon emissions and promoted resource efficiency. China's green financing initiatives, such as the Agricultural Bank of China's bond issuances, exemplify how capital allocation can accelerate the transition to low-carbon economies (Weber, 2016; Tang et al., 2023).

The integration of ESG principles advances financial inclusion and social equity. Microfinance programs in Latin America, like Banco Compartamos, have expanded credit access for underserved populations, fostering entrepreneurship and reducing poverty (Zhou et al., 2020). Impact investing also improves labour standards in vulnerable sectors, aligning economic growth with social welfare (Taghizadeh-Hesary & Yoshino, 2019).

Weak regulatory environments and inconsistent ESG data hinder progress. Emerging markets like India and Brazil face enforcement gaps and fragmented reporting standards, deterring investor confidence (Van Lerven & Ryan-Collins, 2017). Tailored regulatory frameworks and standardized ESG metrics are critical for transparency and risk assessment (Kahn & Yaghoubi, 2020; Mian et al., 2024).

Collaborative capacity-building programs are essential for institutional readiness. The International Finance Corporation (IFC) and UNDP have supported technical training and knowledge-sharing, yet emerging markets require localized strategies to address skills shortages (IFC, 2019; Kurniawan & Kurniawan, 2022).

Persistent barriers include limited access to capital, regulatory uncertainties, and socio-political instability. Investors perceive green projects as high-risk due to underdeveloped financial sectors and governance gaps (Zhou et al., 2020). Financial literacy gaps further impede adoption, underscoring the need for targeted education initiatives (Turner & Lang, 2019).

Conclusion and Policy Recommendations

Sustainable finance holds transformative potential for emerging markets, yet its adoption requires addressing systemic barriers. Strengthening regulatory frameworks through context-specific policies and standardizing ESG data reporting are critical to enhancing transparency and investor confidence. Capacity-building initiatives, supported by institutions like the IFC and UNDP, must prioritize local expertise to address technical gaps. Multi-stakeholder collaboration, including public-private partnerships, can mobilize capital for green infrastructure and renewable energy. Promoting financial literacy and robust impact measurement will ensure investments align with sustainability goals. By prioritizing these strategies, emerging markets can leverage sustainable finance to achieve inclusive growth, climate resilience, and equitable development.

Research Limitations and Scope for Future Research

This study's reliance on secondary data and qualitative analysis introduces potential selection bias and limits real-time insights into evolving sustainable finance practices. The focus on China, India, and Latin America, while illustrative, may not fully capture regional nuances in other emerging markets. Additionally, rapidly changing regulatory landscapes and ESG standards could affect the timeliness of policy recommendations. Future research should prioritize empirical studies with primary data to validate findings, expand geographical coverage to underrepresented regions like Africa and Southeast Asia, and explore the interplay between cultural norms and ESG adoption. Longitudinal analyses tracking the long-term impacts of sustainable finance on inclusive growth and climate resilience would further enrich the field.

References

Ali, S., Al-Nassar, N. S., Sindhu, M. I., & Naveed, M. (2025). Sustainable synergy: Static and dynamic nexus between ESG and BRICS equity markets. *Research in International Business and Finance*, *74*, 102698. https://doi.org/10.1016/j.ribaf.2025.102698.

Ameli, N., Drummond, P., Bisaro, A., Grubb, M., & Chenet, H. (2021). Climate finance and disclosure for institutional investors: Why transparency is not enough. *Climatic Change*, *163* (4), 1733-1755.

Agyemang, A. O., Osei, A., & Kongkuah, M. (2025). Exploring the ESG–circular economy nexus in emerging markets: A systems perspective on governance, innovation, and sustainable business models. *Business Strategy and the Environment*. Advance online publication. https://doi.org/10.1002/bse.4278.

Barney, J. (1991). Firm resources and sustained competitive advantage. *Journal of Management*, *17* (1), 99-120.

Biju, A. V. N., Geetha, S., Prasad, S., Sasidharan, A., & Jayachandran, A. (2025). ESG–firm performance nexus: Evidence from an emerging economy. *Business Strategy and the Environment*. Advance online publication. https://doi.org/10.1002/bse.4152.

Boffo, R., & Patalano, R. (2020). *ESG investing: Practices, progress and challenges*. OECD.

Boiral, O., Brotherton, M.-C., Gilbert-Parisée, D., Talbot, D., & Martinez, I. (2024). Decontesting an essentially contested concept: The standardization of sustainable finance. *Business Strategy and the Environment*. Advance online publication. https://doi.org/10.1002/bse.3972

Campiglio, E. (2016). Beyond carbon pricing: The role of banking and monetary policy in financing the transition to a low-carbon economy. *Ecological Economics*, *121*, 220-230.

Chatterji, A. K., Durand, R., Levine, D. I., & Touboul, S. (2016). Do ratings of firms converge? Implications for managers, investors and strategy researchers. *Strategic Management Journal*, *37* (8), 1597-1614.

DiMaggio, P. J., & Powell, W. W. (1983). The iron cage revisited: Institutional isomorphism and collective rationality in organizational fields. *American Sociological Review*, *48* (2), 147-160.

Eccles, R. G., & Serafeim, G. (2013). A tale of two stories: Sustainability and the quarterly earnings call. *Journal of Applied Corporate Finance*, *25* (3), 8-19.

Edu, A. S., Ofosuhene, E., Agozie, D. Q., Gyamfi, B. A., & Asongu, S. A. (2025). Optimizing sustainable resource efficiency: A fuzzy-set qualitative comparative analysis of sustainable practices in SMEs. *Business Strategy and the Environment*. Advance online publication. https://doi.org/10.1002/bse.4125.

Freeman, R. E. (1984). *Strategic management: A stakeholder approach*. Pitman.

Gangwani, M., & Kashiramka, S. (2024). Does ESG performance impact value and risk-taking by commercial banks? Evidence from emerging market economies. *Business Strategy and the Environment*. Advance online publication. https://doi.org/10.1002/bse.3882.

Goel, R., Gautam, D., & Natalucci, F. M. (2022). Sustainable finance in emerging markets: Evolution, challenges, and policy priorities. *IMF Working Papers* (Working Paper No. 2022/182). International Monetary Fund.

Gucciardi, G. (2024). Do venture capital investments contribute to the achievement of the sustainable development goals? *Business Strategy and the Environment*. Advance online publication. https://doi.org/10.1002/bse.3942.

Hong, Y., Fei, W., Zhijie, L., & Cifuentes-Faura, J. (2025). Private vs. public: Differential impacts of sustainable innovation on ESG performance in the digitalize era. *Business Strategy and the Environment*. Advance online publication. https://doi.org/10.1002/bse.4194.

Hossain, M., Alamgir, M., & Alam, S. (2021). ESG disclosures and stock return: Evidence from emerging markets. *Business Strategy and the Environment*.

IFC International Finance Corporation. (2019). *Green buildings: A finance and policy blueprint for emerging markets*. World Bank Group. https://documents1.worldbank.org/curated/en/586841576523330833/pdf/Green-Buildings-A-Finance-and-Policy-Blueprint-for-Emerging-Markets.pdf.

IFC International Finance Corporation. (2019). *Emerging market green bonds report 2019: Momentum builds as nascent markets grow*. https://www.ifc.org/content/dam/ifc/doc/mgrt/202005-em-green-bonds-report-2019.pdf.

Jamali, D., & Karam, C. (2018). Corporate social responsibility in developing countries as an emerging field of study. *International Journal of Management Reviews*, *20* (1), 32-61.

Joshipura, M., Nasrallah, N., & Kedia, N. (2025). Green and climate finance for sustainability: Hybrid review and framework development. *Business Strategy and the Environment*. Advance online publication. https://doi.org/10.1002/bse.4173.

Kahn, M., & Yaghoubi, S. (2020). ESG disclosure and financial performance in emerging markets. *Journal of Sustainable Finance & Investment*, *10* (2), 239-254.

Kurniawan, R., & Kurniawan, I. W. (2022). Developing innovative financing scheme for leveraging energy efficiency deployment in Indonesia. *Indonesian Journal of Energy, 5* (1), 1-XX. https://doi.org/10.33116/ije.v5i1.132.

Kyrdoda, Y., Balzano, M., & Vianelli, D. (2024). The formation of a sustainable organizational identity: Insights from Brazilian coffee producers. *Business Strategy and the Environment.* Advance online publication. https://doi.org/10.1002/bse.3975.

Luo, M., Lin, J., & Luo, X. (R.). (2025). The impact of digital transformation on the sustainable performance of organizations: A configurational approach. *Business Strategy and the Environment.* Advance online publication. https://doi.org/10.1002/bse.4279.

Malakar, K. D., Kumar, M., Anand, S., & Kuzur, G. (2023). *Climate change and socio-ecological transformation: Vulnerability and sustainability* (1st ed.). Springer Singapore.

Martinez, J., & Williams, R. (2021). Sociopolitical instability and its impact on sustainable finance implementation. *Global Policy Journal, 19* (4), 75-89. https://doi.org/10.7890/gpj.2021.194.

Mian, H. R., Hewage, K., & Sadiq, R. (2024). Responsible financing and investment: Identification, development, and assessment of Environmental, Social, and Governance (ESG) metrics. *Sustainable Futures, 8*, 100246. https://doi.org/10.1016/j.sftr.2024.100246.

Rataj, O., Kemp, R., & Mordaszewska, K. (2024). Mainstreaming innovative circular economy, solutions A comparative study between entrepreneurs in developed versus emerging markets and developing economies. *Business Strategy and the Environment.* Advance online publication. https://doi.org/10.1002/bse.3957.

Siddiqi, R. A., Codini, A. P., Ishaq, M. I., Jamali, D. R., & Raza, A. (2024). Sustainable supply chain, dynamic capabilities, eco-innovation, and environmental performance in an emerging economy. *Business Strategy and the Environment.* Advance online publication. https://doi.org/10.1002/bse.3976.

Sullivan, R., & Gouldson, A. (2017). The governance of corporate responses to climate change: An international comparison. *Business Strategy and the Environment, 26* (4), 413-425. https://doi.org/10.1002/bse.1925.

Taghizadeh-Hesary, F., & Yoshino, N. (2019). Sustainable solutions for green financing and investment in renewable energy projects. *Energies, 12* (5), 840. https://doi.org/10.3390/en12050840.

Tang, Y., Wang, B., Pan, N., & Li, Z. (2023). The impact of environmental information disclosure on the cost of green bond: Evidence from China. *Energy Economics, 126*, 107008. https://doi.org/10.1016/j.eneco.2023.107008.

Turner, D., & Lang, S. (2019). Capacity constraints and the adoption of sustainable finance practices. *International Review of Financial Analysis, 68*, 101-115.

United Nations. (n.d.). *SDGs: 17 goals to transform our world.* Retrieved October 17, 2024, from https://www.un.org/en/exhibits/page/sdgs-17-goals-transform-world.

United Nations Framework Convention on Climate Change. (n.d.). *Key aspects of the Paris Agreement.* Retrieved October 18, 2024, from https://unfccc.int/most-requested/key-aspects-of-the-paris-agreement#:~:text=The%20Paris%20Agreement's%20central%20aim,further%20to%201.5%20degrees%20Celsius.

Van Lerven, F., & Ryan-Collins, J. (2017). Central banks, climate change and the transition to a low-carbon economy: A policy briefing. New Economics Foundation.

Van Lerven, F., & Ryan-Collins, J. (2017). The role of sustainable finance in emerging markets: Case studies and analysis. *Finance Research Letters*, *22*, 200-210. https://doi.org/10.1016/j.frl.2017.06.003.

Vandana, Sangwa, N. R., Ertz, M., & Shashi. (2024). Sustainable and resilient cold chains: Enhancing adaptability, consistency, and digital transformation for success in a turbulent market. *Business Strategy and the Environment*. Advance online publication. https://doi.org/10.1002/bse.3805.

Weber, O. (2016). *Sustainable finance and investment: A global perspective*. Routledge.

World Bank. (2008). *World development report 2008: Agriculture for development*. World Bank.

World Bank. (2018). *Mobilizing private finance for sustainable development*. World Bank.

Zhou, X., Tang, G., & Zhang, X. (2020). Green bonds and sustainable finance in emerging markets. *Journal of Sustainable Finance & Investment*, *10* (2), 145-160. https://doi.org/10.1080/20430795.2020.1750031.

Chapter 12

An Analytical Hierarchy Process-Based Assessment of Strategic Approaches in Green Finance

Shyam Sunder Agrawal[1,*]
Amitabha Maheshwari[2]
Sneha Raghuvanshi[3]
and Amanjot Singh Syan[4]
[1]Mittal School of Business, Lovely Professional University, Punjab, India
[2]Prestige Institute of Management and Research, Gwalior, Madhya Pradesh, India
[3]Medi-caps University, Indore, India
[4]Canadore Stanford International College, Ontario, Canada

Abstract

This research work is devoted to evaluating Green Finance Strategies. For evaluation, a well-known multicriteria decision-making (MCDM) technique, the Analytical Hierarchy Process (AHP), was used, fed by responses to a questionnaire sent to a group of experts. With the help of a literature review and experts' opinions, lists of criteria and sub-criteria, along with alternatives, were created. The identified alternatives were Impact investing, green bonds, sustainable agriculture funds, and renewable energy funds. The research work advocated impact investing, green bonds, sustainable agriculture funds, etc. The research work represents the original work of the researcher for evaluating green finance strategies using AHP. A model has been developed and ranks them based on results.

---

* Corresponding Author's Email: shyamsunderagrawal8@gmail.com

In: Environmental, Social, and Governance (ESG) …
Editor: Veena Grover
ISBN: 979-8-90134-138-4

Keywords: green finance, multicriteria decision making (MCDM), analytical hierarchy process (AHP), ESG, impact investing

1. Introduction

Without green finance - an emerging challenge with rapidly growing recognition - no effort towards sustainable development or climate change reduction can be effectively accomplished (Lee, 2020). Green finance refers to environmentally sustainable investment and business practices, and even though this has always existed - even pre-financial markets - green finance has become a prerequisite for sustainable development and climate-change reduction amongst policymakers, investors and financiers (Nepomuceno et al., 2024). Here, environmentally sustainable investment decisions include environmental, social, and governance problems in a way that allows for long-term growth (Meng & Shaikh, 2023). For a low-carbon, resource-efficient and sustainable economy, investors need to be willing to provide the financial returns (Liu et al., 2020). The international monetary system is crucial for delivering sustainable development. With climate change, environmental degradation, and aspects of social hardship on the rise, the need for long-term investments has also increased (Qin et al., 2021). This research has taken an environmental focus to analyse green financing. The Analytical Hierarchy Process (AHP), a well-known multiple criterion decision-making (MCDM) method, can assist with this (Aliyev et al., 2020).

1.1. Green Finance

The concept of green growth has garnered significant international recognition as a burgeoning catalyst for economic expansion, with the potential to foster both environmental sustainability and economic progress, predating the global financial crisis (Thirumurthy et al., 2022). Green financing plays a crucial role in supporting the growth of environmentally sustainable initiatives. Green finance is typically characterised by its forward-looking approach, as it seeks to promote economic growth, environmental protection, and the advancement of the financial industry (Algarín et al., 2017). Green finance is considered a form of targeted funding that specifically supports green economic activities. These activities may include export financing, financing for Small and

Medium-sized Enterprises, and financing for IT ventures. The concept of green finance can be categorised into two main divisions: The two main areas of focus are (1) securing funding for green growth and (2) securing funding for the prevention of environmental costs (Arda et al., 2025). The aforementioned encompasses, with greater specificity, the realm of indirect financing within the capital market, encompassing green loans as well as direct finance markets, exemplified by the creation of the green index and the initiation of the green fund (Chien et al., 2021).

Previous literature[1] has documented that market returns exhibit negative skewness and asymmetric volatility, which is a tendency for volatility to rise with negative return. When calculating the impact of national elections on crashes, this research adopts a narrow, euphemistic definition of the word "crash," associating it solely with conditional skewness of return distribution, in which conditional skewness is interpreted as a measure of the crash.

1.2. Objectives of Research

The following points represent the objectives of the present research work:

a) Evaluation of priorities of green finance strategies; and
b) Ranking of green finance strategies.

2. Review of Literature

The present section portrays the contributions of researchers to green finance and concludes with the investigated gaps in the research, as presented in upcoming sub-sections.

2.1. Contributions of Researchers to Green Finance

Sustainability, the environment, reducing carbon emissions, and adapting to a changing climate all fall under the umbrella term "green finance," as defined by Noh (2018). In addition to these studies, a review of the literature in the following section demonstrates that researchers and academicians have made an effort to investigate the effects of GF on sustainable development, green development, innovation, energy efficiency, the adoption of renewable energy sources, environmental sustainability, and carbon dioxide emissions (Rasoulinezhad & Taghizadeh-Hesary, 2022; Fang et al., 2022). In addition, some research has analysed the effects of digital banking on energy-environmental performance. According to recent research, green financial investment efficiency rose thanks to the digital economy. The banking sectors of countries have begun to contemplate including GF products in their portfolios as a result of the significant expansion of green finance over the last few years (Tian et al., 2022). Corporate social responsibility (CSR) has emerged as an additional motivating element alongside GF (Guang-Wen & Siddik, 2022). By analysing the elements of green financing, Li et al., (2023) help us get closer to our carbon peak and neutrality goals. The purpose of this study is to use the Delphi and fuzzy AHP techniques to identify, evaluate, and rank the variables of GF in a country with a middle-to-high income level, namely China. Akomea-Frimpong et al., (2022) conducted literature research on green finance within the banking sector, taking into account the products and determining factors of green financing (Zaheb et al., 2024). Forty-six studies were reviewed and synthesised using the content analysis method. Banking institutions offer a range of green finance products, including climate and carbon financing, insurance, lending, and infrastructure. Karim (2022) examines the relationship between CO2 emissions and green finance in the top ten economies that promote green financing. In this work, we employ quantile-on-quantile regression to look at the relationship between green financing and CO2 emissions on a quantitative scale (Wind & Saaty, 1980). Our data confirm the general adverse effect of green financing on CO2 emissions; however, the strength of this association differs among the quantiles of both variables. Using regional data from 2010 to 2019 from China, Irfan et al., (2022) apply difference-in-differences, mediation effects, and panel vector autoregression models to empirically test the influence mechanism and policy intervention effects of inclusive green finance on green innovation. The results show that green financing makes a significant contribution to green innovation and that this impact persists when using different estimators. Corporations have consequently redirected their attention from solely prioritising profit to adopting a broader perspective known as the "triple bottom line."

This approach aims to achieve economic, social, and environmental performance concurrently to promote sustainable development. Currently, various sectors of the global economy are actively discussing their strategies for environmental protection. The financial sector is also joining this movement by adopting a 'going green' approach. Several financial service providers, including banks, stock brokerages, insurance companies, and consumer finance companies, have embraced a sustainable approach in their operations (Tara & Singh, 2014).

Studies show that companies can significantly increase stock liquidity by raising the level of their ESG disclosure (Cao et al., 2024). Additionally, we examine and validate using mechanism testing how ESG disclosure affects stock liquidity by boosting media coverage and analyst attention (information effect) as well as reputation (reputation effect). The work contributes to the body of knowledge about the economic effects of ESG information disclosure and stock liquidity issues, both theoretically and practically (Çelikbilek, 2025).

To alleviate financing constraints, green finance has the potential to magnify the peer effect of environmental, social, and governance (ESG) information disclosure. In general, this research contributes to understanding how green finance operates and how companies share information about their environmental, social, and governance (ESG) practices. Furthermore, it provides policy implications for improving these disclosures at the business level (Liang & Yang, 2024).

2.2. Research Gap

The following points represent the gaps in the research:

a) There are very limited researches that focus on the ranking of green finance strategies and
b) There is a minimal number of research papers available that focus on the ranking of green finance strategies.

3. Solution Methodology

In the present research work, the Analytical hierarchy process (AHP) is used. The Analytical Hierarchy Process (AHP) is a structured technique that summarised in Figure 1, enabling researchers to make informed decisions (Holder, 1991). Instead of prescribing an accurate decision, the AHP helps to work out one. Following are the steps of solving a problem using AHP:

a) In the first step, an AHP model showing hierarchies is drawn, consisting of goals, criteria, and/or sub-criteria and alternatives, as shown below.

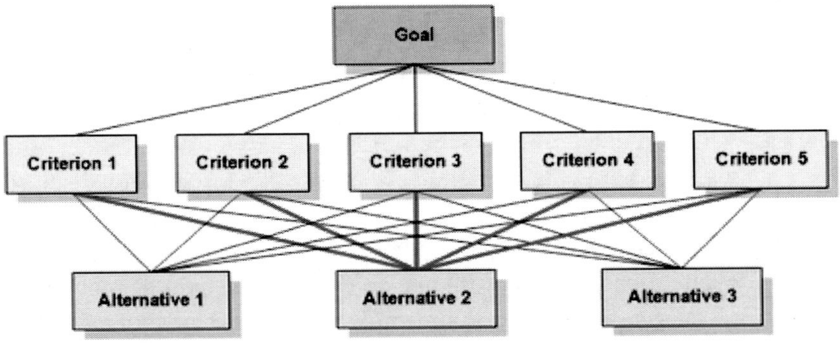

Source: Saaty, 1980.

Figure 1. Hierarchy Structure of General AHP.

b) In the next step, with the help of a pairwise comparison scale, a questionnaire is designed and submitted to experts for giving their responses, consisting of all the possible combinations of criteria and/or sub-criteria and alternatives, from 1 to 9 where 1 for equal importance to 9 for extreme importance of one criterion over another.
c) In the next step, a pairwise comparison matrix is drawn, consisting of criteria and/or sub-criteria and alternatives at the beginning of rows and columns, and responses are marked on it;
d) In the next step, after normalisation of responses, eigenvalues of different parameters are calculated, which are declared as priorities, using consistency ratio (CR), where:

$$C.R. = \frac{(C.I.)}{(R.I.)} \qquad (3.1)$$

where CI is called consistency index:

$$C.I. = \frac{(\lambda-1)}{(n-1)} \qquad (3.2)$$

where gamma is the maximum eigenvalue, n is the matrix size, and R. I. may be found in the following table for the country in week t.

Table 1. Average Random Consistency Index

Size of Matrix	1	2	3	4	5	6	7	8	9	10
Random Consistency Index (R.I.)	0.00		0.58	0.90	1.12	1.24	1.32	1.41	1.45	1.49

Source: Saaty, 1980.

e) On getting favourable values of CR, the rankings of the parameters based on their priority values (highest to lowest) may be suggested.

4. Case Study

The present research work is based on the Evaluation of Green Finance Strategies using AHP. For this purpose, a well-established solution methodology was used, the details of which are presented in Figure 2, as follows.

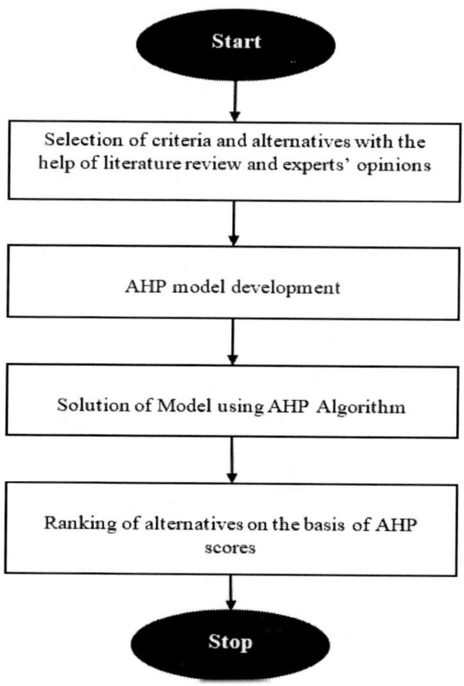

Source: Authors' creation.

Figure 2. Solution Methodology for the Research Problem.

Details of different steps used in solution methodology are presented as follows:

a) First of all, with the help of a literature review (Meng & Shaikh, 2023) and experts' opinions, a list of criteria, sub-criteria, as alternatives was prepared, as presented below

Table 2. Details of criteria, sub-criteria, and alternatives

S. No	Criteria	Sub criteria	Alternatives
1.	Environmental factors	Resource conservation	Impact investing; Green bonds; Sustainable agriculture funds; Renewable energy funds
2.		Pollution prevention	
3.		Environmental impact assessment	
4.	Social factors	Community engagement and human rights	
5.		Income distribution	
6.		Employee satisfaction	
7.	Governance factors	Corporate governance	
8.		Risk management	
9.		Ethics and values	

Source: Authors' creation.

The evaluation of investment alternatives based on ESG factors considers Environmental, Social, and Governance (ESG) criteria, each comprising key sub-criteria. Under Environmental factors, investments are assessed for their impact on resource conservation, pollution prevention, and environmental impact assessment, with alternatives including Impact Investing, Green Bonds, Sustainable Agriculture Funds, and Renewable Energy Funds (Li et al., 2023). Social factors focus on community engagement and human rights, income distribution, and employee satisfaction, highlighting the role of investments in fostering social equity and workplace well-being (Calabrese et al., 2016). Governance factors emphasise corporate governance, risk management, ethics and values, ensuring ethical decision-making and regulatory compliance. This structured approach (Table 2) provides a comprehensive framework for ranking sustainable investment options based on their contribution to ESG objectives.

In the next step, AHP model development was accomplished, as presented in Figure 3.

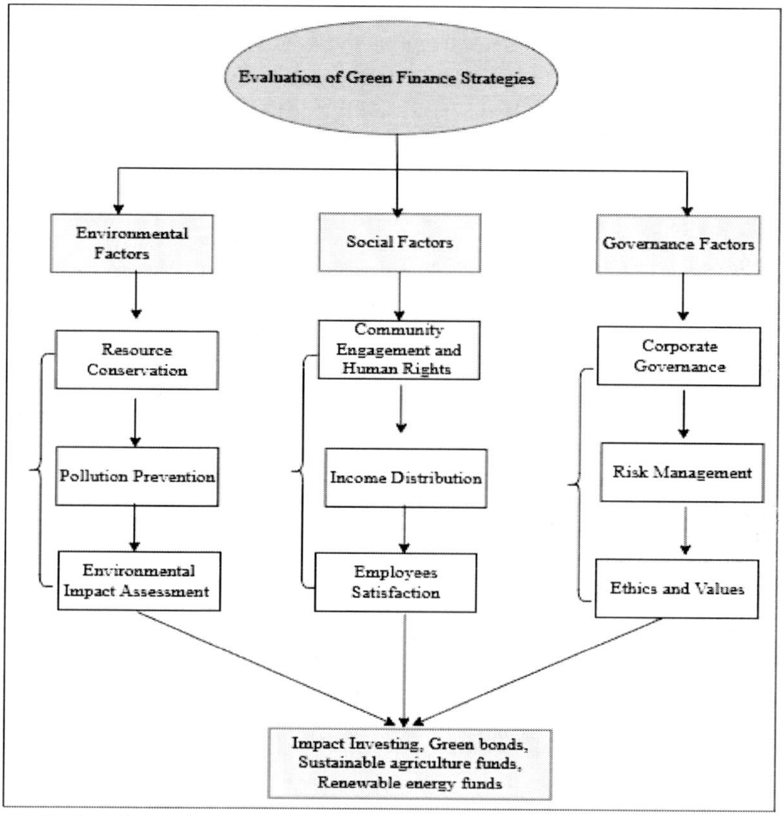

Source: Authors' creation.

Figure 3. AHP model for the evaluation of green finance strategies.

Table 3. Pairwise comparison matrix for criteria

From/to	Environmental factors	Social factors	Governance factors
Environmental factors	1	2	5
Social factors	½	1	2
Governance factors	1/5	½	1

Source: Authors' creation.

In the next step of the research work, priorities of criteria, sub-criteria, and alternatives were determined. For this purpose, first of all, a systematic questionnaire based on a pairwise comparison scale was sent to a group of experts. Their responses were recorded in the form of a pairwise comparison matrix, and then, using the AHP procedure, the local as well as global priorities of criteria, sub-criteria and alternatives were investigated (Chabouh et al., 2024), the details of which are presented as follows.

Table 4. Priorities for criteria

S. No	Criteria	Priority
1.	Environmental factors	0.595
2.	Social factors	0.276
3.	Governance factors	0.128
Consistency Ratio = 0.002<0.1		

Source: Authors' creation.

Table 5. Pairwise comparison matrix for sub-criteria under criteria "Environmental factors"

From/to	Resource conservation	Pollution prevention	Environmental impact assessment
Resource conservation	1	1	1
Pollution prevention		1	1
Environmental impact assessment	1	1	1

Source: Authors' creation.

Table 6. Priorities of sub-criteria under criteria "Environmental factors"

S. No	Criteria	Local Priorities	Global Priorities
1.	Resource conservation	0.333	0.198
2.	Pollution prevention	0.333	0.198
3.	Environmental impact assessment	0.333	0.198
Consistency Ratio = 0 < 0.1			

Source: Authors' creation.

Table 7. Pairwise comparison matrix for sub-criteria under criteria "Social factors"

From/to	Community engagement and human rights	Income distribution	Employee satisfaction
Community engagement and human rights	1	2	1
Income distribution	½	1	1
Employee satisfaction	1	1	1

Source: Authors' creation.

Table 8. Priorities of sub-criteria under criteria "Social factors"

S. No	Criteria	Local Priorities	Global Priorities
1.	Community engagement and human rights	0.412	0.113
2.	Income distribution	0.259	0.071
3.	Employee satisfaction	0.327	0.090
Consistency Ratio = 0.02 < 0.1			

Source: Authors' creation.

Table 9. Comparison matrix (pair-wise) for sub-criteria under criteria "Governance Factors"

From/to	Corporate governance	Risk management	Ethics and values
Corporate governance	1	1	1
Risk management	1	1	1
Ethics and values	1	1	1

Source: Authors' creation.

Table 10. Priorities of sub-criteria under criteria "Governance Factors"

S. No	Criteria	Local Priorities	Global Priorities
1.	Corporate governance	0.333	0.042
2.	Risk management	0.333	0.042
3.	Ethics and values	0.333	0.042
Consistency Ratio = 0<0.1			

Source: Authors' creation.

Table 11. Pairwise comparison matrix of alternatives for sub-criteria "Resource conservation"

From/to	Impact investing	Green bonds	Sustainable agriculture funds	Renewable energy funds
Impact investing	1	1	1	2
Green bonds	1	1	1	1
Sustainable agriculture funds	1	1	1	1
Renewable energy funds	½	1	1	1

Source: Authors' creation.

Table 12. Priorities of alternatives for sub-criteria "Resource conservation"

S. No	Criteria	Local Priorities	Global Priorities
1.	Impact investing	0.297	0.058
2.	Green bonds	0.246	0.048
3.	Sustainable agriculture funds	0.246	0.048
4.	Renewable energy funds	0.209	0.041
Consistency Ratio = 0.02 < 0.1			

Source: Authors' creation.

Table 13. Comparison matrix (pair-wise) of alternatives for sub-criteria "Pollution prevention"

From/to	Impact investing	Green bonds	Sustainable agriculture funds	Renewable energy funds
Impact investing	1	1	1	3
Green bonds	1	1	1	2
Sustainable agriculture funds	1	1	1	1
Renewable energy funds	1/3	½	1	1

Source: Authors' creation.

Table 14. Priorities of alternatives for sub-criteria "Pollution prevention"

S. No	Criteria	Local Priorities	Global Priorities
1.	Impact investing,	0.319	0.063
2.	Green bonds	0.280	0.055
3.	Sustainable agriculture funds	0.242	0.047
4.	Renewable energy funds	0.157	0.031
Consistency Ratio = 0.039 < 0.1			

Source: Authors' creation.

Table 15. Comparison matrix (pair-wise) of alternatives for sub-criteria "Environmental impact assessment"

From/to	Impact investing	Green bonds	Sustainable agriculture funds	Renewable energy funds
Impact investing	1	1	1	2
Green bonds	1	1	1	1
Sustainable agriculture funds	1	1	1	1
Renewable energy funds	½	1	1	1

Source: Authors' creation.

Table 16. Priorities of alternatives for sub-criteria "Environmental impact assessment"

S. No	Criteria	Local Priorities	Global Priorities
1.	Impact investing	0.297	0.058
2.	Green bonds	0.246	0.048
3.	Sustainable agriculture funds	0.246	0.048
4.	Renewable energy funds	0.209	0.041
Consistency Ratio = 0.020<0.1			

Source: Authors' creation.

Table 17. Comparison matrix (pair-wise) of alternatives for sub-criteria "Community engagement and human rights"

From/to	Impact investing	Green bonds	Sustainable agriculture funds	Renewable energy funds
Impact investing	1	1	2	3
Green bonds	1	1	1	1
Sustainable agriculture funds	½	1	1	1
Renewable energy funds	1/3	1	1	1

Source: Authors' creation.

Table 18. Priorities of alternatives for sub-criteria "Community engagement and human rights"

S. No	Criteria	Local Priorities	Global Priorities
1.	Impact investing,	0.378	0.042
2.	Green bonds	0.242	0.027
3.	Sustainable agriculture funds	0.196	0.022
4.	Renewable energy funds	0.181	0.020
Consistency Ratio = 0.039<0.1			

Source: Authors' creation.

Table 19. Comparison matrix (pair-wise) of alternatives for sub-criteria "Income distribution"

From/to	Impact investing	Green bonds	Sustainable agriculture funds	Renewable energy funds
Impact investing	1	1	2	4
Green bonds	1	1	1	1
Sustainable agriculture funds	½	1	1	1
Renewable energy funds	¼	1	1	1

Source: Authors' creation.

Table 20. Priorities of alternatives for sub-criteria "Income distribution"

S. No	Criteria	Local Priorities	Global Priorities
1.	Impact investing	0.403	0.028
2.	Green bonds	0.238	0.016
3.	Sustainable agriculture funds	0.190	0.013
4.	Renewable energy funds	0.166	0.011
Consistency Ratio = 0.061<0.1			

Source: Authors' creation.

Table 21. Comparison matrix (Pairwise) of alternatives for sub-criteria "Employee satisfaction"

From/to	Impact investing	Green bonds	Sustainable agriculture funds	Renewable energy funds
Impact investing	1	1	2	3
Green bonds	1	1	1	2
Sustainable agriculture funds	½	½	1	2
Renewable energy funds	1/3	½	½	1

Source: Authors' creation.

Table 22. Priorities of alternatives for sub-criteria "Employee satisfaction"

S. No	Criteria	Local Priorities	Global Priorities
1.	Impact investing	0.365	0.032
2.	Green bonds	0.277	0.024
3.	Sustainable agriculture funds	0.232	0.020
4.	Renewable energy funds	0.123	0.011
Consistency Ratio = 0.015<0.1			

Source: Authors' creation.

Table 23. Comparison matrix (pair-wise) of alternatives for sub-criteria "Corporate governance"

From/to	Impact investing	Green bonds	Sustainable agriculture funds	Renewable energy funds
Impact investing	1	1	2	3
Green bonds	1	1	1	1
Sustainable agriculture funds	½	1	1	2
Renewable energy funds	1/3		1/2	1

Source: Authors' creation.

Table 24. Priorities of alternatives for sub-criteria "Corporate governance"

S. No	Criteria	Local Priorities	Global Priorities
1.	Impact investing	0.371	0.015
2.	Green bonds	0.241	0.010
3.	Sustainable agriculture funds	0.233	0.009
4.	Renewable energy funds	0.153	0.006
Consistency Ratio = 0.04 <0.1			

Source: Authors' creation.

Table 25. Comparison matrix (pair-wise) of alternatives for sub-criteria "Risk management"

From/to	Impact investing	Green bonds	Sustainable agriculture funds	Renewable energy funds
Impact investing	1	1	1	1
Green bonds	1	1	1	1
Sustainable agriculture funds	1	1	1	1
Renewable energy funds	1	1	1	1

Source: Authors' creation.

Table 26. Priorities of alternatives for sub-criteria "Risk management"

S. No	Criteria	Local Priorities	Global Priorities
1.	Impact investing	0.25	0.010
2.	Green bonds	0.25	0.010
3.	Sustainable agriculture funds	0.25	0.010
4.	Renewable energy funds	0.25	0.010
Consistency Ratio = 0 < 0.1			

Source: Authors' creation.

Table 27. Comparison matrix (pair-wise) of alternatives for sub-criteria "Ethics and values"

From/to	Impact investing	Green bonds	Sustainable agriculture funds	Renewable energy funds
Impact investing	1	1	2	1
Green bonds	1	1	1	1
Sustainable agriculture funds	1	1	1	1
Renewable energy funds	1	1	1	1

Source: Authors' creation.

Table 28. Priorities of alternatives for sub-criteria "Ethics and values"

S. No	Criteria	Local Priorities	Global Priorities
1.	Impact investing	0.297	0.012
2.	Green bonds	0.246	0.010
3.	Sustainable agriculture funds	0.209	0.008
4.	Renewable energy funds	0.246	0.010
Consistency Ratio = …<0.1			

Source: Authors' creation.

5. Interpretations of the Data

The data presented in the tables represent a structured decision-making approach using the Analytic Hierarchy Process (AHP) to evaluate different investment alternatives based on Environmental, Social, and Governance (ESG) factors. The process involves pairwise comparisons of criteria, sub-criteria, and alternatives, followed by the calculation of priority weights and ranking of investment options (Chiu et al., 2021).

5.1. Criteria Weighting (Table 3 & Table 4)

The pairwise comparison matrix for ESG criteria (Table 3) indicates that environmental factors are given the highest importance, followed by social and governance factors. The computed priority weights (Table 4) show:

- Environmental factors: 0.595
- Social factors: 0.276
- Governance factors: 0.128

Since the Consistency Ratio (CR) = 0.002 < 0.1, the judgments are consistent and reliable. The high priority of environmental factors suggests that sustainability plays a key role in decision-making (Chun-Yueh, 2022).

Table 29. Ranking of Alternatives

S. No		Environmental factors			Social factors			Governance factors			Overall score	Rank
	Alternatives	Resource conservation	Pollution Prevention	Environmental impact Assessment	Community engagement and human rights	Income distribution	Employee satisfaction	Corporate governance	Risk management	Ethics and values		
1.	Impact investing	0.058	0.063	0.058	0.042	0.028	0.032	0.015	0.010	0.012	0.318	I
2.	Green bonds	0.048	0.055	0.048	0.027	0.016	0.024	0.010	0.010	0.010	0.248	II
3.	Sustainable agriculture funds	0.048	0.047	0.048	0.022	0.013	0.020	0.009	0.010	0.008	0.225	III
4.	Renewable energy funds	0.041	0.031	0.041	0.020	0.011	0.011	0.006	0.010	0.010	0.181	IV

Source: Authors' creation.

5.2. Sub-Criteria Weighting for ESG Factors (Tables 5–10)

Each ESG criterion is further divided into sub-criteria, and their priorities are calculated:

- Environmental Factors (Table 6):
  - Resource Conservation: 0.333
  - Pollution Prevention: 0.333
  - Environmental Impact Assessment: 0.333
  - (CR = 0, indicating perfect consistency)
- Social Factors (Table 8):
  - Community Engagement & Human Rights: 0.412
  - Income Distribution: 0.259
  - Employee Satisfaction: 0.327
  - (CR = 0.02 < 0.1, confirming consistency)
- Governance Factors (Table 10):
  - Corporate Governance: 0.333
  - Risk Management: 0.333
  - Ethics & Values: 0.333
  - (CR = 0, confirming consistency)

The findings suggest that among social sub-criteria, community engagement and human rights have the highest importance, whereas all governance sub-criteria are equally weighted.

5.3. Comparison and Ranking of Investment Alternatives (Tables 11–28)

The alternatives considered in the analysis include Impact Investing, Green Bonds, Sustainable Agriculture Funds, and Renewable Energy Funds (Göçmen-Polat, 2024). These alternatives are compared against each sub-criterion using pairwise comparison matrices (Tables 11, 13, 15, 17, 19, 21, 23, 25, and 27). The corresponding priority weights of each alternative for each sub-criterion are presented in Tables 12, 14, 16, 18, 20, 22, 24, 26, and 28.

Some key observations are:

- Impact Investing ranks highest across multiple sub-criteria, especially in community engagement and human rights (0.378, Table 18) and income distribution (0.403, Table 20).
- Green Bonds perform well in environmental impact assessment (0.246, Table 16) and pollution prevention (0.280, Table 14).
- Sustainable Agriculture Funds and Renewable Energy Funds rank lower across most criteria.

The Consistency Ratios (CR) for all comparisons remain below 0.1, ensuring the credibility of the rankings (Guang-Wen & Siddik, 2022).

5.4. Overall Ranking of Investment Alternatives (Table 29)

Based on the aggregated priority scores across all sub-criteria, Table 29 provides the final ranking of alternatives:

1. Impact Investing (0.318) – Best Performing Alternative
2. Green Bonds (0.248) – Second Place
3. Sustainable Agriculture Funds (0.225) – Third Place
4. Renewable Energy Funds (0.181) – Lowest Ranked Alternative

Impact Investing emerges as the best investment alternative, given its superior performance in both social and governance aspects, alongside a strong presence in environmental factors. Green Bonds follow closely, indicating their relevance in sustainable financing. Sustainable Agriculture Funds and Renewable Energy Funds score lower, highlighting potential limitations in their ESG impact or financial viability (Meo & Abd Karim, 2022).

6. Results and Discussion

Table 30 presents the results of the research work:

Table 30. Results of the research work

S. No	Alternative	Rank
1.	Impact investing	I
2.	Green bonds	II
3.	Sustainable agriculture funds	III
4.	Renewable energy funds	IV

Source: Authors' creation.

The Table shows that impact investing scores the maximum value of the sum of priorities and secures rank I, while green bonds, sustainable agriculture funds, and renewable energy funds secures ranks II, III, and IV. Investing in harvesting is a strategy that enhances financial gains in businesses that are involved in social or environmental impact, which, in turn, is the most promising strategy for businesses.

Considering the fixed income perspectives, the alternative, green bonds secured rank II, offer a promise of fixed income over time. Alternative, sustainable agriculture funds have secured rank III due to less familiarity of industrialists with the recent technologies of agriculture. In contrast, the alternative, renewable energy funds, have secured rank IV, which may be due to heavy competition among the companies along with continuously reducing rates of such products (Yadav et al., 2024).

Conclusion, Limitations, and Future Scope of the Research

This research systematically evaluates green finance strategies through the Analytical Hierarchy Process (AHP) to select the most relevant investment alternative using Environmental, Social, and Governance (ESG) factors. The analysis found that Impact Investing ranks first, followed by Green Bonds in second place and Sustainable Agriculture Funds in third place. This study emphasised the importance of environmental sustainability and responsible investing in financial decision-making through the criticality of ESG criteria. The model developed presents a structured and data-driven approach to ranking green finance alternatives and provides insights to investors, policymakers, and financial institutions (Aungkulanon et al., 2023).

One of the significant limitations of this research, apart from its contributions, is that it has a specific set of criteria, sub-criteria, and alternatives that may not capture all aspects of green finance. Besides, the research has AHP as its sole methodology, which limits the methodological versatility (Marza et al., 2025). Given that AHP is a pairwise comparison method, there will always be some degree of subjectivity involved in the process, and so results could further be dependent on the experts chosen. What is more, real-time financial market conditions and external economic factors may have been left out of consideration, which is likely to influence the performance and attractiveness of green finance alternatives with time (Rawat et al., 2022).

These findings have important implications for several stakeholders. Investors can use the findings to make informed decisions about sustainable investment options, prioritising ESG-compliant alternatives. Policymakers will find the valuable study in enacting regulations and instruments that promote green financing (Mukherjee et al., 2025). Financial institutions will use the ranking model for sustainable investment products and portfolios. It also provides a framework for integrating ESG into financial decision-making, reinforcing impact-driven investments as pivotal for reaching long-term sustainability goals (Kyei et al., 2023).

Additionally, three future research perspectives are suggested. A more comprehensive study using many criteria, sub-criteria, and alternatives would seek to reinforce its robustness. The reliability and accuracy of the rankings could also be enhanced by expanding decision-making methods to include Fuzzy AHP, TOPSIS, or Machine Learning-based models (Kamaruzzaman et al., 2018). Comparative studies could reveal the existence of regional differences in the green finance strategies of different industries, countries, or economic sectors. Finally, future efforts might track the longer-term financial performance and sustainability impact of these investment alternatives, assessing the real-world effectiveness of green finance strategies (Zyoud et al., 2025).

References

Akomea-Frimpong, I., Adeabah, D., Ofosu, D., & Tenakwah, E. J. (2022). A review of studies on green finance of banks, research gaps and future directions. *Journal of Sustainable Finance & Investment*, 12 (4), 1241-1264, http://dx.doi.org/10.1080/20430795.2020.1870202.

Algarín, C. R., Llanos, A. P., & Castro, A. O. (2017). An analytic hierarchy process-based approach for evaluating renewable energy sources. *International Journal of Energy Economics and Policy*, 7 (4), 38-47.

Aliyev, R., Temizkan, H., & Aliyev, R. (2020). Fuzzy analytic hierarchy process-based multicriteria decision making for universities ranking. *Symmetry*, 12 (8), 1351.

Arda, T., Bayrak, O. C., & Uzar, M. (2025). Analysing coastal vulnerability using analytic hierarchy process and best–worst method: a case study of the Marmara Gulf region. *Arabian Journal for Science and Engineering*, 50 (3), 1851-1869.

Aungkulanon, P., Atthirawong, W., & Luangpaiboon, P. (2023). Fuzzy analytical hierarchy process for strategic decision making in electric vehicle adoption. *Sustainability*, 15 (8), 7003.

Calabrese, A., Costa, R., Levialdi, N., & Menichini, T. (2016). A fuzzy analytic hierarchy process method to support materiality assessment in sustainability reporting. *Journal of Cleaner Production*, 121, 248–264.

Cao X., Mei T., & Li S. (2024). Research on the relationship between ESG disclosure quality and stock liquidity of Chinese listed companies, *Green Finance*, 6 (1), 24-51, https://doi.org/10.3934/GF.2024002.

Çelikbilek, Y. (2025). A Fuzzy Analytic Hierarchy Process Based COPRAS Approach for the Evaluation of the Renewable Energy Sources. *The Journal of International Scientific Research*es, 10 (1), 118-133.

Chabouh, S., Hammami, S., Fessi, H., & Achour, A. (2024). Towards sustainable dialysis modality selection: a multi-expert fuzzy analytical hierarchy process-based approach for guided decision making. *Annals of Operations Research*, 1–29.

Chien, F., Ngo, Q.-T., Hsu, C.-C., Chau, K. Y., & Iram, R. (2021). Assessing the mechanism of barriers towards green finance and public spending in small and medium enterprises from developed countries. *Environmental Science and Pollution Research,* 28 (43), 60495–60510. https://doi.org/10.1007/s11356-021-14907-1

Chiu, W. H., Lin, W. C., Chen, C. N., & Chen, N. P. (2021). Using an analytical hierarchy process to analyse the development of the green energy industry. *Energies*, 14 (15), 4452.

Chun-Yueh, L. (2022). Fuzzy AHP-based prioritisation of the optimal alternative of external equity financing for start-ups of lending companies in uncertain environments. *Sci. Technol*, 25 (2), 133–149.

Fang, Z., Yang, C., & Song, X. (2022). How Do Green Finance and Energy Efficiency Mitigate Carbon Emissions Without Reducing Economic Growth in G7 Countries? *Frontiers in Psychology,* 13, 879741, https://doi.org/10.3389/fpsyg.2022.879741.

Göçmen-Polat, E. (2024). Assessment of Critical Raw Materials by Addressing Sustainable Development Goals Using Fuzzy MCDM Approach. In *Harmonizing Global Efforts in Meeting Sustainable Development Goals* (pp. 164-181). IGI Global.

Guang-Wen, Z., & Siddik, A. B. (2022). Do Corporate Social Responsibility Practices and Green Finance Dimensions Determine Environmental Performance? An Empirical Study on Bangladeshi Banking Institutions. *Frontiers in Environmental Science,* 10. https://doi.org/10.3389/fenvs.2022.890096.

Holder, R. D. (1991). Response to Holder's comments on the Analytic Hierarchy Process: response to the response. *Journal of the Operational Research Society*, 42 (10), 914-918, https://doi.org/10.1057/jors.1991.177.

Irfan, M., Razzaq, A., Sharif, A., & Yang, X. (2022). Influence mechanism between green finance and green innovation: exploring regional policy intervention effects in China. *Technological Forecasting and Social Change,* 182, 121882, https://doi.org/10.1016/j.techfore.2022.121882.

Kamaruzzaman, S. N., Lou, E. C. W., Wong, P. F., Wood, R., & Che-Ani, A. I. (2018). Developing a weighting system for refurbishment building assessment scheme in Malaysia through an analytic hierarchy process (AHP) approach. *Energy Policy*, 112, 280-290.

Kyei, E. Y., Junwen, F., Bo, F., Jamatutu, S. A., Amoako, P. Y. O., & Opoku, P. (2023). Analytic Hierarchy Process Based Comparative Analysis of Green Financing in Developed and Developing Countries: Evidence from China and Ghana. In *Applied Research Conference in Africa* (pp. 343-358). Cham: Springer Nature Switzerland.

Lee, J. W. (2020). Green finance and sustainable development goals: The case of China. Lee, Jung Wan (2020). Green Finance and Sustainable Development Goals: The Case of China. *Journal of Asian Finance Economics and Business*, 7 (7), 577–586, http://dx.doi.org/10.13106/jafeb.2020.vol7.no7.577.

Li, C., Solangi, Y. A., & Ali, S. (2023). Evaluating the factors of green finance to achieve carbon peak and carbon neutrality targets in China: A Delphi and fuzzy AHP approach. *Sustainability*, 15 (3), 2721, https://doi.org/10.3390/su15032721.

Liang Z., & Yang X., (2024). The impact of green finance on the peer effect of corporate ESG information disclosure, *Finance Research Letters*, 62 (Part A)105080, https://doi.org/10.1016/j.frl.2024.105080.

Liu, N., Liu, C., Xia, Y., Ren, Y., & Liang, J. (2020). Examining the coordination between green finance and green economy aiming for sustainable development: A case study of China. *Sustainability*, 12 (9), 3717, https://doi.org/10.3390/su12093717.

Marza, B., Bratu, R. D., Serbu, R., Stan, S. E., & Oprean-Stan, C. (2025). Applying AHP and fuzzy AHP management methods to assess the level of financial and digital inclusion. *Economic Computation and Economic Cybernetics Studies and Research*, 55 (4), 2021, 165-182. arXiv preprint arXiv:2501.10001.

Meng, X., & Shaikh, G. M. (2023). Evaluating Environmental, Social, and Governance Criteria and Green Finance Investment Strategies Using Fuzzy AHP and Fuzzy WASPAS. *Sustainability*, 15 (8), 6786, http://dx.doi.org/10.3390/su15086786.

Meo, M. S., & Abd Karim, M. Z. (2022). The role of green finance in reducing CO2 emissions: An empirical analysis. *Borsa Istanbul Review*, 22 (1), 169–178, https://doi.org/10.1016/j.bir.2021.03.002.

Mukherjee, S., De, A., & Roy, S. (2025). Risk prioritisation in enterprise supply chains: application of fuzzy analytic hierarchy process. *Business Process Management Journal.*

Nepomuceno, T. C. C., de Carvalho, V. D. H., Poleto, T., & Figueiredo, C. J. J. (2024). A knowledge-based directional multicriteria framework with a defuzzified subset of preferences for sustainable banking strategy analysis. *International Journal of Bank Marketing*, 42 (7), 1888-1919.

Noh, H. J. (2018). Financial strategy to accelerate green growth (No. 866). *ADBI* working paper.

Qin, G., Zhang, M., Yan, Q., Xu, C., & Kammen, D. M. (2021). A comprehensive evaluation of regional energy internet using a fuzzy analytic hierarchy process based on cloud model: A case in China. *Energy*, 228, 120569.

Rasoulinezhad, E., & Taghizadeh-Hesary, F. (2022). Role of green finance in improving energy efficiency and renewable energy development. *Energy Efficiency,* 15 (2), 14, https://doi.org/10.1007/s12053-022-10021-4.

Rawat, S. S., Pant, S., Kumar, A., Ram, M., Sharma, H. K., & Kumar, A. (2022). A state-of-the-art survey on analytical hierarchy process applications in sustainable development. *Int. J. Math. Eng. Manag.* Serv, 7, 883–917.

Saaty, T. L. (1980). A scaling method for priorities in hierarchical structures. *Journal of mathematical psychology*, 15 (3), 234-281, https://doi.org/10.1016/0022-2496 (77)90033-5.

Tara K., & Singh S. (2014). Green Banking: An Approach Towards Environmental Management, *Prabhandhan Indian Journal of Management*, 11 (7), http://dx.doi.org/ 10.17010/pijom%2F2014%2Fv7i11%2F59258.

Thirumurthy, S., Jayanthi, M., Swaminathan, M., Duraisamy, M., Kabiraj, S., & Anbazhahan, N. (2022). Multicriteria coastal environmental vulnerability assessment using analytic hierarchy process-based uncertainty analysis integrated into GIS. *Journal of Environmental Management*, 313, 114941.

Tian, X., Zhang, Y., & Qu, G. (2022). The impact of the digital economy on the efficiency of green financial investment in China's provinces. International *Journal of Environmental Research and Public Health*, 19 (14), 8884, https://doi.org/10.3390/ ijerph19148884.

Wind, Y., & Saaty, T. L. (1980). Marketing applications of the analytic hierarchy process. *Management Science,* 26 (7), 641-658, http://dx.doi.org/10.1287/mnsc.26.7.641.

Yadav, S., Pal, D. B., Singh, R. P., Dhakate, P. M., & Giri, B. S. (2024). Barriers to sustainable biowaste-to-energy solutions: an analytical hierarchy process-based method analysis. *Biomass Conversion and Biorefinery*, 1–11.

Zaheb, H., Obaidi, O., Mukhtar, S., Shirani, H., Ahmadi, M., & Yona, A. (2024). Comprehensive Analysis and Prioritisation of Sustainable Energy Resources Using Analytical Hierarchy Process. *Sustainability*, 16 (11), 4873.

Zyoud, S., Omair, S. M., & Jarrad, S. A. (2025). A two-stage model of the fuzzy analytic hierarchy process and the fuzzy synthetic evaluation technique to prioritise sustainable sanitation services under uncertainty. *Scientific Reports*, 15 (1), 3736.

Chapter 13

Sustainable Finance and ESG Investing: A Blueprint for Future Growth in India's Banking Sector

Adwiti Singhal*
Aradhana Madhusudanan†
Vijayalaxmi Rajendran‡
and Amit Kumar‖
School of Business and Management, CHRIST University, Bengaluru, India

Abstract

The paper focuses on sustainability transformation in banking, notably through environmental, social, and governance (ESG) investing. Today, completely profit-focused banks are gradually incorporating sustainability into their basic functions. This is consistent with global initiatives, namely the Paris Agreement, besides the United Nations' Sustainable Development Goals. This reflects a deeper understanding that financial activity must be environmentally friendly and socially responsible. With that, banks can now appraise if the bank's investment is profitable, good, and sustainable.

Reserve Bank of India, being the regulatory authority in India, with the help of the Securities and Exchange Board of India, has also been supportive by laying certain rules that enforce transparency of ESG

* Corresponding Author's Email: adwiti.singhal@bba.christuniversity.in
† Corresponding Author's Email: aradhana88@gmail.com
‡ Corresponding Author's Email: vijayalaxmi.rajendran@gmail.com
‖ Corresponding Author's Email: amit.kumar@christuniversity.in

In: Environmental, Social, and Governance (ESG) …
Editor: Veena Grover
ISBN: 979-8-90134-138-4

practice, encouraging green bond issues. Thus, regulations are seen as bringing Indian banks close to world standards and promoting this sustainability culture. The paper also draws upon the importance of integrating ESG factors into risk management systems to mitigate any financial risks that could stem from environmental and social concerns. It further argues that although ESG practices will be beneficial in improving financial performance, their impact does differ by component and should, therefore, be adopted while working in emerging economies such as India.

1. Introduction

In support, the change seems strongest on the banking side within the mainstream trend towards a shift for the more sustainable kind of industries everywhere. The two decades of evolving dynamic behind and integration within the main sustainable finance practice driver have fundamentally undergone a huge change. This development, on the one hand, made an emerging still-only two-year-ago niche term Environmental, Social, and Governance investing a dominant drive of banking strategy and its performance. It is not a new concept, but in the 21st century, sustainable finance is taking center stage with unprecedented attention. This, however, is changing the way people look at the banking industry because it was more traditionally a profit-driven industry and is now moving towards sustainability as part of business models.

The new concept is that environmental and social concerns have to be totally integrated into financial operations, not only in pure green banking, but also in pure green banking. This is a new form of banking that is still very specialized. Banks are no longer pure agents of moving capital today but themselves 'engineers of change' in sustainable development.

Sustainable finance can trace its roots to a host of global initiatives towards responding to climate change, poverty, and inequality. The Paris Agreement in 2015, generally the United Nations' SDGs, acted as a catalyst to drive the discourse on sustainable finance. It has, thus far, been a map guiding countries and corporations to track their own efforts and realign operations toward achieving the set global sustainability objectives. This, therefore, means integrating ESGs into the lending, investment, and risk management practices from a bank's perspective.

India, with high growth rates, feels that sustainability finance is the only way forward towards realizing national targets. The country has a duality of growth in the context of regular climate change, depletion of resources, and the wage gap. However, Indian banks are increasingly being nudged towards ESG practices; although partly because of regulations, they are also featured in a broader societal shift towards sustainability.

2. New Norm of Banking: ESG Investing

New norms in the banking world come through ESG investing. This refers to investment where the investor considers the environmental, social, and governance aspects apart from financial aspects in making his/her investment decision. Investors are also able to rate their banks by analyzing long-term viability together with the ethical impacts of the bank's investments. It's a very crucial aspect for any organization, yet the ESG factors indicate a more vast view of how good a company is performing and the extent of risk it can absorb.

A few more articles highlight that other than management, finding new opportunities is an aspect of ESG investing. Bank integration into the everyday practice of their operation with ESG factors might release new opportunities for growth, innovation, and market differentiation. There's this growing market of green finance- a category of loans and investments in renewable energy, energy efficiency, and other low-carbon techs that the bank investing in environmental sustainability could capitalize on. Similarly, socially responsible banks can attract a group of socially conscious customers and investors who demand ethical business practices.

The changing needs of stakeholders for increased transparency and accountability in financial institutions to enhance governance. Appropriate risk management by banks would, therefore, enable them to be stable and resilient in the long run. ESG incorporation into bank core strategies would open more avenues to enhance financial performance through reputation and stakeholder relations as well as social welfare addition.

3. Role of Regulatory Bodies in ESG Investing

The regulatory bodies of India have brought in regulations from RBI, SEBI, and many others, announcing that the operating mechanism of banks and financial institutes would bring sustainability into itself either via holistic strategy or integrated offering. These regulations had started to make the banks of India play by the global standard and to make India contribute towards its sustainable development goals.

For example, a company with the top 1000 companies on the stock exchange has to disclose its performance in the area of ESG while submitting its Business Responsibility and Sustainability Report (BRSR), which is yet another big move towards transparency and accountability. Such moves make a bank rate and bring its practice of ESG as well, which would lead to a sustainable banking culture. Another example of regulations that are promoting sustainable finance in India is the issue of green bonds, which are financial instruments supporting projects that have environmental benefits. Such regulations force banks to rate and report on their ESG practices, thus fostering a culture of sustainability within this sector. The introduction of green bonds- the financial instrument used to fund such projects. Banks have also started offering green bonds, which collect funds for renewable projects, all with the objective of turning this country into a low-carbon economy.

It is, however, not simply the regulation that is going to promote the ESG agenda forward. As many articles demonstrate, industry leadership and innovation have their equal share. By positioning themselves as pioneers in sustainable finance, Indian banks have taken a proactive approach to ESG and, hence, are able to position themselves to gain the competitive advantage of sustainable finance. Additionally, Voluntary adoption of global ESG standards (e.g., Global Reporting Initiative, GRI, or PRB Principles for Responsible Banking) by banks can positively contribute to their image and increase international investment interest while also enabling them to align themselves with the best practices in the world.

4. ESG and Risk Management System in Banking

Traditionally, the banking sector incorporated a risk management system largely based on financial risks: credit risk, market risk, and operational risk. However, with ESG increasingly playing a greater role for banks, they have realized that ESG risks can have a significant impact on their financial performance.

Physical damage to assets, supply chain disruptions, and increased insurance costs are environmental risks caused by climate change. This translates to higher credit risks for banks because vulnerable industries are looking to borrow, but these industries may not be able to repay loans. Similarly, social risks like labor disputes or poor working conditions can damage a company's reputation and, with it, the trust and loyalty of customers. There are also possible governance risks, such as corruption or the lack of transparency, leading to legal penalties, regulatory sanctions, and learner confidence.

Therefore, banks need to integrate ESG practices into their risk management system to mitigate the above-mentioned risk. For example, banks can conduct environmental due diligence before giving any loans to companies in vulnerable or high-risk sectors, thereby limiting their exposure to possible liabilities. In addition, banks can also promote good governance practices that enhance their internal controls and help ensure that they comply with regulatory requirements.

Therefore, by addressing ESG risks, banks protect their financial interests while also keeping the rest of the financial system stable. Experts have emphasized that ESG risk management is not a regulatory obligation but rather imperative for long-term sustainability. If banks fail to contemplate ESG risks, they can suffer financial losses, reputational damage, and regulatory penalties in the future.

In conclusion, ESG investing and sustainable finance are ushering in a new era in India's banking sector. Regulatory pressures, market demand, and increasing demand for greater accountability are creating a push amongst Indian banks to integrate their financial strategies with ESG principles, which are explored in this chapter.

5. Literature Review

The integration of ESG into Indian banks has improved their financial performance and allowed them to achieve a much wider social objective concerning environmental protection, social equity, and good governance. The Indian banks have been able to do something about their ESG investments due to which, going by what the future is shaping itself to be like in the name of finance, this will be what the work has much to do with the times ahead.

One of the relations between sustainability performance and financial performance, of which much has been found about emerging economies, including India, is that aspects explored concerning ESG practices that are supposed to have several effects on different financial performance measures. The review of a number of such studies brings forth the very complex interplay between those factors and results, which vary considerably on account of the specific components of sustainability that are being analyzed.

One such interesting article is that of Jyoti and Khanna (2021), who researched the correlation between Indian service sectors listed on the Bombay Stock Exchange in light of the sustainability and financial performance of firms. It raised questions on the point that the environmental scores of these service sector firms had high negative correlations with their corresponding financial metrics like ROA and ROCE. This is also accompanied by the drop in Return on Equity with the social score. At least inferences would be that sustainability practices pursued, at least at the company level under study, haven't yet translated into an improvement in performance. The authors have also stated that more emphasis must be achieved towards the practice in terms of sustainability for better utilization amongst the fast-emerging economies like India, along with research that is less to reports, which has also provided mixed outcomes as well (Jyoti & Khanna, 2021).

This nexus Ilker Yilmaz discussed over corporate sustainability as well as financial performances emanating from five emerging economies that include India too based on Sustainability database ESG scores for fetching relevant reports for sourcing the needed company accounts' extraction that had been done through the use of panel regression models in this analysis. Findings: There was a general positive correlation between sustainability performance and financial performance; discrete scores for environment, social, and governance did not contribute to any value. Thus, it may be said that although an increasing number of companies are embracing ESG activities as a good activity, the dimensions of ESG are not equal and contribute to achieving financial performance, as stated by Ilker Yilmaz 2021.

The 2021 overall review of Bahaaeddin Ahmed Alareeni and Allam Hamdan also directs that the summation of all the ESG positive impacts profitability measures but, on the other hand, shows that some elements are not in agreement to bring in the same impacts. This would, therefore, suggest that although the commitment to sustainability by a firm improves its financial performance, the contribution of ESG practices toward this end is not homogeneous. Several studies in the empirical, meta-analytic, and theory based on an exchange of views concerning debates between business ethics discourse-based corporate governance have offered recommendations; collectively, the reports postulated a positive association relationship among financial and ESG-based companies while there appears to be disagreement at what scale. For example, even though overall ESG scores correlate positively with a few financial metrics, the same might not hold in such regard for environmental and social practice scores. Another effort to present such complexity is through recent study efforts made by Gaurav Jyoti and Ashu

Khanna (2021). The study elaborated on the relationship and connectivity between sustainability performance and Indian service sector firms' financial performances.

Aggregate ESG level is positively and significantly correlated with the chain of financial performance metrics at a 0.01 level of significance, though both environmental and society scores have poor correlations. The governance score has also been positively correlated to all the measures of financial performance. Therefore, it would suggest that governance practices perhaps hold more importance in allowing scope for the improvement of financial results than environmental and social ones. Firm controls consisted of the control variables of the study. A fixed effect model fits according to the results from the Hausman test. Although the results vividly portray a general direction in a positive manner, the low R-squared values indicate a minimal relationship in terms of explanatory power and point towards more significant research about this detailed exploration in dynamics (Jyoti & Ashu Khanna, 2021).

The implications of findings from the study are quite vital for the companies of emerging economies. They further argue that although, from a financial performance perspective, doing good may help, there is a more important task at hand: figuring out which constituents of ESG matter and how the constituents differ in terms of impact. Mixed results indicate that a one-size-fits-all approach is probably not likely to fit the situation. It would be in the best interest of corporations if they tailored their sustainability strategies around the stakeholders that are most likely to yield positive financial benefits in their specific environments.

They also point out how sustainability must be incorporated into corporate strategy. As the business environment shifts toward a more sustainable one, all those firms that do not track along with this shift can only expect to lose by being less competitive. Strong ESG practices have thus far been shown to result in strong company performance, but the mechanism by which this is accomplished often can be quite subtle as many factors intertwine with the financial outcome.

It is found that this relationship of sustainability performance with financial performance indeed turns out to be complex within Indian banks and service sector firms. The existence of evidence says there is an enhancing effect on overall sustainability practice towards financial performance; however, the impacts of all ESG components are quite diverse. Studies, as found available, have been proof that even as environmental and social scores appear not to correlate with financial measures, governance practice still somehow reveals a more consistent positive influence. These firms need to consider while implementing sustainable practices for the perusal of sustainable success. Others in similar directions will be developed and discussed while applied to emerging economies with a focus on deeper penetration into discussions about the interaction of sustainability and financial performance.

6. Conceptual Development

Since the trend toward sustainability affects almost all industries, banking has definitely been transformed to the highest and strongest extent. In this regard, finance and sustainability have transformed and integrated into the fundamental factors for the practice of sustainable finance for a pretty long time. However, it has also brought on the scene a niche concept for almost two-year-old ESG investing as a mainstream feature for both banking strategies and performances in recent times. Although such an ideology of sustainable finance was not around long ago, it still fascinates the unparalleled iniquity of interest in the 21st century. This was the first time that the banks, long considered to be mainly profit-gaining industry, were attempting to incorporate sustainability into their business model. The assumption now is that everything done is financial but will come with environmental and social aspects incorporated within financial activities, not strictly in green banking, which is this new type of banking that remains highly specialized. Banks should not be regarded as merely capital-moving agents anymore but rather as 'engineers of change' in sustainable development.

Sustainable finance emanates from several initiatives around the world that responded to climate change, poverty, and all sorts of inequalities, more specifically, the Paris Agreement of 2015 and, more broadly, the UN's Sustainable Development Goals. They serve as a map for countries and corporations to pursue and track along for synchronizing their activities with sustainability aims at the global level. Therefore, for a bank, this implies incorporating ESGs into lending, investment, and risk management. A country like India, characterized by high growth rates, soon discovers that sustainability finance is the key to reaching national-level targets.

This is a duality because the country then faces growth in normal climate change through resource depletion and the wage gap. However, it is reported that Indian banks are increasingly encouraged toward ESG compliance, not as much from regulations but just as a part of overall societal movements toward sustainability. Sustainable finance and ESG investing have become disruptive paradigms in the entire global financial landscape. Both approaches support investments that bring about environmental protection, ensure social equity, maintain good governance frameworks, and make returns to the economy.

Sustainable finance would be an important instrument for India in making its economic growth trajectory align with the principles of sustainability in reaching the United Nations Sustainable Development Goals by 2030. Banks are agents of change in India, playing a huge role as intermediaries of capital and risk managers who have the power to influence the direction of economic activity toward sustainable resource use and development. The new norm in the world of banks is ESG investing. ESG investing is described as a type of investment where all factors - environmental, social, and governance - are also included along with the financial ones for making the decision for the investment. Today, investors can check for the long-term sustainability of investments as well as the ethical impacts by evaluating the investments made by banks. Profitability is no longer an end, but rather, the presence of ESG factors offers a more holistic view of how well the company is doing and the amount of risk it can take. Most articles have also pointed out that ESG investing is not only about managing but also discovering possible opportunities. Integration of ESG factors into the day-to-day operations of banks can unlock new growth, innovation, and market differentiation opportunities. Such is the example of how the burgeoning demand for green finance-loan category and investment in renewable energy, energy efficiency, and low carbon technology would reap environmental sustainability invested by banks. Similarly, the socially concerned banks can acquire a niche consumer and investor segment interested in ethical conduct in businesses.

Sustainable finance integrates ESG factors into decision-making processes to ensure long-term growth. It crosses over into green bonds, sustainability-linked loans, and ethical banking. It, therefore, implies that major financial institutions in such sectors are seen to mitigate the risks that bring environmental degradation, facilitate community development, and increase transparency in governance. As such, sustainable finance is going to act as an accelerant to handle significant problems that the country faces, such as climate change, poverty, and infrastructural deficits. It is a source of financing climate-resilient projects since it is one of the world's most vulnerable countries to climate change. Most importantly, the gap in investments closed is estimated at over $2.5 trillion per annum worldwide to meet the SDGs.

ESG investing is finding an increasing interest in India with the ever-increasing investor awareness, regulatory push, and international commitments such as the Paris Agreement. Essex and others have been implementing ESG frameworks more for most Indian banks and financial establishments. The lack of standards in metrics, data weakness, and lesser awareness among other stakeholders remain challenges here. Neo-banks, on the other hand, were completely digital platform-based banks that demonstrated extreme agility in embracing ESG considerations. These banks focus transparency on ethical lending and customer involvement as well through technology that facilitates improvement and scale impacts. For example, neo-banks in India provide green financial products, advocate for paperless transactions, and invest more in renewable energy projects (Singh & Agrawal, 2024).

Such existing studies emphasize the transformational capacity of sustainable finance and ESG integration into banking. For example, studies indicate that banks adopting ESG principles generally benefit from improved risk management, increased customer trust, and healthy financial performance (Zafar & Qarni, 2024; Saxena et al., 2021).

For example, ESG-oriented banks in developed nations have shown better performances during downturn periods, which is another latent advantage through the risk reduction of sustainable practices. The uptake of sustainability practices in India has been more gradual, especially within public sector banks. Despite that, public sector banks continue concentrating on the social aspects of financial inclusion and community development rather than the innovation of green products and reporting sustainability by private banks (Saxena et al., 2021).

The Indian government has enacted many policies that indirectly promote sustainable finance and ESG investing. It gives banks the base through which they can align their operations with the overall national and global sustainability goals.

The RBI seeks a percentage share of bank credit in sectors that are aligned with the green goals of the SDG, such as agriculture, renewables, and small-scale units, thus supporting economic inclusion and eco-friendly development (Saxena et al., 2021). Green sovereign bonds in India also fund climate-resilient projects such as renewable energy and transport; it mobilizes the capital that is being put towards environmentally clean projects (Gratcheva & Gurhy, 2024). Initiatives like the International Solar Alliance clearly indicate that India is a committed country to clean energy and provide a blueprint for banks to finance solar and other renewable energy projects (Saxena et al., 2021). SEBI also makes it compulsory for top-listed companies to make disclosures about ESG, encouraging banks to do the same with regard to their sustainability practices (Saxena et al., 2021). Banks are best positioned to spur sustainable development through resource allocation, innovation, and stakeholder engagement. Banks can attract the conscience of green investors through the design and offering of green bonds, sustainability-linked loans, and ESG-focused mutual funds. Banks can finance solar, wind, and other renewable energy projects that reduce climate risks and tap into emerging growth sectors. The extension of credit to the underprivileged and micro-enterprises reduces social inequities and drives economic growth (Saxena et al., 2021). It involves such measures as having dedicated ESG teams, regular training programs, and cultivating sustainability in the institution. Effective governance enables banks to be in control of more risks, hence making them stable and sound in the long term. Embedding ESG in the underlying strategies of a bank opens up opportunities for improving financial outcomes related to reputation and stakeholder networks, as well as social welfare. Technology also plays a great role in promoting good, sustainable banking practices. Digital media enables efficient management of ESG data, facilitates a platform for green financial products, and enhances literacy in finance. Technological innovations such as blockchain increase the transparency of ESG reports; AI is used to assess climate risks and optimize sustainable investments (Singh & Agrawal, 2024; Saxena et al., 2021).

The integration of ESG factors into banking operations boosts the sector's resilience to environmental and economic shocks. Those banks with a diversified portfolio that includes green assets have better prospects to cope with the uncertainty of the markets (Zafar & Qarni, 2024). The ESG investments in affordable housing, education, and healthcare have social equity and community development. The financial products targeted at women entrepreneurs or rural enterprises add value to inclusive growth (Saxena et al., 2021).

The alignment of Indian banks with international ESG benchmarks can attract foreign funds and increase their strength in the League of International Sustainability rankings (Gratcheva & Gurhy, 2024).

Indian banks would advocate for clear and consistent ESG regulations from the RBI and other governing bodies for the full realization of the potential of sustainable finance and ESG investing. Such campaigns should be used to educate customers and investors through transparent reporting. It will provide access to expertise and financial resources through collaborations with international organizations like the Green Climate Fund and multilateral development banks (Saxena et al., 2021). It can design new financial products like green savings accounts, carbon credits-linked loans, and eco-friendly credit cards, meeting the emerging needs of customers (Saxena et al., 2021). The following will be added to metrics if third-party audits and regular public disclosure are sought on the sustainability impacts of bank operations. Sustainability Finance and ESG investing will be a potential roadmap toward growth and resilience for the Indian banking sector. Sustainability principles embedded in the core operations of banks would help build economic growth, reduce environmental risks, and support social equity. This would make the national objectives of sustainability resonate with the global vision. Indian banks promise more than long-term prosperity by helping lead global change in the same direction toward sustainable future growth. A collective effort to embrace innovation, foster collaboration, and make commitments to transparency will help redefine its role as an enabler for sustainable growth.

7. Implications and Limitations

This paper draws many inferences from the research findings on the adoption of ESG practices by the Indian banking sector, but it is not without its caveats. First, working with secondary data and drawing its material from previous literature, the study might miss the capture of dynamic evolutions as they are happening in real-time. Hence, the study reflects trends and issues rising as outlined by previous studies while excluding practices that are ongoing or surfacing today. Such practices in changes over roles that Fintech is playing in expanding further its contribution to ESG integration and lack of comprehensive data pertaining to more insignificant financial institutions and regional rural banks with a resultant over presence in this analysis of larger established ones.

The primary drawback of the framework is that there is no standardization when it calculates the ESG metrics of diverse banks in India. If the definition and the criteria of ESG are not uniform, it really gets very difficult to standardize or compare. On the other hand, the disclosure of ESG through top-listed companies is still very much insisted upon by SEBI but cannot be implemented throughout the banking sector at large. This may open very gaping loopholes in the non-listed, lesser institutions' evaluation. The operational and cultural differences that can be seen in various banks may result in complexity for a one-fits-all ESG approach. The heterogeneity in sustainability reporting renders an impossibility of generalizing to make an inference that would work uniformly for all the banks.

This has nothing to do with other segments such as insurance, asset management, or even microfinance; it is applicable strictly within the banking sector and so cannot be generalized to include results from these sectors. All these are integral elements within Indian financial architecture but work along distinct operational models and regulatory frameworks and are not suitable enough for direct application. This, therefore, aims to put scope over a very thin lens over ESG integration rather than pursuing a broad financial landscape.

Despite all these limitations, the implications of this study are still pretty significant. For example, it asks RBI and SEBI to put robust frameworks with respect to ESG that are uniformly applicable to all financial institutions. In that regard, it would require proper comprehensive disclosures; more transparency and accountability towards the motives of financial institutions would be obtained. Incentives would likely include tax benefits or reduced regulatory compliance costs directed at the earlier adopters aimed at encouraging greater sector-wide participation.

Research leads to innovation and technology that can spur the adoption of ESG. Such innovations usually culminate in technologies such as artificial intelligence, blockchain, and big data analytics. Such technologies have come very critically to streamline reporting on ESG, creating possibilities for better choices within organizations. Blockchain offers transparent records of ESG compliance while creating immutable ones. Undeniably, AI-based systems will be used to calculate climate risk and find investments that align with ESG standards. Providing funding for this technological infrastructure would smooth many operational challenges for ESG integration.

The most important message is stakeholder engagement to enforce ESG adoption. The awareness level is very poor and is one of the major barriers for customers as well as investors. A proper training and awareness campaign, in terms of enlightening values through ESG practices, not only for institutional investors but also for retail customers and banking transparency reporting highly integrated with highly interactive communication strategies, will invite stronger stakeholder engagement for larger participation in sustainable finance.

On this account, more weight is put on the reinforcement of banking capabilities to overcome inner resistance in case ESG is introduced. Therefore, it makes sense to design special teams on ESG, systematized training, and the development of sustainable organizational culture. In this manner, concerned employees will be better empowered with the principles of ESG so that they can integrate lending, investment, and risk management more effectively.

Leadership commitment further translates into mainstreaming ESG practices in the core strategies of financial institutions.

This paper, therefore, presents the potential economic and social benefits of ESG integration for Indian banks. It might make the practices of Indian banks compliant with globally implemented ESG standards, thereby attracting international investments and improving their competitive advantage compared to the banks of developed countries. It can counter the negative factors climate change, resource depletion, and social inequality are bringing in the long run in sustaining the financial sector. It is only possible if policymakers, financial institutions, and other stakeholders coordinate to close the identified gaps and challenge material areas.

Conclusion

Sustainable finance and ESG investing can be a transformative opportunity for India's banking sector because it shifts the value of profitability toward social and environmental responsibility. The more integrated the ESG principles become in banking activities, financial performance will improve, risks decline, and long-run instability can be avoided. The regulatory framework, technological innovation, and stakeholders are the key drivers of interest in ESG principles. Other challenges include non-standardized metrics and incomplete data regarding small institutions. The benefits of sustainable finance, however, justify the challenge.

This would put Indian banks in a niche from which they can spearhead sustainable development by literally channeling resources into the highest social and environmental benefit projects. Thus, the practices of ESG would ensure, in addition to the regulatory mandates that such a system would comply with, clientele relationships with the banks from trust among customers and investors that would enhance reputation and competitiveness in that sense in the market to mainly mainstream Indian banks. And that will attract more investments from foreign shores with a better contribution toward a global, transnational perspective toward a sustainable economy.

This can come only through concerted efforts on such identified limitations and the search for opportunities thrown up by ESG investing. It will be able to facilitate cooperation among the regulator, financial institutions, and other stakeholders to establish the Indian ecosystem of sustainable finance so that it is sturdy enough to support overall economic growth, social equity, and environmental preservation. It is this surviving spirit of ESG principles in the Indian banking sector that will define its resilience and relevance going forward into the increasingly changing landscape of global finances.

References

Alareeni, B. A., & Hamdan, A. (2020). ESG impact on performance of US S&P 500-listed firms. *Corporate Governance, 20* (7), 1409–1428. https://doi.org/10.1108/CG-06-2020-0258.

Alam, M. M., Atan, R., Said, J., & Zamri, M. (2018). The impacts of environmental, social, and governance factors on firm performance: Panel study of Malaysian companies. *Management of Environmental Quality, 29* (2), 182–194. https://doi.org/10.1108/MEQ-03-2017-0033 *(Corrected ordering of authors as listed in your original source).*

Amutha, K., & Kalpana, S. (2015). *Landscape of green finance in India*. In *Inducing green practising strategies for a sustainable future* (p. 18).

Badhe, M. D. A. (2011). *Role of urban co-operative banks in sustainable development of India*. Department of Economics, Solapur University.

Birindelli, G., Dell'Atti, S., Iannuzzi, A. P., & Savioli, M. (2018). Composition and activity of the board of directors: Impact on ESG performance in the banking system. *Sustainability, 10* (12), 4699. https://doi.org/10.3390/su10124699.

Boiral, O., Brotherton, M. C., & Talbot, D. (2024). What you see is what you get: Building confidence in ESG disclosures for sustainable finance through external assurance. *Business Ethics, the Environment & Responsibility, 33* (4), 617–632.

Brooks, C., & Oikonomou, I. (2018). The effects of environmental, social and governance disclosures and performance on firm value: A review of the literature in accounting and finance. *The British Accounting Review, 50*, 1–15. https://doi.org/10.1016/j.bar.2017.11.005.

Chelawat, H., & Trivedi, I. V. (2016). The business value of ESG performance: The Indian context. *Asian Journal of Business Ethics, 5*, 195–210. https://doi.org/10.1007/s13520-016-0064-4.

Gratcheva, E., & O'Reilly Gurhy, B. (2024). *Sovereign environmental, social and governance investing: Chasing elusive sustainability* (IMF Working Paper). International Monetary Fund.

Green Finance Institute. (2019). *Sustainable banking and ESG integration: Best practices and case studies*. https://www.greenfinanceinstitute.co.uk/reports/sustainable-banking-esg-integrationbest-practices.pdf.

Jaiwani, M., & Gopalkrishnan, S. (2023). Do private and public sector banks respond to ESG in the same way? Some evidence from India. *Benchmarking: An International Journal*. Advance online publication. https://doi.org/10.1108/BIJ-05-2023-0340.

Jyoti, G., & Khanna, A. (2021). Does sustainability performance impact financial performance? Evidence from Indian service sector firms. *Sustainable Development*, 1–10. https://doi.org/10.1002/sd.2204.

Saxena, D., Dhall, N., & Malik, R. (2021). Sustainable banking: A roadmap to sustainable development. *Corporate Governance and Sustainability Review, 5* (3), 42–56. https://doi.org/10.22495/cgsrv5i3p4.

Singh, S., & Agrawal, M. (2023). *Neo banks and sustainable finance: A comprehensive analysis of ESG integration and impact*.

Steuer, S., & Tröger, T. H. (2022). The role of disclosure in green finance. *Journal of Financial Regulation, 8* (1), 1–50.

Sustainable Banking Association. (2021). *Annual report on ESG integration in neo banks*. https://www.sustainablebankingassociation.org/reports/2021-annual-report.pdf.

United Nations Principles for Responsible Banking. (2020). *Principles for responsible banking: Implementation guide and framework*. https://www.unprinciples.org/publications/principles-for-responsible-bankingimplementation-guide-and-framework.pdf.

Yilmaz, I. (2021). Sustainability and financial performance relationships: International evidence. *World Journal of Entrepreneurship, Management, and Sustainable Development, 17* (3), 537–549. https://doi.org/10.1108/WJEMSD-10-2020-0133.

Yu, Z., Farooq, U., Alam, M. M., & Dai, J. (2024). How does environmental, social, and governance (ESG) performance determine investment mix? New empirical evidence from BRICS. *Borsa Istanbul Review, 24* (3), 520–529.

Zafar, M., & Qarni, M. O. (2024). Uncovering diversification benefits: Return spillovers in USA ESG and non-ESG oriented banks. In *Proceedings of the International Conference on Business, Economics, Law, Language & Psychology* (pp. 328–329). Social Science and Humanities Research Association.

About the Editor

Veena Grover

Gold Medalist, UGC (NET)-qualified and university topper in Economics with over 23 years of experience in teaching, research, and academic leadership. She is currently serving as Professor and Dean (IQAC) in Lloyd Business School. She is a seasoned academic professional, extensively involved in NAAC and NBA accreditation processes, ensuring institutional quality and standards. Her research expertise lies in micro finance, healthcare, international trade, sustainability, macro economic variables, and innovation strategy. She has published 40+ research papers, 30+ book chapters, 15 patents, 6 books, presented papers at numerous conferences, and supervised PhD thesis projects. She is a reviewer of many reputed Scopus Indexed journals. She has also completed Innovation Ambassador certification (Basic+ Advanced) under the Institution's Innovation Council, an initiative of the Ministry of Education's Innovation Cell. She is known for driving educational excellence, inspiring faculty, and promoting student success. She has been committed to advancing research, implementing sustainable strategies, and fostering global academic collaboration.

Index

M

O

P

R

S

T

W

More information about *Veena Grover* can be found at

https://novapublishers.com/writer/veena-grover/